Behind the Sequins

SHIRLEY BALLAS

Behind the Sequins

BBC BOOKS

1

BBC Books, an imprint of Ebury Publishing
20 Vauxhall Bridge Road,
London SW1V 2SA

BBC Books is part of the Penguin Random House group of companies
whose addresses can be found at global.penguinrandomhouse.com

First published by BBC Books in 2020

www.penguin.co.uk

A CIP catalogue record for this book is available from the British Library

ISBN 9781785945113

Typeset in 11.5/19 pt Bembo Infant MT Std
by Integra Software Services Pvt. Ltd, Pondicherry

Printed and bound in Great Britain by Clays Ltd, Elcograf S.p.A.

Penguin Random House is committed to a sustainable future for
our business, our readers and our planet. This book is made from
Forest Stewardship Council® certified paper.

To my amazing and beautiful mother, Audrey. You truly have always been a shining star in my life. I love you to the moon and back.

Contents

Prologue

What Dance Requires

What makes a perfect Ballroom dancer? As with everything else in life, there's no such thing as complete perfection in dance, only a series of hopefully perfect moments. You can study, train, practise, find great teachers and learn their lessons, but at some point, you must prepare yourself, body and soul, surrender to the process and simply enjoy yourself.

In many ways, dance is like everything else in life, and yet it has a magic all of its own. It is demanding of you. It requires musicality, technique, synchronisation, coordination, and the discipline of constantly practising and perfecting.

Technique is just the beginner's framework. To communicate through dance, you have to learn how your body works, then decide how best to tell your story. Some people are naturally born performers who can walk straight on to a dance floor and shine, while others have to learn and work hard at it.

The work required to look effortless on the floor is immense. Underneath the beauty, the poetry, the strength, the glamour and romance are hours, months, years of training, preparation, blood, sweat, tears, thousands of hours of individual effort and extraordinary teamwork. And for what? Two minutes of intense beauty. It is very, very difficult, and if it looks like you're working hard, you're not working hard enough.

Lots of students believe that dancing only requires a few key skills, that there are only a couple of boxes to tick, but it's a lot more complicated. It demands authenticity, reading, watching, understanding, study and learning the lessons of others. Most importantly, it requires courage.

There is no such thing as the perfect dancer, but any true dancer must have a huge heart and be prepared to reveal it.

Introduction

I knew joining *Strictly Come Dancing* was a very big deal. Not just for me but also my family, my students, my rivals in the dance industry and all those who had previously followed my path to the top of the dance world for 30 years.

I'd discovered it was also incredibly, sometimes surprisingly, important to the fans of the show, the millions who'd tuned in for every Rumba, every Waltz, every smile, every tear, through all the years that *Strictly* had become such an unmissable highlight of the country's Saturday-evening television schedule.

In May 2017, when it was first announced I would replace Len Goodman, everyone seemed incredibly excited for me. I was going to be the head judge on the country's biggest entertainment show – not bad for a 57-year-old woman who'd never appeared on British TV before! However, I quickly discovered that everyone was also a little nervous for me, particularly whenever they lowered their voices, which I soon realised meant they were about to mention Len's footwear. 'Big shoes to fill' was the phrase I heard most often.

Now here I was, taking part in my first ever live show. I'd already danced a Samba with the professionals and that had gone wonderfully, far better than I could have hoped, considering it was years since I'd performed in front of an audience. Nevertheless, I knew my real baptism of fire was still ahead of me. I had to walk across the glittering dance floor to where the hosts Tess Daly and Claudia Winkleman were standing, waiting for me. I'd already had a bit of drama backstage. For that evening, my very first night as a judge, the wardrobe ladies had given me a beautiful long evening dress, with black and white stripes and little white petals at the top. It was so tailored, they'd had to squeeze me in, and in fact, it was so tight the zip broke, so they'd had to quickly sew me into it, finishing just seconds before I was due to walk on. I love that dress – wearing it that night is a very special memory, and it still has pride of place in my wardrobe.

I smiled at the audience as though this was just like any other Saturday night for me and finally I took my place with the rest of the judges on the panel. On the outside, I was desperately trying to look natural, as though I didn't have a care in the world. On the inside, all I could hear was my heart pounding in my ears and my knees knocking.

I gazed down under the panel and imagined Len's shoes there on the floor, and in my head I placed my dainty slippers next to them. There was no filling Len's place and I'd already decided not to try. I could only bring my own.

Throughout my first few weeks on *Strictly*, in truth, I was over-awed. If it looks simple being a judge, believe me when I tell you, there's an awfully long list of things you have to remember. Even walking on is a high-wire act in itself. You only have so many seconds to get to your seat, and I always seemed to get there late, which meant I was flustered right from the beginning. Once you're in your seat, you have to work out where to look, what to say, when to press your scoring button, plus all the time you're very aware it's going out live to millions of people at home, so there really is no place to hide.

The format is the same for every couple who come on and do their number. For me, judging the dance routines is by far the most straightforward part of the programme – after all, that's what I've been doing professionally for decades. The minute each couple has finished their dance, that's when I have to press my scoring button so the score can go up to the computer and be programmed to show up on people's TV screens – when the couple are upstairs with Claudia and the whole *Strictly* entourage.

The reason we have to press our score buttons so promptly is so there's no confusion later. Well, of course those first few weeks I kept forgetting to press my keypad. Nicola the floor manager would call out from the production gallery, 'She hasn't pressed her button, press the button, oh my god, she hasn't pressed the button.' She had to keep frantically gesticulating to me. I thought she was just waving at me to be encouraging, so I was happily smiling back at her, and all the while she was having kittens! It took me about three weeks to get everything together – the paddle, the key pad, the cameras – and the more I was trying to do it right, the more I was perspiring and losing my train of thought. All those years of dancing in front of the world's harshest judges hadn't prepared me for this. Trust me, it was a hundred times more nerve-wracking.

People don't believe me, but when you're dancing in competitions as I'd been doing for all those years, it's a lot easier to concentrate on your routine. Once you step out on to the floor, it's just you and your partner in a world of your own. Everyone's watching, but you can lose yourself in the music and relax in your own little fish bowl. On the other hand, when you're a judge on *Strictly* you're in a similar fish bowl, but you have to watch the routines, hold the paddles and give constructive criticism, all in front of around 15 million viewers. You can never lose your concentration for a second.

I worried constantly about getting it right, but what I discovered was that viewers are very forgiving; not only that but actually they seem to enjoy it when things go a bit awry. I guess it shows them we're real. I found this out one evening when the computers went down for the results, and we four judges were all scrabbling around with our pieces of paper like we were at our local bingo hall.

After you've pressed your button, you have to prepare your critique. You don't know what any other judge is going to say, so sometimes you might have a really good thought in your head, and the next second you hear it come out of the mouth of the person just before you. That means you have to think on your feet while the dancers are waiting with Tess, and come up with something else equally valuable to say instead. And you have to say your piece in crisp short sentences, because you each have only about 15 seconds to speak, so you have to mentally edit what you're going to say to get your message across. I always ask myself, 'What did they do well?' 'What could they improve for next week?' I keep it in mind to be as encouraging as possible about what they've achieved, because I know they've been practising all week, and yet everything boils down to those two minutes on the dance floor. Trust me, I've been there enough times to know what that feels like. So I like to offer some encouragement as well as some constructive criticism to help them progress on their journey.

Then it's time for the big one, the paddle. At first, even something as simple as that turned out to be a challenge. I know what you're thinking – how hard could it possibly be? Well, at first, whenever I lifted it up to give my score to the camera, I was always covering my face. I eventually discovered you have to hold it in just the right place under your chin. And all the time this is going on, there are three or four cameras in front of you, so you have to remember exactly where to look.

I know it doesn't sound like a lot, but I'll not lie – those first few weeks on *Strictly* were all a bit overwhelming or, quite frankly, terrifying.

All the time I was trying to learn the ropes, I was feeling acutely aware of what a responsibility, as well as a privilege, it was to be part of such an enormous show. But I knew it was a really big deal, so if I hadn't been nervous, I believe there would have been something wrong with me. Once I started to get a handle on everything, it was exhilarating.

I got the *Strictly* job at 57, exactly 50 years after I got my first set of dancing shoes. I'd been a professional dancer, teacher and coach for 40 of those years, and knew my way round every ballroom, every competition, every dance routine anyone cared to throw at me. There wasn't a question about dance I couldn't immediately answer, but this TV business was a whole new ball game. I remember those first few weeks. Any time I wasn't trying desperately to remember what it was I was meant to be doing, I sat there, gazing around at the orchestra, the familiar staircases, the glittering dance floor and the famous faces around me. I felt like a tiny fish in a huge ocean, wondering, 'Which way do I swim?'

The answer was upstream for sure, but then again, I'd been doing that all my life.

CHAPTER 1
The Quickstep

'A dance identified by its interpretation of up-tempo music, bright and bubbly, making excellent use of feet and ankles to change speed with hops, skips and jumps, steps and swing actions, requiring a dexterity of skills. It is full of optimism and energy.'

'Shirley Rich, piss poor broke, without a pot to piss in.' That was how the girls at my school used to describe me, which wasn't at all nice to hear, even though it was a pretty accurate description of the best part of my childhood.

It wasn't always that way. My first memories of this world are like something out of a fairy tale, living in my great-grandfather's house at the top of a steep hill. It was a genteel old Victorian home, beautifully kept, and at the bottom of the hill was the sea, which could be blue on a summer's day. We were in New Brighton, right in the heart of Wallasey, on the topmost tip of the Wirral, halfway between the golf club and the River Mersey.

I've called lots of different places home in the years since then – Wallasey, Yorkshire, London, Manchester, Texas, London, California and now finally, London again – but the Wirral is always in the bones of me, and I'm happy to say that I come from that part of the world, along with some pretty impressive people I've always admired. Though you'd never guess it from her posh tones, Glenda Jackson was born here, as was cricket legend Ian Botham. James Bond himself Daniel Craig went to school here, as did the politician John Prescott, and our former Prime Minister Harold Wilson was head boy a long time ago at Wirral Grammar School for Boys.

Even closer to home, master baker Paul Hollywood is, like me, Wallasey born and bred, so to speak. Nigel Lythgoe, someone who, like me, has built a career on dance, was born just up the road from me. Years later, our paths would cross in LA, but that's a story for later. All the local people are incredibly proud of this impressive amount of homegrown talent, and they're right to be. It's not bad for a tiny peninsula about 15 miles long and 7 miles wide, tucked in between Wales and Liverpool.

From the topmost north corner of the Wirral, you can look across the Mersey and see north Liverpool gazing back at you. If the clouds part, you can see further up the coast to Southport. And if you're lucky enough to be there on a really clear day, you can see all the way to Blackpool. From where I was standing on my local beach as a child, it looked a million miles away. I had no idea then that it would become such a central place for so many of the most important events in my life.

For everyone living on the Wirral, the debate has long raged about whether or not we're allowed to call ourselves 'Scousers', and there are all sorts of old wives' tales to explain why we can't. Some say you have to be born within hearing distance of the old one o'clock gun down at Morpeth Dock, while others say you need to arrive in the world within sight of the Liver Building. That second one always confused me as, before the area got more built up, you used to be able to see the Liver Building from miles around, from spots far beyond the city, and easily from over here on the Wirral. But anyway, I'm happy to count myself an honorary Scouser if I'm allowed, even if my friends from over the water still think I'm a 'wool' – or 'woolyback', to give me my proper name. Historically, this was the name they gave to people coming in from out of town, although the origin of the word remains a bit vague. They were either delivering coal and wearing sheep fleeces, or working on the docks and ending up covered in wool after carrying bales around. Whatever the true story is, I'm very proud of all my connections with Liverpool, but to my bones I'm a Wallasey girl.

All the locals in Wallasey like to complain about living there, mostly about the weather and the wind coming in off the sea that can turn a 5-minute walk into a 20-minute battle, but the truth is that, of the thousands of people who live there, very few ever want to leave the place. And why would they? Wallasey is a beautiful spot, surrounded on every side by the sea and stunning, sandy beaches. Plus, it's a very close community, where people are either taking the rise out of each other, or promptly stepping in to help a neighbour.

I know people over in Liverpool think of us woolybacks as all quite posh. That's probably more true the further south you get, in towns like West Kirby and Heswall. Up here on the northern tip, it's a bit more mixed. New Brighton, where I started out, used to be 'the Blackpool of the Wirral' – with its beach, its pier, its open-air pool, it was one of the biggest holiday destinations of the northwest.

I was born at the Highfield Maternity Hospital in Wallasey, on 6 September 1960. My mother has always remembered me as 'that baby, the one making the noise', trying to stand up in my pram, pulling all the blankets off, screaming the place down.

My first home was my great-grandfather's nice house, and there were a lot of family members tucked up in it. My great-grandfather had originally owned a big dairy, which is where his children had all grown up. He'd later sold up and made quite a bit of money, before he moved and bought a fish and chip shop.

After my great-grandfather lost his wife, he didn't like living on his own so he moved back in with his son Frank, Frank's wife Daisy and their daughter Audrey – that's my mum.

Then my great-grandfather bought this big house at the top of the hill and that's where we all ended up. He had loads of room, so when my mother got married and my brother and I came along, it made sense for all of us to live there as well.

Daisy, my grandmother, had been brought up on a farm, and she was a great cook, while my grandfather Frank had previously trained as a cabinet-maker. Frank used to travel from his family dairy to her family farm to collect the milk, and that was how they originally met. I remember him as a very strict and stern man, while Daisy wouldn't say boo to a goose. But they were my grand-parents, and I spent the first three years of my life feeling secure and in the nest of a big family home. My mother was one of five children, so there were always plenty of people around me.

Plenty, except one ... You've probably noticed that I've not got round to mentioning my father just yet. That's because he was hardly there during those first years, and then, by the time I was two years old, he'd left us completely.

He was called George Andrew Rich, and everyone called him 'Andy'. My parents had met when my mum was a schoolgirl. He was a handsome young man who used to come by to deliver the school milk – fun, good-looking and just a few months older than my mum.

Later, they worked together on the buses, where my mum was a clippie and my dad was a conductor. Apparently, he cut a bit of a dash back in those days, jumping down the stairs, swinging around the pole and impressing everybody, or the young girls at least. My parents fell in love, got married, and before long, my brother David entered the world.

My father's mother was married twice and he had one sister and four half-sisters. His father was from Birkenhead, his mother from Secombe, and my mother always got on well with his side of the family, which proved to be a lot better than how well she got on with her actual husband.

They'd probably married far too young, and it was a very volatile relationship from the beginning. Apparently, he always liked a drink, and he also turned out to be that classic male combo – a man who was possessive with his wife, but also maintained his right to keep an eye out for other ladies. He'd disappear out for 'half an hour with the lads' and come back 'later' – sometimes hours, sometimes days, sometimes even weeks – drunk, tapping on the window, demanding to be let back in. He was just your classic two-bit, poor-effort husband. He wasn't really cut out for marriage or parenthood, even though he tried marriage four times in total and ended up with four children.

My parents were married for six years, although they only lived together for four. I was two years old when they went their separate ways. My mother never married again, although she's never been short of attention or company.

The whole time I was growing up, my mother never once slagged off my father to us, even though he gave her plenty of reason. Sunday after Sunday, he would tell her, 'I'm coming to pick up the children and take them out,' so she'd get us all ready, washed and ironed, brushed, suited and booted, and then we'd sit there all day, waiting for him to show up, listening out for every knock at the door, jumping up to the window to see if we could see him coming up the path, for hour upon hour. I can remember my brother and I would sit chatting while we waited, and then as the hours passed, we'd grow increasingly quiet, both nursing our disappointment. He wouldn't turn up, and then we wouldn't hear from him for another six months. Then, he'd turn up again out of the blue as though nothing had happened.

On one occasion he did turn up, my father gave us each a pound, and then the next day he took it back before he left. He used to tell us other times, 'Your Christmas present is in the mail,' but it never arrived. Each time, we got really excited until Christmas Day itself, and it was only at the end of the day that we'd finally give up hope of it somehow turning up.

One morning, my father turned up on our doorstep and announced, 'My mother has cooked you Sunday dinner.' We got excited, scrambled to get our best clothes on, then got in the car with him and drove to Secombe. All the way there we were buzzing with excitement – for us this was a proper treat – until we got to our grandmother's house, and it was instantly clear she had no idea we were coming.

She was a very nice woman, and when she saw our faces that day she did her best to patch something together for us. She ended up dividing her own meal into enough for three more people, and that meant I didn't get a roast potato on my plate. For some reason that has always stayed with me. Even then, I knew in my head it was only a potato, but somewhere in my heart, it seemed to sum up to me all my father's big empty promises. My strongest memory of my dad throughout those years is that sense of waiting, wanting and being promised something that never came.

He didn't give my mum much, if anything, towards child support, nor did he feel any sense of responsibility about making her life just a little bit easier, never offering her a break from looking after us, for example, so she could have a few hours to herself to put her feet up. He was just an irresponsible, selfish person.

In fact, sometimes, he could be downright nasty. I was very young when I once heard them have an argument, and this prompted him suddenly to say quietly, 'I wouldn't mind if two men kicked you to death.' As a young child, hearing my own father say this to my mother terrified me. It was a horribly violent thing to hear anyway, but, even by that young age, I had started to realise that my mum was my only lifeline, and for my father to threaten her made everything I knew feel really fragile. He may not have meant it at all, but I had no way of knowing whether my father's words could come true or not, but the thought of it scared me for a long time, and added to the sense of dread I started to feel whenever he turned up, never knowing what kind of mood he was going to be in. To my young mind, he started to carry with him an aura that was very sinister and threatening.

My father ran a pub in Secombe for a while, then the next we heard, he was off to live in Yorkshire, and from that day until now, he barely featured in our lives. During all those years, we received a few unexpected visits and phone calls, as unpredictable as ever, but apart from that, he completely abandoned us. These days, nearly six decades on from all the pain I felt, I wouldn't say he's a significant figure in my life, but we are cordial and, at the end of the day, he'll always be my dad. There's a lot of water under that bridge. Growing up, my heart was always a little sad whenever I heard other girls call out, 'Daddy', as I knew I would never experience that simple and secure feeling conveyed with just one word. I was never Daddy's Girl.

My closest, oldest friend Karen Hilton is one of the many girls I grew up with who has a great dad, and he's always treated her and her sister Cheryl so well that it taught Karen to expect that kind of treatment from every other man in her life. Karen was simply her dad's queen, and just by behaving so well towards her, so consistently, he taught her what to look for in a husband – trustworthiness, reliability, putting her first, all the important things.

Those were Karen's standards, they were always high, and fortunately, her wonderful husband Marcus met those standards, and they have been very happy together in nearly 40 years of marriage. In contrast, my lack of a strong paternal figure meant my standards in men were always a bit shaky. My mother always tried to fulfil the role as best she could, to be a mother, a father and a friend to me, everything I needed, but it was hard. I felt my brother also needed my dad, but he just wasn't there. I ask myself if we'd have been better off if he'd just disappeared completely, instead of being like a flickering light bulb that you couldn't rely on. It was his unpredictability and the empty promises of love that shook me up and had such a long-term effect on my sense of self and well-being.

By the time my dad left, my mother was used to looking after her children on her own and getting on with things by herself, so she didn't miss his support at home. Instead, I think the whole experience of his behaviour and then his departure made her determined to be extremely independent. After we were born and she went back to work, the list of her jobs became legendary. She worked in a teashop, a restaurant, a greengrocer's and a sweet shop. She got herself a job in an office for a wholesale chemist, and for a while she worked in the department store Lewis's in the city. Later on, she earned herself some extra money in the evening working behind the bar at the Melody Inn Club, a local nightclub, ten minutes on the bus from our home, and also waiting tables at Finnegan's Steak House. If there was one thing my mother learned as a result of her short, not entirely sweet marriage, it was to never rely on anybody else for money. She instilled in me from an early age that nothing in life comes for free, that you earn your own money, you ask for nothing and you make sure you owe nothing in return.

My mother was determined to do it all herself, to give us everything she possibly could and to fill the gap left by my father's absence. She became increasingly strong over the years, and she was also fortunate to be armed with a brilliant sense of humour that got her through many a tough time. My mother isn't the gushy sort, she didn't used to share her emotions as I was growing up and she doesn't do it now, but she amazed me then and she still does. She was simply born with resilient bones, and I will feel forever blessed and fortunate she passed them on to me. From where did we inherit them? Well, funny you should ask . . .

• • •

One of the many wonderful things to come out of my joining *Strictly Come Dancing* was that I was invited to take part in *Who Do You Think You Are?* – the BBC genealogy series that takes a different celebrity each episode and traces their family tree. I'd never really known much about my ancestors; I'd only heard the kind of family rumours that everyone hears, such as that my great-grandmother Clara was a real party girl who had abandoned her family, and that there might be some black heritage somewhere along my father's line. Digging into my family history, I was quite nervous as I really didn't know what to expect. Back when I was growing up, my father had always given the impression there was some ominous family secret that nobody wanted to talk about, and so I was anxious that I might accidentally unearth something awful. The producers warned me that the process could be surprisingly emotional, digging up all the ancient family stories, but when they said that, I just gave them one of my looks. I'm made of tough northern stock, and it was going to take more than a few old photographs to get my bottom lip trembling. Little did I know how strongly what I discovered would affect me.

First, we went up my mother's side of the family tree. It was her grandmother Clara who everyone said was a party girl, and there was talk that she'd abandoned her three young children, flown the coop and disappeared to try her luck in America. I'd always heard this story when I was growing up, and I had wondered about her a lot, where she disappeared to, and why. I'd also heard that she'd asked her daughter Daisy, my grandmother, to go overseas with her, but that Daisy didn't want to go. As part of the TV programme, I found some pictures of a young Daisy looking sad, and that upset me just for starters. Apparently my grandmother was very shy and nervous as a child, which chimed with my memories of her in later years. There was also talk that Clara's husband George had died of a broken heart, which is a bit hard to imagine in this day and age, although who's to say? Could someone be so heartbroken that their immune system fails them, or they stop taking proper care of themselves? I think there's actually a lot we don't know about the human heart and all its strengths and weaknesses.

I'd always found my family's version of Clara's story astonishing, particularly after I became a mother myself. From that moment, I could never imagine for one minute being able to head off for a new life and leave my little boy behind. It just seemed unthinkable. Well, as with all things, the truth turned out be a little more complicated.

Yes, Clara *was* married to my great-grandfather George Sutton, and she *was* very outgoing – apparently she was fond of a trip to the local pub, which probably raised a few eyebrows back in those days. It's a shame she was judged so harshly for being a woman true to herself, but she was clearly born a bit ahead of her time.

What the historians on the programme helped me discover was that Clara appeared on the local census of 1911, along with her children, but there was no sign of her husband George. Instead, that same census found him in hospital in Liverpool, already very ill with cancer. We also found his will, in which he left all his money and worldly goods to his mother Elizabeth, and nothing to his wife Clara. There was no mention of Clara, so they'd clearly separated at this point. He died five years later aged only 36, leaving all those children, including my poor grandmother Daisy who was only nine at the time, in the care of his mother. It seemed that, from then on, Clara just disappeared from our family history, apart from all the stories and rumours about her that got passed down to me.

Personally, I don't think Clara was the party girl she was always made out to be. I think she probably realised that she wouldn't be able to provide for her children, especially now she was a single woman and at a time when there was no welfare state, and she probably judged that they'd have a better chance of a good life if they stayed with their grandmother. How must she have felt, giving them up? I just couldn't imagine it. What we found out made me think very differently about Clara. The more I discovered about her, the deeper the connection I began to feel with her – more than I could ever have imagined. I was just sorry that I'd grown up with such a wrong impression of her, and carried it around with me all my life.

It turned out Clara did make that trip to the US with her second husband, Arthur Spiddle. They settled in Boston and adopted a small girl called Dorothy.

Life went terribly wrong for Clara, though. In 1928, she filed for divorce, which back then was very badly thought of, and her affidavit made for grim reading. My voice actually broke as I had to read it out loud on camera. Soon after their marriage, Arthur Spiddle 'drank spirituous liquors to excess and on many occasions threatened the libellant [that was Clara] with bodily violence, put her in fear of her life, said that a married man had a perfect right to be improperly intimate with a woman not his wife, and that by reason of this constant ill-treatment the libellant has been forced to seek medical treatment'. I could just imagine the scenario, and the despair she must have felt.

Fortunately, Clara got the divorce, which in those days would have been very difficult, and she also secured custody of her daughter, before her story took an even sadder twist.

The historian Fern Riddell helped me find more records that revealed Clara died in an institution that had the initials N.H.S.H., which stood for 'New Hampshire State Hospital'. By now, I was starting to fear the way this story was going. Fern had to very gently explain to me that NHSH was a psychiatric hospital, and that Clara spent the last 17 years of her life there, before dying of syphilis. The syphilis she caught from her husband, and I learned that if it goes untreated, it can appear in the patient as dementia, causing you to lose your mind as much as your body. I could barely believe what I was reading. I completely forgot the cameras were still rolling, and just sat there. I couldn't even speak.

My heart ached for my great-grandmother and all that she had to go through. My only consolation was knowing that somewhere along the way, she'd adopted Dorothy and kept hold of her, proving she still had a huge amount of love to give, but, oh my goodness, how she must have suffered.

What was so sad about finding all this out was my knowing that none of her family had the remotest idea, and we'd spent years talking about 'party girl Clara'. She was never the party girl that just abandoned her family, she was somebody quite different entirely, and she deserved all our love and respect.

There were even more surprising revelations on my father's side of the family. His background had all been a bit vague for me, but what little he had said on the subject had always convinced me there was something I wasn't being told. There were a few family whispers, though, that I had black ancestry, so I was very curious to find out the truth about my roots.

For the programme, I phoned up my father, but he refused to help me. All he said was, 'Let sleeping dogs lie', which made me think there was definitely something worth uncovering, but also made me feel very nervous. Instead, I went to visit his sister, my Aunty Barbara, and she showed me a lovely picture of my grandparents, Nelly and George Rich. George was a very hardworking man, a stoker who used to shovel coal. He spent time in the Royal Navy and also fought as a boxer, so he was very fit.

His father, my great-grandfather, also called George Rich, was born in Cape Town in South Africa. He came over to Great Britain, where he met his wife Elizabeth, and they settled in Birkenhead, Cheshire.

To continue researching this part of my history, I flew off to Cape Town, where I spent some time walking the streets, imagining that I was retracing the footsteps of my ancestors. I'd visited the city previously, but it had never occurred to me for one minute that my own heritage would be found there.

I started this part of my journey at the National Library of South Africa in the centre of Cape Town, where I discovered the biggest surprise of all: George's birth certificate revealed he'd been born to John and Mary Elizabeth Rich, and he was baptised in a local Anglican church. The city was a British colony in those days, so it was very common for people to join in Anglican worship.

Then I learned that my great-grandfather George had a sister called Caroline, and when we got hold of her death certificate, there was an even bigger surprise waiting for me. Two words jumped off the page – 'Mixed race'.

I couldn't believe my eyes. I'd always heard the family rumours, but it was still absolutely mind-boggling to see it in print. That meant Caroline had one white parent, one black, which meant so did her brother George

I followed the trail back in time, all the way to another Caroline. She was my 4x great-grandmother and had had three of her children baptised on the same day in 1850. A local Christian missionary reported that he had converted the whole family from their original religion. Sure enough, when I found this Caroline's parents on the register, the writing was very faint on the old paper, but another surprising word jumped out at me, and that was 'Malay'.

In nineteenth-century Cape Town, 'Malay' was a catch-all term for people from Indonesia, India and other parts of Africa. And 'Malay' didn't just mean 'not white'. It also meant Muslim.

In Cape Town, the poorest of the poor were often Muslim, and I also discovered from local records that Caroline had been a hardworking washerwoman, based in Bo-Kaap, home to the city's Muslim community for more than 300 years. This is a very popular part of the city and when I visited, I could see why, with its colourful houses all painted in lime green, yellow, sky blue and lipstick pink. Five times a day, you can still hear the call to prayer from the minarets of the seven mosques in the area. Bo-Kaap has a life all of its own, and I could well imagine my ancient ancestor working night and day with her laundry, typical of a Malay profession back then.

Cape Town's Malay traditionally originated from slaves, mainly from Indonesia, Malaysia and West and East Africa, including Madagascar, where Caroline was born. It is very possible that her parents arrived as slaves, and she could likely have been born into slavery herself. She was just one of a long line of strong, tireless women in my family, striving to get money and to survive. My heart was heavy for her tremendous workload, and her history of slavery. But I was proud of her, and she left me inspired.

The discovery of all this family history so late in my life was pretty overwhelming for me. The fact that little Shirley Rich from the Wirral had a Muslim great-great-great grandmother, and my 4x great-grandmother was even born into slavery, well, it just showed me how small the world really is. I felt sad that life was so tough for both Clara on my mum's side and Caroline and *her* mother on my father's side, but they clearly had a lot of spirit about them, and the will to survive and make the most of it. Without them, there'd be no ME.

I will always be grateful for the chance I had to find out all this information about my family tree. And of course, just as for everyone else who takes part in that TV show, for me there were tears, there was pain and a tremendous amount of heartache. At the same time, I felt a huge amount of pride in the history of my family.

It gave me insight into where I might have got my own survival instinct, as a child growing up in tough circumstances. I feel fortunate that I've got this from both sides of my family, and I like to think I've taken a little piece of each and every one of my ancestors and carried them with me all the way through my life.

• • •

One of the first big changes in my life came when my great-grand-father announced he was going to get married again, to a woman called Dorothy. She had been married before and several of her husbands had died. When my great-grandfather met her, the next thing he told his family was that he was selling the house, which meant it was time for the rest of us to move.

This was crunch time for my mother, having to decide whether to move in with other members of her family, or try her luck on her own. While she was still working it all out, she went to stay with a friend of hers and I went with her. My brother David stayed with the rest of the family as he had to go to school nearby. David fretted more than me at our parting. He always needed to be with my mother, while I was a bit more independent.

My grandparents Daisy and Frank moved down the road to Ellesmere Port, a coastal town, with a port, funnily enough, orig-inally built because of its position where the River Mersey met the Ellesmere Canal. Technically, it's in Cheshire, but to every local and visitor alike, it has always been better known as one of the doorways to the Wirral. We used to visit my grandparents often, and they invited my mother and her children to move in with them, but my mother realised that if she didn't make the break from her own mother at that point, she might never do it, and so we were off ... down the road to the Leasowe housing estate. It wasn't what my mother had asked for, it was just what she was given, and it already had a reputation for being a bit rough around the edges, but I think my mother was ready to move and be properly independent from her parents.

David was four and I was two when we moved to the estate. They used to say that once you got on to that estate, you never got off it, and sure enough, we soon met people who had been there all their lives. You go to school there, it's where the shops are; it's a tight, closed community with its own unwritten rules and codes. There's a comfort and familiarity that comes with living on that estate, but also the sense that everyone who crosses your path already knows your business. My mother's always been a very private person and I know at first she found it hard to adjust.

There's a wariness, maybe even a suspicion too, for any outsiders, which was how we were regarded, even though we were really only from down the road. Initially, David got very badly bullied because they said he wasn't from that area, and that caused my mother years later to say she regretted bringing us up there. To this day, though, she still lives around the corner on the edge of that same estate, and she's also made dear lifelong friends there, so some good always comes with the bad.

Each council flat came in a block of nine. There were blocks everywhere, surrounded by houses, and the blocks were almost identical – towering, forlorn slabs against the sky, everywhere you looked. In each of the blocks, you'd walk up concrete steps between all the floors – no lifts anywhere – and each of the floors had three flats in a row. Our flat was in the middle.

Once you walked into the flat through the front door our tiny narrow hallway led straight through into a tiny kitchen. We didn't have any heating, nor was there any washing machine, fridge or phone. I remember we managed to get ourselves an Osocool, one of those little mobile fridges you still sometimes see these days on campsites. It didn't have any electric power, it was just a metal box covered in plaster of Paris with a sort of well at the top. You poured water in the well and it kept the rest of the box cool, so you could keep your butter from going soft. It was all battered up and beaten out of shape when we got hold of it, but as far as we were concerned, we thought we'd won the pools!

Next to the tiny kitchen was our lounge. It had a great big window where we could gaze out over a good deal of the housing estate. There were two bedrooms, one for my mother, one for David and me, although most of the time I slept in with my mum. Going to the bathroom was like venturing out on an Arctic expedition. The only outdoor space we had was the coal shed we shared with the other residents on our floor, and we used the coal for our tiny fire in the lounge; it was the only heating we had in the flat, and we loved that fire. We would huddle around it to watch TV, play games and just share time together as a family.

I always remember the flat being very cold, apart from this one tiny warm spot by the fire, but one thing I can say for our home, it was flawlessly clean and neat as a pin, because my mother wouldn't settle for anything less. I can remember walking home with my friends and we'd spot her hanging out of the window, standing on the ledge and leaning right across to clean the glass from the outside. My friends thought she was bonkers, but she just couldn't stand to see any marks on those windows. It was the same on the inside of the flat. She'd polish our tiles so thoroughly that if you walked across them in your socks, you'd risk slipping and breaking your neck. There's something to be said for living in a small home – it makes you compact, disciplined, always tidy. It wouldn't have mattered where she lived, my mother has always had the highest standards when it comes to keeping order, making everything immaculate and running a tight ship. Our flat was small but spotless.

When David and I wanted to go and play outside, we'd go to the big lawn out front that my mother could see from her big lounge window. That's where all our friends would congregate, play marbles or just hang out with our friends from the estate – people like Danny McGarry, who was one of my best friends and very first love, and Susan Barrell.

For years we coveted the council houses opposite our block. They came with three bedrooms, one bathroom, a separate dining room, a kitchen, a lounge and a long hallway. From where we were sitting, we'd stare across enviously and think, 'They're just great.' Then, a few years later, we actually got the opportunity to move into one that was right opposite our flat, which promised a massive, massive upgrade for my family. We still didn't have a washing machine or a fridge, but guess what – we actually got ourselves a phone, and it was bright red.

The day we moved in was a glorious occasion, and a lifelong lesson for me in appreciating even the tiniest improvements in your life. If getting our little Osocool fridge had felt like winning the pools, moving into our house was like winning the rollover lottery!

We certainly knew as a family that we didn't have much, but what we had we took care of and, comfortingly, everybody else on the estate was in the same boat. Nobody had much, but what they had they shared in times of need. Everybody used electric meters – you'd put coins in to feed 'the leccy' which meant, quite simply, if you had no money you had no power. Often, you could be watching something on the TV, and the picture would suddenly disappear until you found some more coins from somewhere to go and feed the meter. Fortunately, there was always somebody nearby with a spare coin. There was a proper sense of community all around us. People often went to each other's homes to spend time together, have a cuppa – everyone loved tea on that estate – and a biscuit. If you were fortunate enough, you could go to Sayers and get a cake, which was something I always looked forward to with my mother and brother. My mother always chose the strawberry tart, while for my brother it was always the chocolate éclair.

Although we didn't have holidays, we had lots of Sundays out at the baths, either in Derby or New Brighton. My mum would always pack us a sandwich, but when we got there, I would go around chatting to all the other families. They asked me, 'Where's your mum?' 'She's over there.' 'Where's your dad?' 'He's dead and gone to heaven.' As a young child, my father was so completely out of my life by then, it sort of made sense to say that instead of trying to explain. Of course, everyone felt sorry for me and I'd return to my own family armed with lots of food.

We were rich in so many ways when it came to the important things in life, the sharing and caring of others, everyone rallying around in times of need. Times were definitely tough for the three of us, as they were for many families on the estate. My mother, like many parents around her, had no choice but to go to work. It wasn't uncommon for women on the estate to make a bit of extra money by babysitting, handing out leaflets, all sorts of little jobs, anything to bring in some extra cash to keep us children clothed and fed. The women I knew all had this in common, doing their best to provide for their families. Nobody was competing, what you don't have you don't miss, and nobody knew any different.

I asked my mother years later why she never went to her own parents, or possibly her grandfather, to ask for some assistance from them, some money to help pay the bills, because I always thought they were reasonably well off, and owned their own homes. I never felt that anyone asked my mother if she was okay, or if she needed any help paying her bills – not that she would have accepted any help from them, mind you, she was far too independent-spirited for that. She just told me, 'I didn't want to owe anybody anything,' but for me, it always seemed we were very much on our own. My mother's attitude for as long as I've known her was to work hard, earn your own way, and if you give something to somebody, don't expect anything in return.

I remember my mother being deeply excited when she got a job at the local nightclub, the Melody Inn. She loved it there. She was good at her job as a barmaid, she got to know lots of people, and this is where she met the lady who would become her very, very best friend, Mavis, who I got to know as my Aunty Mavis. She soon became like a second mother to me. She still lives around the corner from my mother, and is in both of our lives on a daily basis. Mavis's partner at the time was a man called Steve Butterworth, and in turn he became my 'Uncle Steve'. He often stepped in to help us – for example, when my mother needed help speaking to my brother. Years later, Steve came down to London to help decorate my house, he even lived with us for a while, and I can say hand on heart, he never, ever once let me down. He was there for me until the day he died, one of the few truly reliable men in my life.

With our mother away at work day and night, David and I were left more often than not on our own in the flat. We were only four or five years old, but we never had somebody sitting with us at home. Instead a series of people popped in to check on us when they could, but for the rest of the time, we were left to our own devices.

Our front door was made of wood, with smoked glass for the top third. Every day throughout those years, somebody would come knocking, while David and I were there on our own, and it always scared us, not knowing who it was or what they were after. We'd run to hide in a corner, and peer up at the top of the door, where we would see the dark silhouette of an unknown figure on the other side of the glass. It was always terrifying, not knowing whether it was a friend, someone we could trust, someone my mother owed money to, or worse.

On the evenings my mother had to work at the Melody Inn, a lady from the next-door flat, Mrs Dewey, started coming in to sit with David and me. I liked Mrs Dewey a lot – she was a keen seamstress, and she used to like making tiny clothes for all my dolls and even my teddy. These days, almost six decades later, he's still in the same outfit she made for him all those years ago!

Mrs Dewey didn't have a TV herself, so she loved coming in to sit with us. She would bring with her a big bag of sweets, and David and I would fight over them because sweets were few and far between back then. She watched TV while we fought. Then she'd tuck us up in bed, leave and lock the front door behind her. She lived on one side of us; Dot Barrell, my friend Susan's mother, lived on the other, and much later in the evening, long after Mrs Dewey had left, it was Dot who used to come in to check we were still safely tucked up and that everything was okay in the flat, because we were still extremely young.

Many years after this period, long after I moved away, I would suffer with terrible nightmares and wake up screaming and crying, with hot sweats. It frequently happened and it went on for years, long after I had married and become a mother. I used to fear the dark, and always slept with a light on. Wherever I went in the world, regardless of whether I was in my own house or staying somewhere else, I never slept in complete darkness. I was too afraid of this recurring vision of a dark figure hanging over me, someone in a big black cloak looming at me out of the shadows, and I never understood where it came from. This fear meant I was deprived of many, many nights of sleep because I'd wake up in horror, and then sit trembling, trying to work out exactly what it was that I was so frightened of. It lasted for years and years of my life and it was paralysing. I still sleep with the lights on somewhere to this day.

It was only when I eventually sought counselling that I discovered what it was. With the help of my counsellor, I had to go back through my life, until I finally I realised what that shadow had been.

When Dot Barrell came in to check we were both safely tucked up and asleep, I would be semi-conscious and hear these footsteps coming into our flat. I didn't want to open my eyes, so instead I used to freeze in terror, praying for the footsteps to go away. All those years of nightmares, and it was just my friendly neighbour leaning over me to check I was okay! It wasn't the devil, it wasn't any bad thing, it was actually an angel, and as soon as I realised, I never had the nightmares, the tremors or sweats again. It was banished from my body and my system forever, but not before it had gone on for years.

School was Birkett Primary, a hop, skip and a jump from our house on the estate, barely a hundred yards from our front door. I loved going to school. I loved to learn and to be around other people, and I tried extremely hard. For me it was a place to apply myself, but I always felt my brother saw it more as a place of surviving as best he could. He showed signs early on of being a very intelligent young man, but the problem was that, because he suffered from being bullied by people on our estate, he just didn't apply himself.

Although, looking back, we had a lot less money than most of the other children, at the time it didn't bother me. As far as I was concerned, our house was always super-clean, my mother was always organised and we had neat, tidy clothes, so there was nothing for me to be embarrassed about. It meant I went to school suited, booted and ready for the day while I sensed my brother was always a bit more sensitive to any criticisms about our financial situation.

Every school child of that era got a school dinner plus half a pint of milk, but as a single-parent family, we qualified for free school lunches even during the holidays. We'd go in just for the meal, while all the other kids who had dads and decent money coming into their homes didn't qualify, so instead they lined up at the gate to poke fun at us. I didn't mind, but obviously my brother did. He would feel embarrassed about standing in line for the lunch, he didn't want to go in for the free food, but me, well,

I worked out exactly which part of the queue to stand in to make sure I got the biggest amount on my plate. I figured out that if you stood near the end, they were trying to get rid of the food, so you got a bigger helping. I loved my food!

Some of the other kids outside would scream, 'You're on the welfare.' I didn't understand why people would laugh at us for getting a free meal, but I was never going to give those kids the satisfaction of making me feel bad. Instead, I used to shout back at them, 'I'm getting a hot dinner. You're getting a cheese butty. Who's winning here?'

My brother David was a very beautiful child. He was good-looking with skin that was like porcelain and, as I say, incredibly bright. I think that if we'd lived anywhere else in the country, things would have worked out differently for him. Instead, growing up on the housing estate, he had to learn to fend for himself from a very young age, and I think that the estate kind of swallowed him up. By the time he was a teenager, he had transformed himself and learned survival skills that made him appear tougher. Again, this made me think that, for David, it wasn't about living on the estate, it was about surviving it one way or another. He quickly became known as a king on the estate, and thus was nicknamed Kola. Nobody crossed my brother. I think they all knew he had a purpose in life and that was to work for the underdog. This was his payback for the years he had been bullied as a small child, and I felt he became a person who was there for other people going through the same thing. His best friend Phil was just one of many people David taught how to stick up for himself.

I was always a little bit nervous of my brother. With my mother so often out at work, he became one of my main carers when I was very young. He was only 18 months older than me, but sometimes he seemed a lot older. If I was ever out of the house past six o'clock or if I was hanging out on the school field and he spotted me, I'd get extremely nervous of him tearing me off a strip, and I would run home. What I only realised later was that he didn't want me hanging out on the estate and being drawn into anything that might turn into something bad, because he knew a lot more about what went on across the estate than I did. His priority was my safety, and that meant he'd do anything to stop me loitering on street corners. At the time, I thought he was a pain in the butt, but when I look back, I realise he did me the greatest favour. He knew the kinds of things that went on around us, what people got up to when they were left to their own devices, and he wanted something better for me. Family was everything to him, he only wanted the absolute best for me, even if sometimes he terrified the living daylights out of me.

I moved up to St George's Middle School, which has the impressive claim to fame of being the first building in the country to be solar-controlled. One of my favourite subjects there was English, where I was always quite good at writing, not spelling. I loved home economics, where I especially enjoyed learning how to crochet my own blankets. I also enjoyed cookery classes, which will be strange to read for anyone who knows me, because these days, I can barely boil an egg, but at the time I loved it. Maths ... well, not very good, but I can add up my own money; what more do you need? History and geography weren't really my thing, but I could always lay things out beautifully with nice handwriting, and my mother would help me with drawings. I always wanted my work to look the best, as I was already competitive even then. If I didn't get an A for a project, I would sulk. I was always pushing myself to be better, and often that meant working to be put up a band in school, where I always started out somewhere in the middle. Whatever it was, I did to my best ability, and I was encouraged by my mother in everything I did. Despite our lack of funds, she was determined I should have a go at anything and everything I fancied, which meant she took me off to tap and ballet when I was as young as two. Then I got to try tennis and swimming, the Brownies, volunteering for the Red Cross, even chess! Anything that was going I wanted to be part of, things like the school choir, the school drama club, although when it came to the latter I would sulk if I wasn't given the main role. I was always the one putting my hand up the highest to volunteer. My hand would stay up so long that often I'd have to hold it up with the other one because I would get tired.

My mother taught me to have good table manners, to conduct myself correctly, to remember to say please and thank you on every occasion. Soon she felt I was picking up a real Leasowe twang in my voice, and she decided she wanted to send me to elocution lessons, so off I went. The lessons were in Moreton Cross, where I walked to on Saturday mornings for an hour's lesson every week, something my mother considered a good investment. This probably accounts for why, these days, I speak with an accent somewhere between Leasowe and 'posh', depending on whose company I'm in. I still remember the poem I had to remember for my lessons – it was called 'The Fly' by Walter de la Mare. I had to recite it for an exam, which I took at the Bluecoat Chambers in Liverpool. I've never forgotten how my knees knocked as I walked into that huge place, full of what seemed like hundreds of other children taking exams, all of them very well-to-do compared with me. Then, when I started to say my poem, my voice trembled, and the nice lady said, 'Take a deep breath, darling, start again,' so I did and once I felt comfortable, I was able to reel off my poem without any mistakes. I left with a Highly Commended mark, one of my first ever exams. Although I was nervous, I wanted to do well for my mother, who had paid for the whole thing. Even then, I had the feeling I wanted to make it worth her while and ensure I gave her something back in return.

Years later, my mother took me to Harrods and we were walking around the shoe department along with lots of other genteel folk. I shouted across to her in a loud voice, 'Come over here, our mother, let's have a look at these shoes.' I did it in my strongest Liverpool accent, and she visibly shuddered. She looked horrified, and just muttered, 'All that good money wasted.'

Whatever I tried my hand at even in those early days, one thing was always clear: I needed to win. It wasn't even against other children, it was all about achieving milestones for myself, and I set high standards. It didn't matter what it was I was doing, it could have been chess, tennis, Brownies or playing marbles. Even when my brother and I were peeling the vegetables for lunch, I had to be the quickest person who'd ever peeled a carrot. I wanted my mother to tell me I was the best person to ever peel a carrot. Whatever it was, I had to come out on top.

The times I didn't win, I always started crying and getting extremely upset which, probably to my mother at the time, made me look like a brat. But actually, I was just trying to make her proud of me, just trying to be the best version of myself, and if that didn't happen, I'd properly beat myself up. I'd tell myself, 'You're a let-down, you're a disappointment, you're not good enough.'

I always wanted to shine in my mother's eyes particularly, and if I thought I'd let her down, that was the worst feeling in the world for me. She had sacrificed so much, and I couldn't bear the thought of being a disappointment. Sometimes she had tough times with my brother, and I didn't want to be an extra burden. There were times when I would hear her crying and I'd go into her bedroom and she would be upset about something. It could have been something to do with my brother or someone else in the family, but whatever it was, she would berate herself and tell me, 'I don't know if I'm doing a good enough job,' so it was important to me that she felt she was doing all the right things.

She held a birthday party for me once in the flat. After all the games, there was a singing competition with a prize for the best singer. My mother was the judge but she didn't pick me to win; instead she chose my friend Susan Barrell, and I had an absolute fit. I managed to completely spoil the birthday party, and I'm very embarrassed now, but at the time I believed I was the best, and I couldn't understand why my mother hadn't picked me. I can still feel those hurt feelings today that she didn't choose me, even though, remembering it as an adult, it's obvious why she didn't. I couldn't win at everything, and I probably couldn't even sing!

One day, I brought home my school report and the teacher had written, 'I'm so frustrated with Shirley. She cannot accept critisism in any shape or form.' Well, although my mother probably agreed with her, for the first time in my life, but by no means the last, she stuck up for me in her own subtle way. She signed the report to say she'd read it, but she also corrected the teacher's spelling of 'criticism' while she was about it.

With all those activities in my life, how would I know when I found my passion, the one thing that would carry me and offer a place to put all that focus and effort? I truly believe that we all have in us one thing that we don't just *want* to do, but we *need* to do, and if we have the good fortune to find it, we truly are blessed.

I also think we look for things, but actually, they find us. We can search and search, but then one day, something great finds us. We have to recognise that we've found it, then follow our instincts to pursue it, nurture it, water it like a flower, and in return it will reward us, pay us back tenfold, and enhance our lives in ways we couldn't even imagine.

So how did I find mine? Well, as I say, in truth it found me. I was seven years old when I went off to the church hall as normal for my weekly Brownies meeting. I was hanging about in one of the smaller rooms, and I think I might have even been learning how to do CPR, when I heard the sound of music playing, and it became harder and harder to concentrate on what the Brownies mistress was telling us. Standing there in my uniform, the music overtook my whole body. The beat of the music got into my ears and it felt like it was overwhelming me. Where was the music playing? Who was playing it? And could I join in? It was such an enchanting feeling that I was compelled to follow a path to wherever the music was coming from.

I can remember the whole thing as if it were yesterday. I slowly walked over to the adjoining room in the church hall. The door was closed but it had a glass top, so I heaved myself up to look through the window, and there I saw it – the most beautiful sight that I'd ever laid my eyes on in my whole life. It was a dance class.

Couples were moving around on the floor in what looked to me like perfect poetry in motion, but which I later discovered was actually a dance class for beginners. It looked magical and I decided there and then that I needed to be part of that world. Of course, they were all grown-ups and I was seven years old at the time, but somehow that didn't stop me. I stood by the side of the room, gazing at everyone, and then a gentleman wandered over to me and asked, 'Can I help you?'

As though it were the most natural thing in the world, I replied, 'Do you have classes like this for children? I want to come and join the class.' I remember feeling very anxious, but also excited for this chance to embrace something I knew nothing about.

And in one of those life-changing moments, the man said, 'Well, funnily enough, we have a brand new children's class starting on Saturday.'

In that one moment, I knew I had to take part in those classes. Was it fate? Was it a chosen direction for me? Was it something that was meant to be? I'll never know. All I knew was that, from the very first note that I'd heard there at Brownies, that dance music had got hold of my soul and wasn't going to let it go. It seemed I'd found my calling at last, not something I wanted to do, but rather something I had to do. And just like that, I found my thing.

CHAPTER 2
The Cha-Cha-Cha

'A teasing, chase-me type of dance with cheeky, saucy moves. It's a very flirtatious, fun, happy dance, but it requires a deceptively strong technique.'

My first ever dance was the Cha-Cha-Cha, to the tune of 'Wheels'. I swiftly followed this with a Waltz to the tune of 'Moon River'. When I stepped out onto the dance floor aged seven, I knew I had found something that I uniquely loved to do, that I could completely lose myself in, that I wanted to do more than anything else in my life. From the very first notes of that very first Cha-Cha-Cha, I never really wanted to be anywhere else.

There were lots of children in the class, more girls than boys, naturally, which meant I was often paired up with a girl. The classes cost 15 pence an hour and they immediately became my favourite hour of the whole week.

My mother has always said I was a natural performer, ever since I was sitting in my pram Cha-Cha-Cha-ing, screeching and squealing. As a child, I was always the first to get up onstage and start singing, running around, and drawing attention to myself. And with dance I found a way of losing myself inside the music and movement. From the very first class I took, I found I had an innate way of moving to music. It took over my soul. I went along with it like I was a fish in the ocean and my heart definitely belonged in dance. I felt a sense of total unity with the music.

One of the favourite moments of my entire childhood came when I was given my first pair of dance shoes. This was a really big deal, as I knew my mother had scrimped and scraped to afford them, and I didn't want to let them out of my sight. I carried them wherever I went, even to the bathroom, and never left them anywhere, as I was nervous about them getting stolen. I knew if I lost them, I wouldn't be getting another pair. I was lucky that, at this point, Mrs Dewey from next door transferred her sewing attentions from my teddy to me. She made me a beautiful dress for my first medal test, and my mother invited her along to watch. It was beautiful, white with chiffon sleeves, and I felt like a million dollars walking out for my exam wearing it. She also gave me a gold-cross necklace for good luck, and I've kept it with me to this day.

My first dance teachers were Vic Knox and his wife May, along with their assistants, Frank and his wife Lil. Frank was always extremely complimentary towards my dancing, as was his wife. He told me I was a natural dancer, whatever 'natural' means. I felt instantly comfortable and had a natural instinct for moving to music, as though somehow I knew the steps before I was shown them.

For a child practising Ballroom dance, there's nothing sensual about it, there's no intimacy between couples, that all comes later. It's more like pure movement to music, innocent and magical. You're learning all the different characters of the dance. For a child like me, an eager exhibitionist, it was hugely fun, learning how to coordinate my arms and legs, making sure my head was pointing in the right direction, remembering to smile and learning all the different routines.

Studying all the different techniques appealed to my sense of thoroughness and competitiveness. I wanted to get everything just right, so all the hours of the week I wasn't at school, I'd be practising in my room, in the kitchen where my mother was trying to cook or in front of the TV while my brother was trying to watch. From that very young age, it was all I ever really wanted to do. I wouldn't say it came easily to me, but nothing ever has. Instead, I loved it so much that I was prepared to put in all the hours, day and night, whatever it took, to be the best that I could possibly be.

I can say, hand on heart, that nothing else ever distracted me. I didn't listen to pop music, I didn't go to youth clubs and I stopped hanging out on the estate, much to my brother's delight. So my life consisted of dance, then school work and chores, in that order. I had a school friend called Lesley Burrell who helped me tremendously. She used to say, 'If I can help you with your schoolwork while you go off and dance, let me know.' We had similar handwriting so the teachers never guessed.

Ballroom dancing was massive back then, for adults obviously but also for children. On the TV, *Come Dancing* was the only thing I watched religiously, once a week. The show had been running for nearly two decades when I started tuning in, and was still incredibly popular. I used to love watching Peggy Spencer. I remember she always showed such commitment to the art of dance, and she had a beautiful voice. She was famous for her formation teams, and they were a sight to behold.

I'd sit and watch *Come Dancing* without blinking, and then go into school the next day and try to get the other children in the playground to copy the routines I'd watched and memorised. I would run around arranging people into teams, organising them and trying to create my very own Penge formation team. Then I'd be the judge! The children who weren't involved in my antics would stand around making fun of me. They tried to make me feel bad, but I didn't care. I was in my own little bubble, and all I wanted was to see my formation team in the playground doing as I told them. The seeds of my future career were being sown. Was I looking to be something special? Hmmm, perhaps, but at this point I didn't know what that something was.

I realised even then why those children were irritated by me putting my formation teams together in the playground. This was a kid from the estate, she had free school dinners, then her mother sent her for elocution lessons and she started talking posh, now she'd started making her own dance formation teams ... I'd started talking differently, now I was moving differently. Let's face it, I was a show-off, and they weren't having it.

'Who do you think you are?', 'You come from the housing estate', 'You haven't got a dad', 'Crawl back under your rock where you came from' ... That was what I heard all day. That's why when people are mean to me on social media these days I'm a *little* bit resilient to it. What they don't realise is, by the time I was ten years old, I'd heard it all – language, bullying, nasty comments, the lot.

By the time I'd changed schools and gone up to St George's Middle School, I probably had more enemies than friends. One time in PE, I was trying to do the high jump when I fell and hurt my foot. I got taken off to hospital, and it turned out I'd broken it. For a dancer, breaking your foot is a disaster. I started fretting: would it heal? Would it affect my future? Would I still be able to dance? So I was already worrying a lot by the time they put me in plaster and sent me home on some crutches. The next day, I was hobbling around at school when one girl came up to me. She was smiling and I thought she was going to be a bit sympathetic, but instead, she said, 'That's it. That's the end of your dancing. You'll never be able to dance again. Your foot's going to fall off.' Of course, I believed her and as a result had lots of sleepless nights until my foot was properly better. It was only when I finally put it back in my dance shoe that I was reassured it was going to be okay, but there were lots of tears and drama for my mother to deal with until that point.

On another occasion, the same girl who was always making fun of me didn't bother to insult me verbally. This time she just beat me up. She came from Moreton, from a much posher house than mine, and she was a bit of a ringleader at school. I wasn't the only one she picked on, but I knew she had it in for me. One day, I had a feeling she was waiting for me somewhere outside, in the field between the school and my home. Sure enough, I was in cookery class when one of my friends told me, 'She's gathering people in the field. I think she's planning to beat in your brains.'

Cookery was the last lesson of the day, and I can remember trying to hang about in the classroom as long as I could, tidying up, offering to help the teacher, too scared to leave, until the teacher finally said, 'Shirley, you really do have to go home.' Well, it turned out I was right to be scared. As I approached the field, I could see this huddle of lots of people. Then this girl decided to jump out at me and start beating the holy living shit out of me, leaving me with bruises and great patches where she'd pulled the hair out of my head. She was a much bigger girl than me, but I tried to defend myself as best I could, and in the end, I managed to give her a good wallop back. There were lots of kids shouting, 'Fight, fight, fight.' We were eventually separated by a parent who'd spotted us, and I came out with a huge black eye. I was always a bit scared of going to school after that, and the fight instilled in me the fear that bad things can happen very quickly out of nothing.

Looking back, I think people around me were just bored. There always seemed to be drama and trouble in our neighbourhood, lots of the kids already smoking from a young age, often stealing their parents' cigarettes. Even I, old goody two shoes, nicked my mum's money once or twice, and let's face it, she had little enough money that she pretty soon noticed when it was gone. I used to go to church every Sunday and, one time, she gave me money for the church collection and I went off and spent it on sweets. That time, my mum got the preacher down to our house and I got a proper telling-off, which put a swift end to my life of crime. Plus, there were all the usual trips to the sweet shop, where half the kids were trying to steal the sweets, and the other half were spies paid for by the shopkeeper to keep an eye out. I wasn't really a bad kid, but just by association, you could find yourself getting into trouble.

For the most part, though, I was saved from all of that by dance, and also by my brother keeping an eye out. He loved it that I danced, that I'd found something that might one day get me off the estate and away. If he came across me anywhere I wasn't meant to be, he'd shout at me, 'Get yourself home. You're going to be a dancer. You're going to get off this estate and make something of yourself.' At the time, I thought he was being a bit of a bully, but of course I realise now he did me the most wonderful favour. David always wanted more for me than he did for himself, and when I did make something of myself, there was no one prouder. He didn't have a jealous bone in his body. He came to as many events as he could to watch me dance, and he'd always tell his mates on the estate about his sister winning a competition, while they stood listening, standing there in their leather jackets and bovver boots.

My mum always gives herself a hard time, even now, wondering if she did enough for us. Sure, we didn't get to go on big holidays like some of the other kids, nor did we have a chest freezer full of food like my school friend Hazel Cook's mum – I admit I was always a bit jealous of that! – but she gave me something far more important. Through her own example of working hard for an honest day's pay, she gave me the tools that got me where I am today. She gave me my work ethic, and that is more valuable than any chest freezer or a trip to Wales.

As I got more heavily involved in dancing, my mother took on more and more jobs for extra money to help me with my private lessons, dresses and shoes. There were people around asking her, 'Why are you giving her all this?', 'What are you doing?', 'What are you throwing away your money for?', 'She'll never amount to anything. It's a waste.' But my mother always said, 'What else can I do? You have to back your children. As long as she walks that distance to the church hall in the rain or the snow, as long as she shows that desire and commitment, I'm going to keep her busy, I'm going to help her.' She said afterwards, 'I did take a big chance, looking back on it, but I got lucky. I backed the right horse.'

My mother would always point out to me, 'I know you must really love your dance lessons, Shirley. You make excuses to get out of everything else, chores, school lessons, everything, but never your dancing.'

So that was how she knew it was something really special to me, and why she supported me like that. And in return, my determination to do right by her and not let her down, as well as learning from her the importance of hard work, meant I did carry on making that journey to class, come rain or shine. To save money, I often walked instead of taking the bus, carrying my little red case that contained my shoes, clutching it close to me at all times, always paranoid I was going to leave it somewhere.

I used to watch my mother work an extra shift, counting her money, and I knew she was constantly calculating in her head, 'How can I get that new dancing dress for Shirley? What does David need? How can I make it all work?'

It made me determined to pay my own way as soon as possible, so I followed my mum's example and picked up some odd jobs wherever I could. When I was about 11 years old, I started washing hair in a salon for a couple of pounds on a Saturday – the lady who owned it also used to give me free fish and chips for lunch – and I got some odd shifts at Finnegan's Steak House in Hoylake where my mum worked, waiting tables, cleaning up, whatever they needed. I was willing to do anything and everything for pocket money until, hopefully, one day I would get a break in my dancing.

What did I think a big break looked like? What was I actually dreaming of? And how was I going to get there? Well, at the church hall lessons, I'd been paired with another little girl called Irene

Hamilton, and we'd started taking part in dance competitions, just small local events, where we usually came in third or so in the under-10s. This was where I first met my lifelong friend Karen Hilton, because she always used to beat us with her sister Cheryl.

It was very rare that Irene and I got first place, but occasionally, when no one else turned up, we did, and that had started giving me hope that people might notice me. My mother was immensely proud in her own way, but she never gushed. Even when she watched me dance she tried to give me constructive criticism, never praise, that was just her way, so I guess even though I'd found my passion, I was still looking for approval wherever I could. That was really all my big dream consisted of at that point, just a big bucket of praise and approval.

Irene's parents were keen dancers, too, taking part in all the local social classes. Her family had a fridge but, more importantly, a car, and her mum and dad, both keen dancers themselves, loved it when Irene and I started to compete. They began to take us to competitions a little bit further afield, places like Butlin's Minehead and Butlin's Bangor. We visited many different Butlin's camps.

Irene and I were trained by Vic and May Knox in the church hall, as were her parents, but, although the dancing was a wonderful part of my life, it was a very adult environment for little girls taking their first steps into the world. For this reason, my mother jumped into action and, along with Irene's parents, they decided to move us away from the church hall and into Liverpool, where they found Margaret Redmond's studio.

Irene and I danced for a while under Margaret's tutelage. This meant moving from a social dance teacher to a competitive teacher, a whole new ball game. Margaret taught Latin dancing to the best couples in the north of England, and Irene and I were both so very, very excited. Her studio was in Crosby, a nice leafy spot on the northwest side of Liverpool, along the coast towards Southport, so to get there, I had to rely on Irene's parents to give me a lift.

After several months under Margaret's supervision, she could see the talent that we girls had, and she suggested to Irene's parents that we should both get little boy partners. Irene and I enjoyed dancing with each other so much, having a real laugh, that the prospect of not dancing together was a little bit intimidating at first. But then we got the offer of two boys, so we went for the try-out.

One of the boys was called David Fleet, one of Margaret's most experienced boy dancers. He had the full backing of his parents, and I know that Irene's parents hoped that David would pick Irene. They talked about nothing else in the car on the way there, and it was clear they had him in their sights for their daughter.

Shortly after the try-out, we got a phone call from Margaret to say that David had picked me. This was pretty unexpected. I had nothing, Irene had all the resources, the helpful parents, the car, but the best boy picked me. And that was it. Irene's parents were more than upset and, understandably, the outcome of it was no more lifts for me. I had to start finding my own way to Margaret's studio and back.

The prospect of me travelling all the way from Leasowe to Crosby was daunting. It was something my mother had to take her time thinking about, her 12-year-old daughter finding her own way there and back, sometimes at night and on weekends. There was no one to take me. My mother couldn't, and no one else in our family stepped up. It was down to me, and only me. I wanted to dance more than I wanted anything else in my life. I never stopped to think of the risk of travelling in the dark. My mother was concerned, but I didn't let up: 'I want to do it. Please let me do it, Mummy.' I was on at her constantly, until in the end she gave in. We just had to get organised to make it all work.

My trips to Margaret's were like a military exercise. I used to walk from our house to the bus stop, catch the bus to Leasowe train station, hop on the train to Liverpool Central, get off the train, run across the city to Ribble bus station on the other side of the town, make sure I got the right bus from about 30 buses all sitting there, then get on the Ribble bus to Crosby. It took about two hours in total.

The worst bit was coming back home in the dark, when I used to run from the Ribble bus station in the pitch-black to get to the train station in time. As I ran down the streets, I can remember the sweat pouring down my back, being alone running in the dark, full of anxiety, heart pounding. At that time, with no internet or social media, you didn't hear all the millions of bad stories the way you do nowadays, but I was instinctively nervous and vigilant of everyone around me on the buses and trains. I was 12, and I wouldn't dream of letting a 12-year-old travel on their own like this nowadays, but back then, the idea of missing a lesson with Margaret was unthinkable, so I just did what needed to be done.

It was required of a dance student back in those days that you learned all ten dances, five Latin, five Ballroom. The Latin set comprised the Cha-Cha-Cha, the Samba, the Rumba, the Paso Doble and the Jive. The Ballroom set was made up of the Waltz, the Tango, the Viennese Waltz, the Foxtrot and the Quickstep.

In those days, you could specialise in Latin, you could specialise in Ballroom, or you could dance all ten dances. These days, the last group are called the 10-Dancers, they're not total experts in any one section but they're very fit and versatile. Then you get the specialists, those dancers who've gone up the ranks in either Ballroom or Latin. There have been hardly any world champions in both styles, as they require very different skills. How do you choose Latin or Ballroom? You don't, it chooses you. You naturally start getting better in one field or the other, your results become consistently better, you go up the rankings, and the other one falls away. Either Latin or Ballroom chooses you, and that's it for life. At this point, I had no idea which way I would end up going, although at the beginning, I was probably leaning towards Ballroom. The ten dances were a lot to learn, but I loved them all in different ways.

As David and I struck up our partnership under Margaret's expert eye, my mother grew increasingly concerned with all my travel, particularly as the winter months set in, and I was going all that way in the dark. She spoke to David's mother, and it was agreed that I would get the bus there on a Friday, and then stay over with his family. We would practise on the Friday night, have a lesson on the Saturday, enter a competition on the Sunday, then I'd somehow find my way back to Wallasey in the evening, just in time to fall into bed and go back to school the following morning. I never knew on Sundays how I would be getting home that evening, and it was at times like this I felt so keenly the absence of a father who would have made it his business to get me home safely.

Margaret was an extremely popular teacher, with a huge number of pupils. Part of her regime was that we all had to compete on a Sunday, whether these events were close by or far away. She frequently had to hire a coach, with 52 of her young students filling up all the seats. On the way there, we'd all do our own makeup and our own hair. The girls would help each other occasionally to put little slides in our hair and things like that, but make no mistake, we were all out to win. We each had the same goal, and it felt like the ultra-competitive bus.

From the moment we set off, I had the additional but familiar worry of trying to work out how I was going to get home, and the further we went from home, the more panicky I felt. Fortunately, at least I knew there were lots of other people looking out for me. As well as Margaret keeping her eye on me, two couples, Zoe and Charles, and another pair, also called Frank and Lil – all under the tutelage of Margaret – always went out of their way to make sure I got home safely.

Margaret was a woman of great authority. She was the best teacher I could have had at that age, and from her I very quickly learned a lot about the quality of dance and, equally importantly, how to behave in the ballroom.

As well as the education she gave me in the advanced techniques of dance that enabled me to improve my dancing very quickly, she taught me a lot about being competitive. She showed me how to dress professionally, how to do my hair and my tan. She was tireless in and out of the dance studio. With her unique teaching ability, she took me from being a medallist to becoming an advanced junior dancer, and she made it clear she believed in my talent, which at that age is everything. She instilled in me a lot of hope for my future.

What made Margaret so special was she had time for each and every one of her students, working out what made them tick, what they needed, so she could get the best out of them. It was her attention to detail, not only in dance, but in every aspect of her life, that I watched and tried to copy for myself. I loved spending time with her talking about everything, but her biggest passion of all was always dancing.

Although I've had many lessons all over the world in the years since, I can say hand on heart that Margaret was instrumental in helping me become the dancer I am. What a woman, and what a stroke of luck that she came into my life when she did. Things could have been very different for me, otherwise, and I carry her biggest lesson with me to this day. She told me at our very first lesson, all those years ago now, 'Listen carefully to the music, Shirley. Learn your technique. Marry the two together and perform from your heart.'

Through all these years, the different places I've lived, the jobs I've had, Margaret has remained in my life. People all around continue to tell her it's time she put her feet up, but she's still hard at work. To this day, she continues to teach, and the new generations of young dancers are just as lucky to have her as I was.

David Fleet's parents were also very good to me. It was completely the norm for dance partners to stay at each other's houses, so they opened their doors to me, but they were also very kind and always went the extra mile. I used to bunk down in his older sister Irene's room and we'd gossip away into the night and talk about dancing.

It was an eye-opener, learning to dance with a male partner after all those years pairing up with Irene. David was very experienced, and much better than me when we started. He'd been extensively trained throughout his career, so dancing with him was like dancing with a prince, and I started rapidly improving. I was like a sponge, absorbing lessons and knowledge from everyone around me.

When I moved to Margaret's studio, I started having some clothes specially made by her mother, who was a wonderful seamstress. One day, my mother told me that she'd saved up enough money for me to splash out on a brand new beautiful ball dress. It was absolutely beautiful, pink with flower buds, all stuffed with cotton wool, then painted and sewn on by hand, just stunning.

Then David's sister Irene made the nice gesture of helping me to pay for some rhinestones to add to the dress, which helped give it lots more bling. From then on, whenever I wore that dress, I felt incredibly special and princess-like and I'm glad I got to enjoy that feeling – at least, while it lasted, which wasn't very long.

• • •

I danced with David for two years in total, and we did fairly well together. The highest we ever achieved was a fourth place in the north of England junior Ballroom finals, and the semi-final of the junior Latin Championships. These finals took place in the Tower Ballroom at Blackpool, a venue very familiar to me long before it became such an important part of *Strictly Come Dancing*. That was where I'd always gone to see all my absolute heroes on the dance floor, people like Marcus Hilton (who later married my best friend Karen) and Janet Wild. There were so many amazing children on the scene back then, and now I got to join in with them.

David was lucky enough to have the benefit of more money for dance lessons than I was used to. His family was able to afford separate Ballroom and Latin lessons for him. I couldn't even think about that, although I was always very grateful that Margaret used to make her lessons with me stretch just that little bit further.

I know it is possible to become a great dancer without ever taking one private lesson, as long as you have the discipline to do it. Years ago, when Russia was behind the Iron Curtain, they had no teachers and all their dancers learned their craft from videos. Later, when the Berlin Wall came down, some of the best dancers in the world came from Russia and they were dazzling. However, when you're starting out on your path as a dancer, lessons with a good teacher can inspire a lot of confidence, and the amount of hours we could get was very important to us.

So yes, David and I were doing quite well, but, even back then, I had a longing to do better than just 'quite well'. When I was 14, I came across the Lunts, a big dancing family from Liverpool. I got on with all of them, including their son Neil. He was older than me, but we were fond of each other, in fact I adored him and he was actually one of my very first kisses. One day, he told me, 'My whole family thinks you've got more talent than you're showing, and we believe you have great potential. I know someone you'd be good with, and he's looking for a partner. He's the ex-junior British Ballroom champion and his name is Nigel Tiffany.'

Straight away, my ears pricked up. Ever since the day I started out, I've always followed the rule: 'Surround yourself with people better than you so you can learn from them.' And Nigel Tiffany was certainly that. As soon as Neil mentioned him, it flashed through my mind, 'I want to be more than I am, and this is a true champion,' so of course I said yes to the try-out without even thinking or first conferring with my mother.

A try-out in the dance world is a funny thing. It's the industry equivalent of a blind date, where each partner gets to size up the other and see if they like what they see. One of the partners is generally more experienced and more in demand, so they'll no doubt be the one that gets to decide whether a partnership will happen. Plus, it's always under the supervision of a dance teacher or coach, also looking intently on, checking for the level of chemistry between the couple, or for any potential pitfalls. It's basically like introducing two pandas in a zoo to see if they'll mate – except you're the panda and you're doing the Cha-Cha-Cha.

I was a student of Margaret Redmond's, and Nigel was one of the star pupils of a rival studio run by George and Pat Coad. He'd been dancing with a girl called Kim Bygate, and they'd done very well, making it all the way to becoming British champions, which for juniors was basically like being crowned world champions, because there wasn't anything bigger. As far as I was concerned, he was in the big league, and now he was looking for a new partner.

When I asked my mum about the try-out, she was quick to point out the problems – we had no transport, no resources, it was a long way between our house and Nigel's home in Shipley, West Yorkshire, so was there really any point in even starting out on this path? But Neil Lunt was insistent on making it happen. He said, 'Why don't you go for the try-out and see what happens?' He even offered to pick up both my mother and myself and drive us all the way to the session at George and Pat's studio in Maghull, on the other side of Liverpool.

I walked up what seemed like a hundred stairs with my mother, and caught my first glimpse of Nigel. He was a few years older than me, stick-thin and looked like a proper Ballroom dancer. I was struck by the way he held himself, the turn of his head, everything.

His parents were with him, as well as his coach, George Coad. None of them knew me, and I was very nervous. Nigel had won every trophy there was to win, and there I was, a complete nobody with one fourth-place ranking to my name. But he was friendly, smiley and gentlemanly, and dressed properly in a suit, shirt and tie. That showed me he was treating the try-out with a lot of respect and it gave me some confidence. Also, I noticed he had a very kind face.

George put on a Waltz and started teaching us as a group. Immediately, I realised I was dancing at a whole new level. As Nigel took my right hand to hold, I felt the security of his beautiful body, his straight posture, his soft but powerful frame. It was like falling into the arms of a Rolls-Royce. As he took me into our first natural turn, he gave us such a swing that I tripped over my own shoes and nearly fell over. It was astonishing, that first time I had the chance to dance with someone so good, someone truly brilliant at his trade. He had a great ear for music too. Every beat of any music has three parts, and usually dancers opt to move somewhere in the middle, but Nigel seemed to have so much time he could leave every move until the final part of the beat. He just made the whole thing feel effortless, and I was in awe of him.

While I was busy being swept away, my mother was sitting outside, busy being not remotely carried away with the romance of it all. Instead, she was spelling out our situation in alarmingly clear terms, telling Nigel's parents exactly what we could and couldn't afford in the way of lessons, transport, costumes and competitions.

There was a huge disparity in how much we could each manage. Nigel had a Ballroom teacher as well as a Latin teacher, so me pairing up with him presented quite an intimidating prospect for my mother and her chequebook. I had to feel for her! Here she was, seeing that I was having the dance of my life, but having to weigh up wanting to fulfil her daughter's dream with the reality of life. It must have been very hard for her, and eventually she told them she could afford one private lesson a week, a few trips here and there, but that was definitely the sum of it.

When Nigel and I finished our dance, he seemed as keen as I was to give it a go, so he persuaded his parents to help out as much as they could, and before my mother and I had got back in Neil's car, the deal was done.

It also meant saying goodbye to David, which wasn't an easy conversation at all. He was really upset, his parents were very cross with me, and his sister Irene was furious. She was so mad with me, she asked me to hand over my lovely pink Ballroom dress that she'd helped create. When I got it back, I discovered she'd removed all the rhinestones we'd spent hours putting on. It was the only dance dress I had, so I had to keep wearing it, complete with all the glue stains where those lovely gems had once been.

In my heart, I felt very grateful to David's family and it was hard for me to move forward like this, but in my head, I knew I was searching for something greater in life, and my instincts told me I was taking the right path towards it.

My part of the new deal with Nigel was to travel every weekend to his home in Shipley. If I thought I'd been making an effort to get to Margaret Redmond's studio in Crosby, my journey to Shipley was like a polar expedition. Back on the bus from home to the station in Leasowe, the train to Liverpool, a second train to Manchester, then a third train to Shipley, where one of Nigel's parents would meet me off the train.

Once I got there, it was the same routine that I'd had with David. Practice on the Friday night, a lesson on the Saturday, travel to a competition somewhere on the Sunday, then I'd begin to make my long way home. After only a few weeks of this, my mother and I realised that it just wasn't possible for me to spend such a huge amount of time travelling every weekend. I was exhausted by the time I got to Shipley, and started dreading that trip in both directions, fearing those long, dark hours on the trains and buses by myself. Before long, Nigel's parents came up to Wallasey to discuss the situation with my mother. They suggested I move into their home with them, which I would be sharing with Nigel, his two siblings plus their parents − six of us cooped up in their little council house on a hill.

I'd been doing quite well in school, staying on track for my O-levels, but my drive and passion for dance were far stronger than my enthusiasm for my education, so when it was suggested I move, I was desperate to pursue it. My mother was very worried about my schooling, but once again she could see that I was prepared to do anything to chase my dream. It was like I was being carried off on a wave, and my mum could see that.

Later, when I asked her why she'd been prepared to let me move away from home aged only 14, she remembered how hard it had been. She told me, 'You were just so fixed on it, and I didn't feel I could get in the way.' Plus, she admitted she didn't think I'd last long with it all, and secretly hoped I'd soon come back home.

My mother liked Nigel a lot – later on, she always said he was one of the nicest men she'd ever met, and she wasn't wrong. She also had long chats with his parents, she realised they were quite strict and ran a tight ship, so she knew I'd be in safe hands. She was just a bit worried about me changing school so close to my exams, and it turned out she was right to be. Off I went to Shipley, where I shared a bedroom with Nigel's sister Carol, while Nigel shared with his brother David.

Nigel and I were soon off competing all over the place – Coventry, Birmingham, London, Wales – as I swapped my seat on Margaret Redmond's bus for the passenger seat of Nigel's yellow Mini. There were hundreds of juniors in the north of England, all wanting to do well, so there were lots of competitions all over the north to keep us busy.

In the beginning, all went well. Nigel and I were slowly going up the rankings, and I seemed to fit in well with his family's routine. The only setback was my schooling. The move to Yorkshire played havoc with my education. I didn't know any of the faces in my new school and I couldn't seem to pick up the curriculum. Overnight, I went from being an average student to somebody struggling for the lowest of grades. Nigel was already working for the Bradford & Bingley building society and used to give me a lift every day to school. I started bunking off and sleeping all day in his yellow Mini instead of going to my classes. Well, unsurprisingly, I fell further and further behind, which I know was a huge source of worry to my mother. That was all a bit of a disaster, but all I could think about at the time was dance, dance, dance.

I missed my mum an awful lot. Very rarely, due to finances, she made the trip to Yorkshire to visit, and occasionally we met up at competitions if we got the chance, but really my world had come to revolve around Nigel and his family. My mother paid Nigel's family £5 a week for my keep and lodging, but his mother was pretty strict with me, and I never felt she was particularly keen on me. I realised at the time, though, that they were on a tight budget too, just like my own family.

I wanted to let Mum know I was okay, but Nigel's mother put a lock on the house telephone so I couldn't call home. I was so desperate to speak to my mum that I managed to figure out a way to get round that one. I used to wait until everyone was in bed, then I'd creep downstairs, unlock the phone with a hairclip and slowly dial the number for my mother's house so that nobody could hear me. I was petrified of being caught, but I was still only 14 years old, and I was desperate to hear my mum's voice and let her know I was alright. We always kept it very short and to the point, but it was enough just to hear her say hello down the phone line, and I found it very soothing. The whole time I was in Yorkshire, she remained my anchor.

• • •

When I reached the age of 16, I couldn't wait to leave school. I soon got a job as an office junior, making coffee and filing, opposite where Nigel worked, earning the princely sum of £16 a week. Soon after I started, the company boss suggested I went on day release to college to learn Pitman's shorthand and typing. I got through the first exams but I had to keep practising my typing to get my next certificate. Nigel's sister Carol was also studying secretarial skills, so she had her own typewriter at home, but Nigel's mother wouldn't let me practise on it. She told me in no uncertain terms, 'That's Carol's typewriter.'

Fortunately, Nigel had my back. We cut up all the letters of the alphabet into squares and laid them out on the floor like a typewriter keyboard, and I bashed away at them instead. Nigel even sat behind me, covering my eyes so I had to imagine where the keys were, and that's how I learned to touch-type. It might have been unconventional but it worked a treat. I passed my exams and I got my promotion.

I was quickly turning into a kind of Cinderella figure, though, getting different treatment from the rest of the family. Sunday night was bath night, when they filled up the tub with hot water. Everyone took their turn to have a bath in the same water, and I always seemed to go last, which meant the water was always black with filth by the time I got in. I used to sit in the bath, hugging my knees, hardly daring to move among all the muck.

My mum also gave me a spin-dryer so I could quickly sort out my washing for the week, but Nigel's mother wouldn't let me use it because of the price of electricity. To be fair to them, they were already saving every spare penny for Nigel's dancing and they had other children to provide for. My being there no doubt added a large burden and it was good of them to have me in the first place.

There was no doubt who the boss was in that house – little Mrs Tiffany, a tiny woman with her big, jet-black beehive hairdo. I was a bit terrified of her the whole time I was living with them. Nigel was always very diplomatic about the fact I didn't get on too well with his mother – he just said it was two big personalities in a small house!

Nigel and I used to have a laugh, though, and a little spark of attraction between us quickly grew into mutual devotion. When we weren't dancing, we'd go out together for trips across the moors, where we had our very first kiss. We started 'stepping out' together when I was aged 15, then by the time I was 16, we were completely in love and talking about getting married. Off to the moors we'd go, where we'd lie on the grass, holding hands, gazing up at the moon and planning our lives together. As well as being a good dancer, Nigel was sweet, polite, a few years older than me with a wise head on his shoulders. He always looked after me and I thought he was lovely.

We first got intimate together on a dance trip to Pontins – who said romance was dead? We weren't intending to tell his parents, but they accidentally found out when they unpacked his dance bag back at home, and out fell the condom wrapper. So embarrassing! They were furious with both of us, properly bent out of shape by the whole thing. They told me they planned to tell my mother, but I managed to get in first with a quick phone call to Wallasey. Unsurprisingly, my mother didn't bat an eyelid, checking quickly that I'd been 'sensible enough to use protection'. It takes more than that to shock her. With a few exceptions in my life, she's always remained as cool as a cucumber whenever I've had to break the news of my latest debacle!

Soon after that, Nigel's parents did accept us as a couple in love, but I never found it very easy to be with them. I'm not sure his mother ever really approved of me, which was fair enough. Nigel was his mother's golden boy, she would shower him with gifts and money, she thought the world of him. I'm sure, if she were honest, I was the opposite of the kind of girl she had in mind for him, so she probably wasn't the happiest mother in the world the day we announced our engagement.

It was the hot summer of 1976 and I was 16 when Nigel proposed to me, during another lovely day out on the moors. He presented me with a ring that he must have saved up for – £125, a huge sum back then – and it was a beautiful single solitaire. We celebrated with a little party at a restaurant for our family and friends, and that was it, our future looked certain. I look at the photos of us from that day now and realise I'm looking at the faces of two children – happy, but completely untouched by life. Was I in love? I was 16.

Before long, however, that familiar sensation started niggling away at me, the feeling that there must be more out there for me. Nigel and I were doing well, but not well enough for me. I was still in a rush, still hungry to do better. We travelled to Great Yarmouth for a dancing event, where we met a couple called Chris and Dawn Vickers. They'd recently moved down to London and were full of enthusiasm for the huge dance scene down there. I realised that was where we needed to be as well if we wanted to take our dancing to the next level. About a week later, I sat down with Nigel and said to him, 'Let's move to London.' What was I thinking?

I should add, this didn't come completely out of the blue. By this point, we were already travelling down there once a month for a private lesson with a brilliant teacher called Nina Hunt. The city was the mecca of the country's dancing world, and if we were going to take our careers seriously, I realised we needed to be down in London to train.

We planned to make our move south. Nigel's career was going a bit better than mine, so he had more to consider, but he put in a request at work for a transfer to London, still with the Bradford & Bingley, and he got lucky with one almost straight away. It got even better – his job in the south was a promotion and it would come with a rent-free flat, so that was a huge weight off our minds. Nigel had to wait a few weeks for his transfer, so in the October following our engagement, I went down ahead of him and rented a tiny room above The Nest restaurant in Norbury, south London, tucked in between Streatham and Croydon. Nigel drove me down south with my few bags, and then headed back to Shipley to complete his last few weeks of work up there, leaving me to find my way about. This was my very first home in London, and it wasn't exactly luxurious.

Well, actually, it was the opposite. For a start, you had to walk through the kitchen of the restaurant beneath to get to the stairs. Often when I came in late at night, I'd stumble across the rats that were always hovering around the bins, or I'd catch them pulling at the rubbish bags and gnawing on the leftovers. To this day, any smell of cooking grease takes me straight back to that time.

My room itself was beyond filthy, and full of cockroaches and other unspeakable things crawling around under the wallpaper.

I could hear them moving around when I tried to sleep at night and it made me freeze, scared they were going to somehow break through the wallpaper and climb up onto the bed.

The best thing about living above The Nest restaurant was what sat opposite it. Out of my window, I could see straight across the road to the Top of the Stairs dance studio, where I knew Mick and Lorna Stylianos ran one of the biggest teaching and social venues in the whole of London. Most evenings, I would sit at my window and watch great queues of people waiting to go inside. It was the time when the film *Saturday Night Fever* had just come out, so you can imagine what they were all wearing, and from where I was sitting, it all looked incredibly glam! I loved watching everyone from my perch at the window across the road, thinking, 'One of these days, I'll be able to afford to go in there myself and have a lesson with the legendary Mick Stylianos.'

While I was dreaming of more dancing, I was picking up some valuable life lessons during those first few weeks in London, including how to cook on a small budget. I went to the market at the end of the day when the prices came down, found out what meat was just on the turn so I could pick it up for a few pence, then I prepared everything in a pressure cooker so a little went a long way. My mum was also sending me what little spare cash she could to keep me going, plus some boxes of biscuits from Cadbury's, where she now worked. However, I knew I desperately needed to get a job if I was to stay in London and give our big plan a shot.

The city itself I found completely overwhelming. I was used to travelling everywhere on buses and trains, so getting to grips with the public transport in London wasn't a problem, but the crowds were a proper shock to my system. After my time in the quiet and peaceful Yorkshire Dales, all I could see were masses of people rushing everywhere, squashing on to tubes and buses, shouting at each other in loud voices and, wherever I went, there was the smell of people eating chips. I found the whole experience exhausting at first and was always quite relieved when I got back to my little room above The Nest.

It was several weeks before Nigel returned and we were off on the next step of our big adventure. Off we went in his yellow Mini to settle into the Bradford & Bingley flat in George Street, Croydon. After my little cockroach-infested room, this felt like a palace, the complete lap of luxury. The very first morning we woke up there, Nigel set off for his first day at his new job – he didn't have to go far as his new office was right underneath the flat. We'd figured out that, for our plan to work, I needed to get a job as soon as possible to pay my share of our dance lessons, plus our food and living costs. I was fast running out of money and knew it was up to me to fulfil my part of the bargain, otherwise we'd have to return back up north. That was unthinkable. My dream would be over before it had even begun.

So I was feeling pretty desperate as I got ready to present myself at the local Jobcentre, clutching my Pitman Grade 2 qualification in my hand. It was late afternoon when I got there; the lady behind the desk was clearly preparing to shut up shop for the day, and she was very abrupt. She quickly said she had no jobs that were suitable. When I asked what she did have, she said nothing for someone with my qualifications. I asked again, what did she have? She ummed and ahhed for a bit, looked me up and down, then finally mentioned one secretarial role for which she told me sternly I was underqualified. By now, I was feeling desperate. 'Send me anyway,' I said. 'No,' she said, but finally I was able to convince her to give me the address. I think she just wanted to go home.

Off I went to Parsons & Whittemore Lyddon Limited, pulp and paper merchants, where I was introduced to Simon Byrne, the gentleman needing a secretary. He invited me into his office for an interview, and my heart was pounding. I knew I was underqualified, but I also knew I couldn't go home without a job offer in my hand. We chatted for a while, during which time my lack of office experience became increasingly clear. He was polite enough, said they'd be in touch, but when he tried to say goodbye, I clutched at his sleeve. 'You don't understand how much I need a job,' I said, and he stared at me. I think for the first time, he could see how panic-stricken I was, and how much I needed him to take me on.

Well, the gods were smiling on me that day. Mr Byrne took pity on me, which is how I became one of the firm's four secretaries, and without doubt the most inept member of staff that had ever crossed his doorway. I earned £60 a week and shared a tiny office space with three other women, all twice my age, very experienced and all of whom thought it was disgraceful that I'd been given this job for which I was clearly underqualified. However, they soon became my reluctant lifesavers, showing me how to use a Golf typewriter and checking my spelling whenever I tried to type a letter. What was Eric Morecambe's famous line about his piano skills? 'I'm playing all the right notes, but not necessarily in the right order.' Well, that was what my typing was like, but where there is a will, there is a way.

Poor Mr Byrne ... he could never find any 'filing' I'd done for him, and when I tried to take shorthand while he dictated a letter, that was also a disaster, as I had to ask him to slow down. It would have been quicker for him to sit down and just type the bloody letter himself, but he never complained. I stayed there for six months in total, and it was probably the longest six months of all of their working lives. I could overhear all the other women's grumbles and complaints about me, but I chose to ignore them as I was so grateful to have the job. Mr Byrne never told me off, though, and I'll always be grateful he gave me a chance.

By now, Nigel and I were living hand to mouth in the flat, working hard, practising our dancing and trying to learn as much about the industry as we could. We took what few lessons we could afford because money was tight, and we were trying to make ends meet. I was 17, he was 20, and life felt tough in the financial sense, but otherwise pretty sweet – after all, we were engaged and in love. What more did we need?

And that was how things were when, six months after we'd moved to London, while I was sitting at my desk at Parsons & Whittemore Lyddon, typing away as usual, Nina Hunt telephoned. Nina was one of my two Latin dance teachers at the time. The other was the world-renowned Walter Laird, who quite literally wrote the book on the techniques of Latin dance – his Laird Technique still remains the benchmark for the training, testing and examining of every Latin student, from beginner to world champion. Nina was more of a specialist in choreography, so between the pair of them, Nigel and I were in very safe hands.

That day in my office, without any preamble, Nina cut straight to the chase: 'I have a question for you.'

To this day, I don't know why, but I stopped breathing from the moment she began talking. It was as though my subconscious had been waiting for this moment, and somewhere in my core, I knew that whatever Nina said next would prove to be of huge significance in my life.

'Do you want to get married and be a secretary for the rest of your life, or do you want to dance?'

I couldn't reply, but Nina kept speaking regardless, almost telling me off. 'Can you hear me, Shirley? Are you paying attention? Shirley! I have an opportunity for you!'

My heart began beating so loudly, I could hear it thumping in my ears. Nina Hunt operated at the highest levels of our industry, and I was shocked and surprised that she thought me special enough to even telephone, let alone to consider me 'for an opportunity'. I was struggling to breathe. I hadn't consciously ever been expecting this call, and yet ... had I?

Once again, as soon as Nina started speaking, I knew instinctively I was about to reach a very important fork in the road, so I tried desperately to calm myself down, to breathe normally and try to take in everything she was telling me.

I just said, 'I'm listening.'

She carried on: 'I have a prospect for you. He's ranked seventh in the world as a professional, Shirley! Not an amateur! He's not in the final but he's about to make it there. He's as ambitious as you are, and he's looking for a new partner. His name is Sammy Stopford.'

CHAPTER 3
The Tango

'A passionate dance portrayed by its musical signature, which is staccato and legato timing and requires a control over the body weight to show both foot and body speed. An exciting and explosive dance that still retains the contrast of a haughty Panther-like stealth.'

'Do you want to be engaged to Nigel and have that ordinary job, or do you want to be a real dancer and have a try-out with Sammy Stopford?'

That was the stark choice my teacher Nina Hunt gave me on the telephone that day, and it was clear she wasn't going to give me much more than a minute to think about it.

I could hear my heart beating loud in my chest, and I went so quiet that Nina thought I'd hung up. She shouted, 'Are you listening, Shirley?' I squeaked, 'Yes, Nina.'

What was I meant to say? Here I sat, 18 years old, living in London and engaged to a man I believed I loved, and now here I was, being asked to try out for a partnership with a man I'd never even met.

I had so many thoughts racing through my head, I asked Nina if I could have a think about it and call her back. She said bluntly, 'You have until the end of the day to make up your mind.'

She was about to hang up when she added, 'Oh, and whatever you do, don't tell Nigel.'

I was flummoxed by this whole turn of events. I immediately called my mother, who gave it to me straight. She already thought my young life was turning into a bit of a rollercoaster, and she told me to think long and hard. She pointed out, 'You have a reliable job. Are you going to give that up? You have a nice young man. What about him? And how on earth are you going to make a living as a dancer? You need to get a real job!'

I didn't know the answer to any of her questions. All I knew was that the prospect of being paired with one of the country's best dancers sounded too good to be true – which was why I called Nina back and told her I'd come along for the try-out.

Sammy Stopford was a big deal. I had never met him, I'd only ever seen him from a distance, but like everyone else in the dance business I knew all about him and his success. He was one of our industry's biggest characters.

Sammy was only four years older than me, but he'd already become very established as a professional. He was ranked seventh in the world as a professional Latin dancer, while I was a paltry 96th in the world as an amateur. If I were to partner up with him, it would mean me bypassing the normal amateur route for 16- to 18-year-olds and going straight into professional competition. This was unheard of in our industry, and just one of the factors that made this idea of Nina's such a daunting prospect.

Sammy was also a hugely successful teacher, drawing the best dancers in the north of England to him like a magnet. His studio was massive and already producing some great success stories. He was a man in demand and, more importantly for me, going places, and those places were in Latin dancing, my first true love.

Meanwhile, Nigel and I were doing okay in dance competitions, getting reasonably good results, but never becoming champions.

Of course, we were still engaged and got on very well together. I struggled with myself, as I felt I was still in love with Nigel, and now here was Nina pressuring me to make a decision about our future in just a few hours. My relationship with Nigel explained Nina's final instruction to me on the phone that day when I called her back, 'The try-out's tomorrow. It might not work, so I say to you again, don't say anything to Nigel.'

Too late! I was so excited, I could barely speak to Nina, and by the time I went home that night, I'd realised that whatever happened with Sammy, Nigel and I couldn't dance together anymore – we were just going in different directions. It was time for me to roll the dice and take a big gamble on my future.

I wanted to be honest with Nigel and tell him the truth about the call from Nina, and what I'd agree to do. When I got home, he was ironing, and I said I had something to tell him. He carried on ironing and said, 'Okay, tell me.' I asked him to sit down and when he finally saw that I had something serious to say, he did. I told him about the try-out but I was quick to add, 'I still want to be with you. I love you. I just want to have the chance to do Latin, and that means dancing with someone like Sammy.'

Nigel was always incredibly reasonable and mild-mannered, it was one of the reasons I always felt so relaxed with him, but on this occasion, he instantly became furious and upset. In no uncertain terms, he made it clear he didn't want me to go to the try-out, even though I tried desperately to explain how much I loved Latin and this could be my opportunity of a lifetime. He wasn't having it and instead gave me an ultimatum that shocked me.

'If you go to that try-out, you may as well leave right now,' he said. 'If you go along and meet Sammy, our engagement goes too.' Just like that, it was all over between us.

I couldn't believe what was happening. It was pitch-black outside and I had no idea where I was going to go. There was no rhyme or reason to it. I was giving up my life with the man I loved on the basis of one phone call from Nina Hunt. Now it seemed that, whether I succeeded at the try-out or not, my whole life was about to change either way. I acted purely on instinct, based on the fact I was prepared to give up anything for this opportunity.

With tears pouring down my face, I put all my clothes into a pair of black sacks, while Nigel stood and watched me. There was a lot of shouting on both sides, but the decision was made. It was horrible seeing Nigel so upset and I hated hurting him and seeing all that pain on his face. I had no idea if I was doing the right thing. I had a longing for something else in my life, and it felt as though this might be the doorway to it. I was always searching, and it brought me constant turmoil.

I had nowhere else to go, so I had to phone Nina – she was equally furious that I'd told Nigel about the try-out as she'd known this was exactly what might happen, but she took it upon herself to find me somewhere to stay, and that's how I ended up lodging that night with another girl, called Denise Weavers, and her grandma. Denise was already well established as a world top-ten amateur dance champion while I was a nobody, and that night she found herself sitting down with a stranger she'd never met, doing her best to console me over my traumatic split from Nigel. I felt awful, full of pain and doubt about what I was doing. Denise and I bonded that night in the most unexpected of circumstances, and she is still one of my best friends to this day.

The following afternoon, I went by tube to Nina's studio in Balham for the try-out. Sammy was there with his teacher, Bob Dale, and it turned out they'd driven down from Manchester in Sammy's pea-green Volvo car. Sammy had loads of jewellery gleaming around his neck. I had no jewellery to speak of and I certainly didn't own a car, so my 18-year-old self was quite taken with all of this, but Sammy instantly terrified me, and I couldn't hide the fact that I had started to shake to my bones. I was also feeling very distracted when I met them because, just as I was walking into the studio, I'd spotted Nigel outside. He'd turned up and was standing over on the other side of the road, trying to find out what was going on. The whole scenario was more than I felt I could cope with. A big part of me wanted to run over to Nigel and ask him to take me back, while another part wanted to jump on a train and run back to Wallasey. But there was a third part of me that said, 'Go into the studio and meet Sammy' and, on that particular day, it was that part that won.

Sammy had told Nina he needed a partner – 'a girl who's in the top six, either professional or amateur, someone of similar level as me, someone who's hungry for it.' He actually had another couple of girls in mind, but Nina was like a dog with a bone, and that bone was Shirley Rich. When she had first suggested me, Sammy had scoffed, 'Shirley who?' – he was convinced this was a huge waste of everyone's time. Eventually, he had agreed to the try-out, if only to keep Nina happy. He was holding no illusions it would work out, though, and he didn't seem very impressed as we said hello for the first time and shook hands. He even told me, 'I don't know who you are or where you're from. You've only got this try-out because Nina thinks you might be a good fit for me.'

I was already feeling pretty inadequate when I walked in, and Sammy's first comments made me feel totally worthless. It was clear he knew he was a big cheese with his choice of girls at that point, many of whom would have twisted my right arm off to be where I was. His manner and reputation were equally intimidating as we prepared to dance the Rumba. I could feel my hand sweating as I put it in his and more beads of perspiration trickling down my back. My legs suddenly became so heavy under me; I was worried I wouldn't be able to move them, let alone dance. The only thing that propelled me forward was remembering how much I'd already given up just to be here with him, and I was determined to give it my best shot.

I moved towards him, gave him my hand, took two back basic steps to start and ... 'I'll take her,' said Sammy.

How did he know so instantly? By then, Sammy had had hundreds of girls and boys pass through his studio, so he could weigh up people's strengths and weaknesses with a glance. He realised I was the right weight for him, the right height for him, the right partner for him, literally in less time than it's taken me to write this sentence.

He could have cast me aside equally quickly. Instead, he said, 'Pack your bags, dear, you're coming with me.'

• • •

Just like that my life was forever altered! My head was spinning with the speed of it all and I felt extremely confused. I couldn't comprehend what had just happened. I was emotionally torn apart – on the one hand, thrilled by the prospect of this larger-than-life character considering me worthy of being his partner, and on the other, terrified by the thought of leaving behind everything I knew.

All this time, I was aware of poor Nigel sitting outside in his yellow Mini. I was in this studio with a stranger wanting to take me up to Manchester, and it was as though I was having an out-of-body experience and looking down on somebody else's life. I realised that, if I accepted this offer, my life would change irrevocably, but I didn't really get the opportunity to dwell on it. No one ever asked me, 'What do you think?' or 'How do you feel about all of this?' I had no idea where I was going to live or what any of this new plan looked like. All these things were running through my mind, as well as the fact that the man I loved was sitting outside, waiting to see if this try-out was a failure.

It wasn't an easy decision to just leap into the unknown but, in Nina's studio that day with all the grown-ups standing around making plans, it seemed as though the decision was being made for me. Nina was queen bee, a teacher at the very top of the industry, while Sammy seemed stubborn and very sure of himself. I didn't know him from Adam, I just knew he was super-strict and even a bit scary. I was the only one quaking in my boots and wondering what exactly just happened.

Whatever love was for a teenager, Nigel was it for me. We'd met when I was 15, we'd danced together, made love to each other, moved to London, struggled together, and now here I was – about to give all that up, and for what? I had no idea. All I knew was that if I went through with Sammy's plan, I was going to break Nigel's heart and mine as well. I knew I was chasing my dancing dream, but I was already feeling the huge personal cost.

In contrast to me, Sammy seemed to know exactly what he was doing. First, he took me round to Denise Weaver's to pick up my belongings, my whole life squeezed into those four black plastic sacks. Then we went over to my office at Parsons & Whittemore Lyddon so I could hand in my notice. I'd expected I'd have to work a few more weeks for them but, to my surprise, they let me pack up my box and leave that same afternoon. Simon Byrne said, 'You go, darling. You go and be that dancer I believe you can be.' At the time, I was so grateful and thought how sweet he was in letting me go, but years later I realised how happy he must have been to see the back of the worst secretary he'd ever had in his life. In fact, they all gathered to wave me off!

I got back in Sammy's car and set out for my new life, my completely unknown new life with Sammy Stopford. My dream had always been to live in London, and here I was heading back up to Manchester, the city I'd been informed was my new location. I was about to set up in a new home, with new people. I had absolutely no idea what to expect. The further away from London we went, the more my heart was torn apart. I felt heavy with sadness for Nigel all the way there, but I knew somehow I'd sealed my own fate.

The first day I met him, we stayed with a friend of his, and Sammy and I shared a room from that very first night. He seemed to make every decision for the pair of us, and in an instant I'd somehow become both his dancing partner and everything else that went with it. Back in the day, without exception, everybody seemed to have a relationship with his or her dance partner, and it seemed as though Sammy and I were going to be no different.

Who was I to question Sammy Stopford? He made every decision regarding my life, and one of his first decisions was that he and I would be a couple. Looking back, I was a real baby to be in that situation, but what do you know when you're young?

Back in Manchester, my new home turned out to be a strange and over-cluttered house that Sammy shared with a friend of his, Bob, and several other young men, all male dancers intent on making it to the top. There was a lot of testosterone in that house, against a background of gold-crushed curtains, a hothouse of plants and pots everywhere, and a poodle called Kiki, whom Bob adored.

It was an end-of-terrace house. I can remember taking my first steps over the threshold of this strange place, and saying to myself, almost out loud, 'What are you doing, Shirley?'

The only answer was, 'I want to dance. I need to dance. I have to dance.'

Every other rational consideration got dismissed, and I increasingly felt I'd backed myself into a corner. There was no turning back.

In the space of those 24 hours, I'd left the man I loved, I'd met Denise Weavers, who was to become a lifelong friend, I'd had a try-out with a man I didn't know, I'd given up my job, had the decision made I was going to move to Manchester, and I'd moved into a house full of boys, into a room where I had no private space. No wonder I was a bit shaken. Looking back, I realise what a strange set-up this was for a young girl on her own and just why my mother was so concerned.

How did I cope with it all? When you came from where I came from, on that housing estate, I guess you took everything in your stride, and you just did what you believed you needed to do to get on. The very first thing I did when I got in that house was get my bleach and Marigolds out and clean our room thoroughly from top to bottom. I don't think Sammy had ever seen it so clean.

Besides Sammy, Bob's housemates included Danny Bell, Wayne Newhouse and Donnie Burns, who is now president of the World Dance Council and considered one of the most influential figures among the men at the top of our industry. I got along very well with Danny and Wayne. Donnie was an extremely competitive man. He and his partner, Gaynor Fairweather, were trained by Sammy, and, under his tutelage, they got to be the amateur world champions. I can't say I always felt the most comfortable around Donnie. We were very different characters and he was much more extroverted and sure of himself than I was as a young girl.

I was never going to start playing house with everyone in that place. When I arrived, I had zero cooking skills, something that hasn't changed to this day. Bob doted on his poodle Kiki, he used to boil up some liver for that dog every day, and leave it in a pot on the stove. Because I had no idea what to cook for Sammy's dinner, I would take some of Kiki's liver, add to it a packet of Smash potato and corn, and serve that up. He didn't really mind what he ate, but Bob was furious I was depriving Kiki of his feast.

Bob and Sammy were extremely close. Sammy had experienced a very testing childhood, and when he was 14, Bob had thrown him a lifeline. From my perspective, it seemed that Sammy felt he owed Bob everything, and there was a strong alliance between them. Bob trained Sammy from scratch, and had given him this unique and fantastic eye that he used to great effect in his teaching. Like me, Sammy had had a very tough start in life, but I felt this was what had made him strong.

My mother isn't one for change, it always takes her a moment to process, so she didn't say very much when I told her what happened. I may have been her daughter, but I don't think she'd ever come across someone like me in her entire life. She was genuinely flummoxed by all the changes going on, and I believe she was also completely mortified by what had happened with Nigel. She'd always had great love for him, plus she was always the one asking me, 'How exactly do you plan to make a living?', 'Where are you going to live?', 'Are you safe?', 'Who is this man?', 'Why are you leaving the man you love for your job?' These were all perfectly reasonable questions for a mother to ask her daughter, and I still wasn't sure how to answer any of them, I just knew I wanted to dance.

My life changed overnight, with Sammy leading the way. I never felt particularly happy with him, but I was a bit lost in my completely new life, and it was a comfort that at least somebody seemed to be holding the map. I couldn't say whether or not I loved him, it was just that he seemed to have all the answers. Although we shared a room, I think I looked on him more as a big brother, or even a father figure, a guide and a teacher. Right from that first day through all the years we were together, we had a strong connection and we grew to love each other, but I don't think we were ever *in* love, and we never properly dated. I don't think either of our hearts ever fluttered the way they do when you first meet and fall head over heels. Nonetheless, over the course of the next few months we were inseparable, united by our passion for dance and for making it to the top. The personal relationship between us came as a result of that, not the other way round.

Before he'd met me, Sammy was already making his living teaching and demonstrating with his former partner, Lyn Aspden, but he had not yet made it to the final. Plus, he already had a big studio in Wythenshawe where he rented space, and he was a successful teacher with lots of students on his books – several of whom were champions across all the divisions. Sammy was an absolutely outstanding teacher. He taught me how to teach, just as he taught me everything else about the industry.

Sammy was always one of those people who were going to succeed in life, no matter what, in whatever field he fell into; he just had a knack for getting the best out of every situation he was put in, and the situation here was dance. Later on in his life, he would put his finger into all sorts of other pies, like real estate, with the same success. Nowadays, Sammy says he saw a similar strength in me. Back then, he seemed very confident, set on his path to the top of the industry. The fact that he was so assertive could make him come across as condescending and strict, and he certainly shouted a lot. He was absolutely used to getting his own way. They say when you're green, you're growing. Well, I was as green as Kermit the Frog, I was definitely growing, and Sammy saw that in me.

From those very first days, we never stopped. We met in the April and our first competition took place in the October. He took me to the Blackpool Dance Festival in May, at the Winter Gardens. As soon as we got there, Sammy sat me down and barked his instructions, 'Look at those girls. Do not take your eyes off them. Particularly look at Hazel Fletcher. Look at those legs and feet. This is what you have to be able to live up to.'

I sat there for hours, staring at the other dancers, too petrified that Sammy would think I wasn't focused or driven enough if I moved. I didn't even dare go to the toilet, and I thought I was going to pee my knickers. I watched that competition. It was the top six professionals in the world, the crème de la crème of Latin American dancers. Everyone on the dance floor was an idol of mine. I hadn't even made the top 96 of the amateur rankings at that point, and I was being told, 'This is what is expected of you. You have to deliver.' It was terrifying. If I could have run away at that point, I would have. I felt like I was going to have to dance for my life.

In June, I took part in my very first demonstration. It came out of the blue, after about only eight weeks of us dancing together, with Sammy announcing we had it booked for the Friday. I told him, 'I don't think I'm ready,' but he was emphatic. I was ready and he knew it.

I'll never forget it, for a couple of reasons. The first was that Sammy didn't tell me where we were going, and he took me into a building I didn't recognise from the back entrance. As we walked through, he said, 'Now we'll find out if you're ready. Now we'll find out whether you can sink or swim.'

Well, blow me down if we weren't back at the Winter Gardens in Blackpool! As I stepped out into that world-famous ballroom, my heart was pounding again. I knew I was being set a test, but, as soon as the music began, I forgot it was the Winter Gardens. I forgot everything except the music for the Rumba, which was 'Autumn Leaves', and I lost myself in it. I swam. Not for the first or last time in my life, dance provided a place of escape for me. I felt safe out there. Nobody could tell me off. Sammy whispered instructions under his breath, but for those few brief minutes, I chose to ignore him.

The second reason I won't forget it was that, for that first demonstration, we were paid £45 between us, which was huge amount of money back then. Compared with the wage I'd been making down in London, it was very good money. I'd been dancing for years, but that was the very first time I thought I might have a chance of making a proper living from doing what I loved.

I was equally terrified when Bob Dale told me I'd be teaching my first lesson. I was instructed to teach the Waltz to an older gentleman, a nice man called Mr Nymph. I must have practised every step of my lesson for a week, but my stomach was churning. Sammy had no sympathy for me. He'd never had a shoulder to lean on, so it didn't occur to him that I would need one. I realised that, whatever we did, it was always going to be make or break for me. After my relationship with Nigel, where we balanced dance with having a laugh, the new regime with Sammy made me feel very lonely. I didn't feel I had any allies in our house, where I quickly learned to keep my mouth shut because everyone repeated everything, and World War III could explode out of nothing.

Instead, I took to phoning my mother for regular chats. I didn't care what we talked about. Just like before, it was soothing to hear her voice and talk to someone I knew cared about me.

My lesson with Mr Nymph was a success, he was very pleased with what he learned, and for that I got £5 for half an hour. At first, I found teaching a terrifying experience. I remember clutching that £5 note when Bob finally put it in my hand. I quickly started to figure out that if I got busier with teaching, I could do quite well. It was possible to earn in a couple of days what I had previously earned in a week. So I set out to learn my trade, to study the technique book under the tutelage of Bob Dale and Eric Hancox.

I was qualified at a very young age in both Ballroom and Latin, and I was soon up and running. Teaching came very naturally to me, more naturally than competing. Without my realising it, all my years studying under wonderful teachers had given me the tools to become a good teacher myself. I fast realised I had a good eye for how it was all put together.

It seemed as though, from the age of 18, I had jumped on a hamster wheel with Sammy and never stopped, and that I found stressful. I had to develop, not to the standards of the industry, but to the standards of Sammy Stopford, which was a higher bar altogether. He had a no-nonsense approach. He wasn't sympathetic about the fact that this was all brand new to me and I was still finding my feet. If I showed signs of stumbling, he'd shout, 'Get on with it.'

Each morning, we practised for three or four hours, then in the afternoons we taught lessons to make our money. At weekends, we'd go to London for private lessons ourselves, or get ready for competitions or demonstrations.

He never told me at the time, but it transpired years later that, a few months after our first dazzling encounter at Nina Hunt's studio, Sammy had been harbouring some serious doubts about me as a partner. At the time, he'd even confided in a friend of his, 'She's not delivering, she's not quick enough. I'm never going to win with this woman. I've made a mistake.'

Fortunately, his wise friend advised, 'Cut her some slack, Sammy. She's come from the amateur division to the professional overnight, she's the youngest person to do it, and it's a completely different environment. She's being swallowed up by an industry she knows nothing about. You're a big cheese, and you can be intimidating. It's not good for her confidence. Give her a break.'

Thankfully, Sammy listened and started training me properly. Where he'd been used to bossing his students about and dictating everything they did, he started treating me a bit more as an equal and I was able to soak up everything he had to offer as a dance teacher. He taught me everything about the industry and how it all worked. He showed me how to be a great teacher myself, taught me all the fundamentals and then shared how to put it all together to be a great competitor.

The only problem was that I realised almost from the beginning that an essential ingredient was missing from our lives. We never seemed to make time for ourselves. In the house, there was always someone else there. I was a very young girl, but we never, ever went out, and we never had a normal date night. I'd had date nights and walks on the moors with Nigel, so I knew what having a normal boyfriend felt and looked like, and I knew this wasn't it. Instead, it was all about dance and me learning all the things

Sammy had to teach me. I was the underdog, and he remained the big cheese. He was very strict with me and started to feel more like a teacher and big brother than a boyfriend.

Over many months, if I told Sammy I fancied a night out – and this was a time when discos were all the rage – he told me he didn't want to go anywhere. Instead, he'd clean my shoes and I'd go out instead with someone else, one of the boys from the house or another friend, while Sammy stayed home and watched TV. I was like a boiling pot that never got the chance to let off any steam. I couldn't ever say anything, because what did I know? I was just that pissant from a council estate who should feel lucky to be there. It was up to me to fit in.

I was always very grateful that Bob Dale gave me a place to live, because at the time I had absolutely no money, but after several months of my living there, it was clear that he and I were starting to chafe on each other's nerves. Whatever the topic of discussion was, he didn't seem to like it if I voiced an opinion, and he would invariably take Sammy's side. I often suspected that Bob was a little bit jealous that Sammy had been hanging out with him for so long, and then suddenly there was this new person taking up Sammy's attention. The men in that house had known each other for a long time, so they inevitably formed one group while I considered myself the outsider.

One day, after yet another argument in the house with Bob taking Sammy's side and shouting at me, I decided I'd had enough and that I didn't want to live there anymore. I insisted on Sammy driving me home to my mother's house in Wallasey. He dropped me off and went back to Manchester. We both sat it out for a week or so, before there was a knock at the door. Sammy was on my mother's doorstep with Bob at his side. Bob actually apologised to me, and stressed that he wanted me to carry on dancing with Sammy. Well, this was a turn up for the books! I thought about it and eventually said I'd give it one more go, but privately I told Sammy I'd only come back on one condition: that we left Bob's house and got our own place. I felt that if we were to have any hope at all of dancing, or even being a real couple and learning how to love each other, we needed our own space, away from all those other boys and away from Bob's constant gaze.

I told him, 'I can't live in that house anymore, with all those men. It's up to you.' For once I spoke my mind and it felt good! Well, Sammy instantly agreed to my request and we started looking for a new place to live.

A short while later, we'd saved up enough money to move out of Bob's house and get a very small place of our own. Sammy had an aunt who wanted to sell her little terraced house nearby for £1,000 so we put our savings together to buy it and finally moved out of that testosterone-filled home.

Once we moved into our own place, I got to pick a small share of the furniture, although I inevitably had a few tussles with Sammy, as he always preferred something that was a deal or a bargain over anything I liked. Sammy was as particular about our new furnishings as he was exacting about his techniques in the dance studio. While that made him a great teacher, I became increasingly frantic in my efforts to keep him happy at home.

I used to share everything with my teacher Nina Hunt in confidence, although years later, I realised that, when it came to Nina, nothing was ever really in confidence. I tried to share with her my concerns about whether this partnership with Sammy was the right thing for me, and she always said, 'Hang in there, just hang in there, this will be the making of you.' She always advised me to stay in Bob's house, and then when Sammy and I later moved out, she suddenly changed her tune and started telling me, 'You and Sammy should get married. Everybody at your age, Shirley, who's dancing in the top six gets married. You and Sammy live under the same roof. You're together all the time. You should consider getting engaged to him.'

As a teenager, I definitely didn't have any sense of balance, any sense of drawing a line between Sammy the iconic teacher – whose opinion was godly as far as I was concerned – and the partner I barely knew.

My mother certainly had her doubts. For a start, she thought I was far too young to be settling down, that we hadn't known each other long enough and that I'd moved into a strange set-up with Bob and his boys. She thought the whole thing was just bizarre and she was not happy.

Despite the fact that I was living with Sammy, she kept reminding me, 'You don't need to get engaged, you can just live together for a while and see what happens.' Back in the day, an unmarried couple living together was still a little bit frowned upon, but my mother preferred that to the alternative she feared – me making a huge mistake.

My mother was always the voice of reason while I was growing up, while I kept pursuing my biggest, wildest dreams, so over the years I'd got used to being able to talk her round to my point of view about most things, selling her on my plans, and this time was no different. What was different, though, was that this time, as much as I was making such a big effort to convince her, I wonder if I was actually trying to convince myself.

Meanwhile, Nina kept coming at me from the other side: 'You're sharing a home, you're fond of it each other, it's only right.' Then she added for good measure, 'Sammy and Shirley Stopford has a much better ring to it than Sammy Stopford and Shirley Rich.' That seemed to seal it for her. I didn't even ask, 'Is that a good reason for getting married?' Nobody ever mentioned the word love.

Once Nina got an idea in her head, she was like a dog with a bone, and she became fixed on the prospect of Sammy and me getting married. She started mentioning it all the time, to the point where once again, I started to feel the pressure of other people trying to make up my mind for me about my life and where it was going.

Before I knew it, we were somehow engaged, and the sad fact is, I couldn't even tell you now how it happened. I have no idea where or when Sammy proposed. We went off to the pawnshop to buy my ring, because, as ever, Sammy was intent on getting himself a bargain. I have to say, on that occasion he struck gold, as he got me a beautiful ring with six diamonds in the shape of a flower.

On the outside, I was putting on a big face of bravado – 'It's so exciting, we're engaged!' At that age, can you truly say you're excited because you're in love, because you're getting married, or because you want everyone to look at your ring?

On the inside, I knew that so quickly after splitting from Nigel, this just didn't feel right. The truth was, although Sammy and I spent all that time together, we barely knew each other. We were definitely fond of each other though, spending all that time together, but in terms of genuine romantic feeling, it was like throwing two strangers in a room and asking them to build a life together.

Once my mother realised there was no talking me out of it, she insisted on buying my wedding dress. We went shopping together and came home with the most beautiful dress, so we were all set for the big day.

Our wedding was close to the house. Some friends lent us a Rolls-Royce for the trip to church, and I did my own hair and makeup. My brother gave me away. We had our reception at the dance studio, and a lady called Gina Littleton did us proud with a lovely spread of sausage rolls, finger sandwiches, crisps and nuts, huge plates of quiche Lorraine – everything anybody could think of, a huge feast laid out on a red tablecloth. Coming home that night was no different from any other day, with Sammy turning on the TV, and me cleaning the house. We didn't even discuss going on honeymoon because the very next day we were due to go on a dance trip.

I was 19 years old when I got married to Sammy in April 1980. When it came to dancing, we were ready to take on the world together. When it came to love, I knew nothing and I don't think my new husband knew any more than me. Married life was no different for the pair of us; it just meant we had a certificate. We got to be 'Sammy and Shirley Stopford' so at least Nina was happy.

After a year or so, we moved out from that tiny little house to another place, which felt like a mansion – four bedrooms, three bathrooms, the most beautiful home by far that I'd ever lived in and I loved it. It was up on a hill in nearby Stalybridge, an industrial town celebrated as one of the country's first centres of textile manufacturing. I was able to choose a few things for myself to furnish my big, brand new house. But Sammy had trouble settling in and before long he'd spotted another house, a much older one down the road, so before I knew it, we were off again. Sammy was always intent on moving on and, for sure, it meant we got to move up the property ladder once again, but it also meant I never got the chance to settle.

One of my biggest dreams, from way before I'd ever met Sammy, had always been to move to the bright lights of London. I'd briefly fulfilled that dream with Nigel, and then I'd given it all up following that fateful day when I'd tried out with Sammy. My dream had been shattered that day, partly because I'd left a man I thought I truly loved, but also because I had to move back to Manchester and leave London behind.

Over the course of our first year as husband and wife, I very carefully started to feel my own way. I say carefully, because Sammy was very clear about what he wanted to do. I gave my opinion, particularly about my wish to move back to London and concentrate 100 per cent on our dancing, but Sammy also had his own ideas. By then, he was set on our creating our own dance studio, and spent his time researching all the buildings and possible locations for the perfect spot. Before long, he'd found what he considered the right place – I didn't have a say – a building in Droylsden, right by the Robertson's Jam Factory. Even though I desperately wanted to move to London, he was adamant we were staying put and opening this Stopford's Dance Club, and that became a source of contention between us.

Eventually, he opened the studio over two whole floors, which made for a huge project. From the day those doors opened, it was work 24/7 for both of us. My whole life, I'd had a good work ethic, and in Manchester, I'd been teaching long hours and demonstrating in between, as well as running our home. We already had a lot going on, and suddenly we had a whole other mountain to climb.

Sammy always had lots of creative business ideas, and he was very good at delegating, which meant I was just as busy as him. As well as trying to keep our home nice, I was teaching a full day of private lessons as well as running all the group classes in the studios. We had a public bar there, so I had to make sure we were always fully stocked, and that the bar staff knew their jobs. I wasn't afraid of hard work, but my daily schedule became overwhelming, and in between all that, we were travelling up to London for our own dance lessons, so we could start to climb up the competition tree. Eventually, we became so busy that even Sammy recognised I was drowning under the workload, and brought in his brother-in-law, Roy. I got on extremely well with Roy from the start, and he lived with us for a while and became somebody I knew I could lean on.

Although I could call myself a married woman by now, I was still in fact a teenager. An awful lot had happened to me in a short space of time; I was working so hard and for such long hours that I never really stopped to ask myself if I was having any fun. There was just no let-up, no evening when Sammy announced we were going out for dinner, no weekend when he surprised me with a trip away somewhere, no holiday to look forward to, and it started to niggle at me that something was missing from my life.

I used to call Sammy 'Old Reliable' and he was definitely that, checking we had enough money, making sure we had enough work, planning out what we'd do next with our business, all important grown-up stuff. He had a lot of great attributes that I learned from, but for me, if I'm honest, just working all the time started to become incredibly boring, without anything to break it up. I was just a normal 19-year-old who wanted to kick her heels, have her knickers ripped off occasionally and go down the disco! Where were our big evenings out? Our days spent in bed together? Our drives to the beach? We had none of it. What we each had instead was a partner whose passion for dance and ambition to get to the top matched our own.

I really enjoyed dancing with Sammy and, for a while, everything we did seemed to go well, probably because we had, indisputably, one director, him, and one follower, me. As time went on, I started to voice my opinion, and it was clear Sammy didn't like it. If he'd been canny, he'd have let me be the boss in one aspect of our life, whether it be in the studio, or even how our house was furnished, but he was too used to having his finger in every pie to do that, and I was starting to feel my own way and form my own opinions, even rebelling occasionally. I felt as though I had nothing to call my own. Instead, just as I'd worked my arse off to become the little school girl I knew my mother wanted me to be, now I worked my arse off to be the dancer Sammy wanted me to be. I know I said I wanted to dance more than anything else in my life, but this was ridiculous. Note to self: be careful what you wish for.

Perhaps lots of people feel like this when they look back on their life – how do you know if you're ever really doing what *you* want? By taking a break and having a big, long look at yourself, that's how, but that means finding the nerve to get down off the hamster wheel – something I'd never even thought about doing before.

• • •

We entered our first competition together about six months after we first met. It was October, and the annual Latin International Championships, which took place at the Royal Albert Hall.

For as long as I've been in the dance industry, this has been one of the biggest dance events in the world. We went into the event, with Sammy making it clear to me he expected us to make the final. We'd done a whole load of demonstrations by then, and I was worried I wasn't living up to his expectations, so I felt enormous pressure leading up to the event.

We missed out on making the final by one point. I cried afterwards, both because I was disappointed, but also because I was worried about what Sammy would say to me. Sure enough, he turned to me as we were walking back up the stairs from the ballroom, and said, 'That is the last time we ever miss a final. Do you understand me, young lady?' And, sure enough, it was.

If I'd thought I was going to have a bit of a break after that, have some time to recharge, maybe go up and stay with my mum for a bit, I was sorely mistaken. No sooner had we got back to Manchester than all talk turned to what was required for us to do better and get into the final of the UK Championships, taking place at the Hammersmith Palais the upcoming January, but before that, we had the Europeans at the Winter Gardens in Blackpool. Everyone in the dance industry knows all these dates better than they know their own children's birthdays. The championships calendar is like a wheel going round year after year, with so many events in it you can never really catch your breath. My spirit was as competitive as Sammy's, but I also felt incredibly stressed by the pressure of trying to improve so quickly, and my stomach was constantly in knots.

We never missed another final after that in all the years we danced together. Normally, you move up the rankings quite gradually, as someone else retires and makes space. But Sammy didn't want to do that, he said he didn't want to wait for a dead man's shoes; instead he wanted to pip them all off, one at a time, so that's what we did.

Whenever we stepped into a ballroom, we were just in sync with each other and we were able to create exceptional chemistry. We had a wonderful quality of movement, a musicality which meant we both heard the music the same way. Sammy was a soft dancer to dance with, with fine hand movements, but he was also very powerful. He didn't like me hanging on him. If I felt heavy, he just let go of me, which sometimes meant I fell backwards on the floor. He used to say to me, 'I'm not your PLP.' He meant Public Leaning Post.

The kind of progress that normally takes ten years, we achieved in a very short space of time. We were Sammy and Shirley Stopford – 'the non-stop Stopfords' they called us – going from strength to strength and getting busier all over the world. As our profile grew, so did our work schedules.

In Sammy, as well as all his experience, I had someone who knew how to choreograph, which was speedy and dramatic. Now that I know so much more about dance, I realise he was ahead of his time. He had this great insight into dance and what it would become in the future. He could make our routines exciting, although a source of great stress for me was that Sammy always wanted to change them. This even went on backstage in the middle of competitions after he'd watched our rivals in action. It would be like an actor spending six months learning a script for a play, then arriving at the theatre to have the writer rip up all the pages and give them new ones to learn an hour before going onstage.

No excuses were allowed. I wasn't allowed to mess up. I could tell just by the look on his face that he was often mortified with my lack of brainpower as I struggled to learn the new steps. It was very hard to cope with, but it definitely raised my standards.

We had no favourite dance. We were both well trained in the art of Ballroom and those skills definitely served us well, but we decided we wanted to become Latin specialists. By the time I was 19, we were already making all the major international finals. In the history of dance, it was probably one of the most meteoric rises in the industry.

Our most significiant breakthrough came in 1980. Back then, to qualify for the World Championships you had to do well at the UK Championships, which took place every January at the Hammersmith Palais.

Four British couples – two in Ballroom and two in Latin – from that event would have the chance to represent their country. That year, we knew for sure that one of the Latin couples would be reigning world champions Alan and Hazel Fletcher, but the other slot was up for grabs. Who was going to get it, Keith and Judy Clifton or Sammy and Shirley Stopford? We definitely weren't the favourites.

Keith and Judy were incredible dancers, and passed on their love for it to their children, Kevin and Joanne, who everyone will know from *Strictly Come Dancing*. Judy had incredible balance and I used to look at her, thinking, 'I'll never be able to move my legs like that.'

In fact, they were such big favourites on the day that the gossip was that their trainer already had a bottle of champagne on ice waiting for them upstairs. But it seemed our time had come. It was a long day with qualifying rounds in the morning, and the final taking place right at the end of the evening. You had to be mentally prepared as well as physically fit. Sammy didn't like me to drink any water throughout any competition, so I was often dehydrated, which made me feel sick, but it helped me feel we had a sense of discipline. That day, I had the most beautiful dress, couture-made, white with a big circle skirt, and I felt beautiful. Sammy looked great in black. We were slim and fit and it all came together for us that night. Sammy and I came third in the competition but, because the couple who came second, Espen and Kirsten Salberg, were from Norway and qualified under their own flag, Sammy and I became the second British couple to win the chance to compete in the World Championships. It also meant we unexpectedly bagged that last spot over Keith and Judy Clifton. Unsurprisingly, Alan and Hazel Fletcher came first.

I was happy that we'd qualified, but my heart also went out to Keith and Judy, because I knew that they really wanted to go to that World Championships. It was a big shock for everyone, us included, and in fact the Cliftons seemed so surprised I think it may have influenced their decision to retire soon after.

Our success meant we got to go to the World Championships in Australia. Not only was it four couples, two each for Latin and Ballroom, travelling together – that doesn't happen these days, everyone travels on their own – but we also had a camera crew come along to film us all on our journey for a BBC documentary. They followed us through the airport and onto the plane, all the way to the competition. I look back on that time fondly, particularly that journey to Australia, which was one of the best trips Sammy and I ever made in our whole career. This was my first long-haul trip, and I was entranced by the company I was in. These other dancers had been my idols all the time I was growing up, and now here I was, sitting on a plane with them, staying at the same hotel, going out for dinner and sharing stories. I felt like a little girl who'd suddenly been given entry to an elite club. They were at the very top of the industry, and I was on the rise. We finished third overall, second in Jive, a brilliant result.

For a very long time Sammy had wanted to be the best and, with me, he was on the way to achieving it. We were still busy with our demonstrations and our teaching schedules, but we started closing in more consistently on the dancers at the top of the rankings, snapping at their heels just as Sammy had planned.

With the retirement of long-time champions Alan and Hazel Fletcher, we came close to winning the British Championships in 1982, losing to the champions, Espen and Kirsten Salberg, by only a couple of marks. I felt Espen saw that as a sign it was the right time for them to leave the floor, so almost as soon as they won, they retired. That meant that if Sammy and I carried on improving at the rate we'd been doing, we had a clear shot at taking over from them at the top of the rankings. That seemed even more certain in October 1982, when we returned to the Albert Hall and won our first International Open to the World Championships title. From there, it seemed like 1983 was going to be our year, the year when everything we'd ever worked for all our lives was going to come to pass. Everything was coming together.

We started as we meant to continue, with the UK title at the Hammersmith Palais in the January, so we knew we were right on track. Just as Sammy had predicted when he swooped me up at that try-out down in London, just as I'd dreamed of and worked towards ever since that day I'd danced my first Cha-Cha-Cha in the church hall in Wallasey, we were on the path to becoming British Open to the World Latin champions at the Winter Gardens in the May. It was only a few more months away, we just had to stay focused, and in both our heads, I think we were already lifting the trophy.

However, in the meantime, there was just one more demonstration we had to fulfil. I had no way of knowing it, but I was dancing all the way to another life-changing fork in the road.

• • •

Professionally, Sammy and I were in complete harmony and dancing was obviously a huge part of our life, but away from it, we still didn't really have much going on. I was in our studio morning, noon and night, and Sammy was working just as hard as me. We shared the same goals, but as ever, he was definitely the boss and he'd often get cross with me easily.

On only a few occasions did I let my feelings be known. During a demonstration we gave at a studio in Germany, our routine included a dramatic, death-defying trick where I had to lie behind Sammy, while he held me with one hand. Well, he decided I was too heavy, so he decided to teach me a lesson by dropping me, although he said his hand slipped. I was young, I was angry and I felt that he'd let me go, plus I'd hurt my head where it had banged on the floor. Afterwards, I somehow managed to keep smiling, while our hosts gave me this big bouquet of flowers and handed him a magnum of champagne. We got in the lift, the doors closed behind us and we had a huge fight. I battered him with the flowers to the extent that the petals flew everywhere. All I was left with was the stalks. We got back out of the lift, to be greeted by several people, who could clearly see all the flower petals strewn everywhere. Sammy said to me, 'Just as well I had the champagne.'

He was five years older than me, he'd known struggles and strife all his life, and it gave him that same will to succeed that I recognised in myself. He taught me what I needed to know about how to make it in the Ballroom industry, and I'll always thank him for giving me so many invaluable lessons about our trade, but away from work, our relationship was becoming increasingly difficult.

Why was I so frustrated? Because, as you may have gathered, there just wasn't enough love there. I wanted to feel more cared for, more nurtured. For sure, Sammy looked after me financially, but I needed something more. He had never known affection as a child, and I don't think he knew how to show it. In his own way, I felt he loved me, but as the person on the receiving end, I never felt desired by him, our marriage was missing an essential element, and my heart gradually went to sleep.

Without him, I know I wouldn't be where I am. My mum always says, 'He didn't make you, you worked hard.' And Sammy himself tells me I would have likely been just as successful in another field because of my drive, but in my heart I know the depth of his contribution to my life. He understood my background because it was comparable with his own, he got it that my mum had worked three jobs to give me food, that my father had never been on the scene, that I came from a housing estate where no one had anything much so I always had a hunger in me for something more. And he helped me channel all that drive and determination into something else – almost an immunity from fear in the competitive world of dance, which gives you a lot of self-belief and power. We brought out the best in each other during that time in our lives, and I will always be truly grateful that my path crossed with his, because it changed everything.

So, why, with such a strong connection and bottomless bond, did our marriage fail? Well, with the luxury of hindsight, we should probably have had date nights, holidays, private Sammy and Shirley time miles away from the dance floor. We didn't have any of that, but what do you know at that age? Instead, despite our growing success, I kept having the nagging feeling there must be more to life than our endless routine of dancing, teaching, demonstrating, performing, travelling, putting our heads down to sleep and then starting all over again.

From the outside, our lives must have looked incredibly glamorous. We travelled the world together, drove nice cars, had a beautiful home, but at the core of it all, something wasn't right. On the positive side, he was reliable, trustworthy, a hard worker who wanted good things for both of us and he wanted to win with a drive that matched mine, but life is about balance, and I never felt our personal life was a priority. We had a true romance in our Rumba on the dance floor, but no romance away from it; we had more passion in our Paso Doble than we did in our entire private life, and I was lonely. I was starting to wonder what else was out there, and then we made a fateful trip to Canada, where I was about to find out.

• • •

It was Nina Hunt who suggested Sammy and I attend La Classique du Quebec, one of Canada's biggest dance contests. That was what took us to freezing-cold North America in February 1983.

With most dance events, it's just about the main competition, but La Classique is a huge, glamorous spectacle, with everybody under one roof, and loads of different, social events going on all over the place. It's a dazzling prospect, and dancers from all over the world are excited to be there. Karen and Marcus Hilton were there along with us, as was Nina Hunt.

The hotel where it's always staged has a magnificent ballroom with escalators that come down all the way to the dance floor. There's a huge swimming pool, games rooms everywhere, you name it, that hotel's got it.

Sammy and I decided we'd wander into the ballroom and see what was going on. As we made our tour of the place, we saw one

111

of our first ever pro-amateur events, the kind you see on *Strictly Come Dancing*. It was my first experience of great professional dancing with a student, and I was mesmerised. I wanted to know more about it, and I realised it was a huge event, as popular as my championship, I'd just never been aware of it before.

We spotted one couple dancing in this pro-amateur competition, and I pointed them out to Sammy. I thought they looked very glamorous together: she was really pretty and a good dancer, while he was a bit short, but very handsome with a tiny waist and dazzling smile. She was clearly the professional and he was the amateur, but I thought no more about it.

The next day, Sammy and I took part in our championship, and we danced spectacularly well. We headed back up to our room, where we took off our makeup and changed our clothes. Karen called me, 'We're going swimming, Shirley. Do you want to come?'

That sounded like a great idea, but Sammy announced, 'We've got a meeting. Tell Karen we'll be half an hour or so,' so that's what I did. I was ready in my swimming costume and bathrobe when there was a knock at the door. In walked a couple who introduced themselves. She was called Patrea Lockie and his name was Corky Ballas.

I recognised him from the pro-amateur event the day before, even though now he was wearing thick-rimmed glasses, like Coke bottles. They were the couple I'd spotted out on the dance floor, and we exchanged some polite chit-chat. Had he won his event? Yes, he'd won his event. He then said, very formally, 'Patrea and I have never seen dancing like we just saw, watching you two.

My mother is a Flamenco dancer. My father used to own one of the biggest and most elaborate dance studios in the world. If you don't mind, I would like to pay for you both to come to Houston, Texas, next month to dance at the Texas Challenge.'

Sammy went to consult our diary. Now, we were so busy by then, every single week for the next four months or so was booked out, but the only single week we had free during that entire time was the one Corky was talking about. Had it been any other time, we wouldn't have been able to go, but it was clearly written in the stars, or something. Sammy started mentioning all the terms, airfares to be taken care of, but he'd barely started talking when Corky interrupted him: 'The money is not a problem. You name your price, my parents and I will take care of it.'

Even Sammy stopped talking then. Corky added, 'Plus, you'll obviously win the Challenge, so there'll be prize money as well. It could be a very lucrative week for you.'

Well, of course all that appealed to Sammy. He couldn't resist Corky's offer, both of a great trip to Texas and all the financial rewards it promised. We'd be staying in the Westchase Hilton hotel owned by Corky's parents, we'd be driven around like VIPs, we'd no doubt make money in the competition, and Corky said he'd guarantee us teaching money, eight lessons per person per day for a week, whether we worked or not! This all appealed to Sammy's sense of business. He kept checking, 'Whether we work or not, we still get paid?' but Corky just gave the same reply to all his questions, 'Money is not a problem.'

I was getting a bit hot and bothered in that hotel room because it made me uncomfortable talking about money. All I really wanted to do at that point was go and join my friend Karen in the swimming pool, but here we were making this arrangement to fly out to Texas. I began to get so twitchy, Sammy eventually noticed and said, 'You go, I'll stay here and sort out the finer details.'

I made my goodbyes: 'Nice to meet you. What did you say your name was?' 'Corky Ballas.' 'Nice to meet you, Corky, good luck with your dancing, and I'll see you in March.' And that was that. In my mind that day I had my normal life, my husband dealing with our business and my best friend Karen waiting for me at the pool. So off I went and I thought no more about it, little knowing that we'd just agreed to something that would have such a massive impact on the lives of everyone in that hotel room.

It was only when we returned to England that we got our first inkling of how successful the Ballas family really was. Sammy was talking to our teacher, Nina, Hunt, and another industry veteran, Bobbie Irvine, about the invitation, and they warned him, 'Whatever you do, don't take that job.' Sammy asked, 'Why?' They replied, 'He's a good-looking man and his family is very, very rich. Shirley's head may be turned.' But Sammy told them, 'It's all fine. Shirley's head is fine. Our career is on track. This is a great opportunity for both of us. Money. Connections. We're taking the job.'

March came around, and off we went to Texas. No sooner had our plane landed than we were picked up by a helicopter, dropped off on the roof of the Westchase Hilton, checked into a beautiful suite and told to charge anything to our room. It began to dawn on us both that Corky hadn't been lying to us when he'd told us back in Canada, 'Money is not a problem.'

The truth was that Corky Ballas's parents weren't just rich — they were absolutely loaded. His father George was an entrepreneur who'd invented the Weed Eater device for trimming weeds from around the trees — apparently he'd come up with the idea one day when he was watching the big bristles going round in a car wash. It had transformed the lawn mower industry and made him millions. Corky's whole family had helicopters flying them around, huge houses, a great fleet of limousines. It was surreal levels of wealth, compared with anything I'd ever known or even seen. Sammy and I were starting to be able to afford to have nice things ourselves, but this was like stepping into another world.

The morning after we arrived, we were whisked off by limousine to the dance studio, where Corky was waiting for us.

'I don't have a full day of teaching for you both,' was the first thing he said, and of course, Sammy immediately started voicing his opinion. 'What do you mean you don't have a full day for us?'

Corky just smiled. 'Calm down, sir. You will be paid. You don't have to worry about it.' Sammy needed that reassurance. With him, it was always about the bottom line, and I could tell he wasn't happy.

A couple of days had gone by without much teaching, when Corky told us, 'My family would like to invite you out for a meal and to go dancing.'

Sammy replied, 'Well, I'll be happy to go to the meal, but you can drop me off afterwards. If you can supply me with some videos to watch in my room, I'll be really happy.'

Then he added, 'You can go dancing with Shirley. It's not my bag.'

I wasn't even surprised, as that was a typical tableau of our life back in Manchester. Sammy, by his own admission, was quite happy with his own company. He's never been a drinker or a smoker, but give him a big pile of DVDs and he's happy. I was used to it, but now in Houston, neither of us realised, by leaving me completely at the mercy of the powerful charm of a southern gentleman, he had just rung the death knell for our marriage.

That fateful evening, we all went for a lovely meal, then we dropped Sammy off at the hotel to enjoy his TV and videos. Then it was back in the limousine for a big night where my hosts pulled out all the stops. Everyone looked their best, all dressed up in their evening clothes, the women in beautiful dresses, the men in suits, everyone wearing big smiles, delighted to be there. We went to Corky's brother's house first for a cocktail, and then we carried on to a glitzy club to dance. It was just the kind of night I loved, everyone having fun and chatting with each other, just what a good evening out is supposed to feel like, and it was all being offered to me to share. To my hungry heart, aching for some excitement, it was like stepping into a fairy tale.

All of Corky's family were with him, and they seemed as warm, friendly and generous as he was. I couldn't believe how well they all got on together, and that evening, they pulled me into this warm tight-knit family. It was like stepping into a hot, bubbling bath, and I was walking on air the entire night. It felt like the very first time in my life that I was allowed to just kick off my heels, throw my arms in the air, roar with laughter at everyone's jokes and dance purely for the joy of it. It was a completely magical evening, and I'd never known anything like it. I'd taken a step into a totally different world from the one I'd known, and somewhere inside me I already knew it was going to be very hard to find my way back.

There was nothing between Corky and me that evening; he was just one of many people making me feel wonderful about being out on this special night, although of course I realised he had been instrumental in making it all happen, so I felt very warmly towards him. We had a few drinks, nothing over the top, but enough to make me feel just slightly giddy, a lovely feeling. Corky offered to drop me back to my hotel. We pulled up outside and I prepared to say good night. Then, as he started to lean across me to open the car door, he went to kiss me.

I turned my head away and said, 'Corky, I'm married.' But I looked into his big brown eyes, his lovely tanned skin, his huge smile, and something inside me went ping, ping, ping.

Corky replied very formally: 'I appreciate that and I apologise for my behaviour. But if you accept my offer to go out again some-time this week for another nice evening, I shall assume that you too want this to go further.' And off he went. I remember Corky's after-shave that evening was by Paco Rabanne, and whenever I smell that same scent now, I'm always transported back to that evening when I was 'invited' to accept his offer.

I was giddy with excitement, but Corky's invitation also placed me under pressure. Once again, somebody was putting me on the spot and forcing me to make up my mind about something when I didn't feel ready. I went back to my room, where Sammy was already asleep, a pile of videos at his side – a happy man.

Sammy and I spent the next day teaching, then we went out to eat, just the pair of us on our own, and the day after Corky appeared in the studio. Once again, he invited us to another evening of dinner and dancing. And once again, Sammy accepted the invitation to dinner but turned down the dancing. Then they both looked at me.

'Let's just wait and see,' I said.

I sounded calm, but in reality, I was torn up on the inside. Should I go out with Corky for a second evening, knowing where it might lead? On the one hand, I was betraying a man who I knew had given me everything. On the other, if I said no, was I saying goodbye to any kind of life apart from the one I had with Sammy, one where something integral was missing? I wanted to do the right thing, and yet my heart was dragging me in the opposite direction.

Corky and I were already flirting, sharing jokes back and forth in the studio, but I definitely hadn't made up my mind to accept his offer. He said later on that I initiated our connection, throwing eyes at him, that I even offered to get underneath him while he was doing press-ups to warm up for his lesson, but in truth it was completely two-way.

I told myself it was innocent, playful banter between us, but I knew I was having feelings I hadn't experienced before. Everything had a heightened quality to it. My body was full of endorphins and all those feelings that just make you want to jump on top of buildings and skip around instead of walking. I felt like I'd been living in black and white and suddenly I was seeing everything in Technicolor. I didn't know it at the time, but I realised later that this was what falling for somebody was supposed to feel like.

All day long I kept quiet, hoping somehow events would be decided for me, without me having to make up my mind. Finally, as Corky left for the day, he turned round and looked at me. 'What time shall I pick you up?'

I still hadn't come to any sort of decision, but I heard the words come out of my mouth, 'I'll be ready at seven.' I still felt very unsure of what I was letting myself in for, but the die was cast.

The following evening, after another lovely meal out, he dropped me back to the hotel, and we looked at each other. We fell into each other's arms, and that was our very first kiss. He said to me, 'This is going to sound weird, and I know we both have other people in our lives, but the first time I saw you in Canada, I knew I loved you.'

And that was it! As much as he'd fallen for me and my dancing, in return I fell for his smile, his laughter and his complete focus on me. I kept replaying his kisses over and over in my mind. I just wanted to stay there forever with him and his big, beautiful family.

The week passed as I succumbed more and more to Corky's charms. I was wined and dined in the best restaurants across the city. He was very carefree but courteous, generous and complimentary, all the things I'd been missing in Sammy while we'd been busy building up our business and planning dance-world domination. Throughout those heady days in Houston, Corky and I partied, danced and laughed non-stop. I felt I'd become a different person.

In the middle of that extraordinary week, Sammy and I danced the Texas Challenge, the event we'd flown out for in the first place, and the whole Ballas family were there to support us. Considering Corky had a girlfriend and I had a husband, we didn't do a very good job of hiding our feelings. We all went out after the dance event and I had an ice-cream sundae, which Corky started eating off my plate, and his girlfriend called him up on it. Sammy didn't even notice.

As the days passed, I became increasingly emotional about the position I'd put myself in. I realised I didn't want to leave this magical kingdom that I'd somehow found myself in. I had to keep disappearing off to the bathroom when it all got too much for me and the tears started to fall. I knew I had a reliable and promising career I wanted to fulfil, but I could sense my feelings were beginning to grow for this man I barely knew.

All my life, I'd been working so hard – throughout my years at school, during my time with Nigel, then building up the business with Sammy – that I'd never taken any time off for me. I didn't realise how sorely I needed some fun in my life, and now it had arrived along with a heady romance, I was truly overwhelmed. I knew throwing caution to the wind could be disastrous, but somehow I felt as though it was meant to be. Right there, right at that moment, I didn't think I had any choice.

When Sammy and I flew home to Manchester at the end of the week, I felt pure sadness. Corky had given me some music to listen to – back then, it was on a Walkman – and listening to the tunes he'd put together for me, I couldn't stop myself sobbing to the point that even Sammy noticed. He asked, 'What's the matter with you?' I told him I was feeling quite tired, and he bought that.

Up until that point in our marriage, there hadn't been anyone else for either Sammy or me. There was no jealousy and maybe that was the problem. On the rare occasions we weren't working, Sammy liked to relax in front of the TV, while I sat staring at the wall.

A portrait of my grandmother's family, the Suttons, featuring my grandmother Daisy, her two brothers, grandmother and extended family.

My grandad, Frank Standring.

My handsome father, George Andrew Rich, as a young man. He looks like Billy Fury, don't you think?

My mother, Audrey, as a young woman. She is my rock and my soulmate, and the hardest worker I've ever known.

My mum and dad looking glamorous on their wedding day in 1958.

I had singed my hair over the fire just before this visit to Father Christmas in 1961.

A rare picture of me and my dad, on a Sunday outing. My mum tells me I was wearing a designer dress here, but all I remember is that it itched like crazy!

Allied Dancing Association Ltd.

AMATEUR MEDAL TESTS

No. 94   Name of Candidate   Shirley Rich
GRADE   C.B.I.

DANCES	Marks Awarded	REMARKS
WALTZ		
FOX TROT		
QUICKSTEP		
TANGO		
Additional Dance		Pleasing expression
RUMBA	25	examples executed with
SAMBA	25	ease excellent
CHA-CHA-CHA	25	
PASO DOBLE	25	rhythm.
JIVE	25	

MARKINGS

Maximum Marks in all Grades....25

Pass Marks .... 12 to 5 in each dance
Commended .... 16 to 19 in each dance   all grades.
Highly Commended   20 to 25 in each dance
This Result Form is for the use of Teachers only.

Top marks in my dancing test in 1968. Highly commended!

With my first ever dance partner, Irene Hamilton, in our matching canary-yellow dresses.

Dancing with my first male partner, David Fleet, in 1970.
Such beautiful memories and still sporting that yellow dress!

With David and our wonderful teacher, Margaret Redmond.

In step on her way to the top

IT'S BEEN a highly successful year for 20-year-old Shirley Rich in national and international Latin American dancing.

For Shirley, whose mother, Mrs. A. Rich, lives in Cameron Road, Leasowe, came third in the world Latin American professional championhips held in Perth, Western Australia. And she has just won the closed British championships in Blackpool. Earlier in the year she also won the all-England and North of England championships.

Her partner is her husband, Mr. Samuel Stopford, whom she married in the Spring. They met two years ago when Mr. Stopford, who had seen her dancing in a competition, rang her up and asked her to partner him.

Now, when they are not in competitions, they tour giving demonstrations and teaching. They have just spent ten days in America.

Shirley is a former pupil of Oxley Comprehensive School, in Wallasey, and first learned to dance when she was nine at St. Chads Hall with Vic and May Knox. Later she went to the Margaret Redmond School of Dancing in Liverpool, and has also had tuition in London.

She has many awards for ballroom, Latin American

Shirley Rich.

American dancing. She turned professional about two years ago.

She and her husband now live in Manchester and

My first press cutting from a local paper. 'In step on her way to the top'.

Nigel and I used to have a laugh, on and off the floor. The little spark of attraction between us quickly grew into mutual devotion.

Again, with Nigel. This was one of my favourite dresses. It was satin and my mum and I decorated it together with penny sequins – all individually sewn on by hand.

My last major competition with Nigel, 1978.

My first ever photoshoot at 18 with Sammy Stopford.

With Sammy on our wedding day, April 1980. I was a 19-year-old bride.

Our fabulous wedding buffet, put together with love by my dear friend Gina Littleton. The reception took place in Bob Dale's dance studio, Manchester.

My first *Dancing Times* cover, featuring my famous pot-stirrer move – I could manage 50 or 60 spins in a row. December, 1980.

The world famous Stopford's Dance Club. This was next door to the Robertson's Jam Factory in Droylsden, Manchester.

Whatever was going on behind the scenes, once Sammy and I stepped onto the dance floor it was pure magic.

Winning La Classique du Quebec with Sammy at 22. My life was about to change forever ...

Walking down the aisle to meet Corky with my wonderful brother, David, September 1985.

With Mrs Ballas, my *fab-u-lous* new mother-in-law, on our wedding day.

Just married – with matching braces. Departing in Mrs Ballas' Rolls Royce.

My father was a surprise guest at our wedding. A rare photograph of my mum and dad together – all smiles on the day of our wedding.

Corky's father, Mr Ballas – the inventor of the multimillion dollar weed-eating machine that was inspired by this popcorn can.

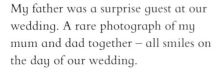

An aerial view of my new home – the sprawling Ballas Estate.

The night before I gave birth to Mark. As you can see from the peach and pink colour scheme, we were all set for a girl, who we were going to name Elizabeth. Then out popped Mark – what a shock!

Corky sent a limo to collect me from the hospital after Mark was born. Sadly, he was nowhere to be seen.

Bouncing back into shape and into the rankings. After having a baby, it was no easy task – it took months of dedication and hard work.

A collection of our Christmas cards throughout the years. What a perm! Everything is bigger in Texas.

Another Christmas, another hairdo. I think Mark is about five here.

A glamorous shoot in Las Vegas. With my very handsome husband, Corky, smoldering for the camera with his dramatic eyeliner.

Performing the Samba on the world's biggest dance tour.
This shot was taken at the Budokan Ballroom in Tokyo, Japan.

My mum was always very fond of Sammy – she knew he took care of me, and that our career was going from strength to strength. But she could tell I was beginning to notice what I was missing, and she did her best to give him fair warning. She told him on several occasions, 'You need to take care of your wife, Sammy,' but he didn't hear it. It meant that, when the prospect of a dazzling romance did present itself to me, in retrospect I was a sitting duck. Yes, a sitting duck.

Now, here I was, back in Manchester, reliving every moment of that crazy, passionate week with Corky, while all the time Sammy was hell-bent on us getting ready for the British Open to the World Championships, due to take place in May, only a few weeks after our return from Texas. Mere weeks before we were meant to take our rightful place at the very top of the dance industry, the position we'd both been working towards all our lives, here I was, with my heart locked on a place thousands of miles away, dreaming of a man I'd only known for a week.

I would have felt under pressure anyway, as Sammy stepped up our training schedule to prepare for Blackpool, and his standards and expectations went through the roof. We spent hours and hours in the studio, with Sammy standing opposite me, taking me in his arms, staring me in the face and demanding my complete concentration. But with what was going on in my head, I found it almost impossible.

In a normal week, I would have found Sammy's intense focus hard to cope with. With my head full of another man and the memory of his eyes on me, it felt like I was having an out-of-body experience. My distraction made for some very long, incredibly surreal weeks before we finally made our trip to the Winter Gardens for what Sammy considered the most important day of our lives, when we would finally become British Open to the World Latin American champions – something, if I was completely honest, by then I'd almost stopped caring about, as awful as that sounds. I was incredibly conflicted the whole time I was meant to be preparing.

I was also completely distracted. All those weeks I spent training with Sammy preparing for the biggest competition of our lives, Corky constantly besieged me with a million phone calls, huge bunches of flowers that arrived at our door almost every day with no name on the card, tapes with more music on them for me to listen to and think of him, plus constant declarations of love.

Of course, Sammy didn't notice a thing. In the evenings, he would sit down in front of the TV and I'd sneak out of the room and make a reverse-charge telephone call to Corky. I'd talk to him for an hour and half, whispering all the kinds of things new lovers do, then finally hang up the phone and walk back into the living room. Sammy would still be in front of the box. He hadn't even realised I'd gone!

Later, Corky received a lot of the blame for wrecking my partnership with Sammy, but the truth was I was miserable in my marriage. I think, in his own way, Sammy really loved me, but he just never expressed it in a way that meant I could feel it. Afterwards, it was easy for Sammy to say I left him for a millionaire – ironic, really, after that first meeting in Quebec when it had been Sammy who'd found the prospect of our trip to Texas so financially appealing. But it wasn't Corky's money that drew me to him. It was his charm, his good humour, his lust for life, his good manners, his frequent phone calls, his complete and total interest in everything about me. Corky was a charming southern gentleman who knew just the right things to say to a lady, and he instinctively understood how hungry I was for someone to lavish that kind of attention and affection on me.

Just before Sammy and I travelled to Blackpool for the 1983 British Open to the World Championships, Corky called me on the phone and said over and over again, 'I really love you. We're meant to be together. I want you to be here with me. I want to be with you forever.' With his words ringing in my ears, I did my best to concentrate on what was expected of me in the competition, but I could barely even focus long enough to pack my bags. I was trembling as I folded my clothes for the main competition – including a beautiful pink and cerise dress, with pink and aurora stones. I always felt lucky in pink.

These championships are gruelling – five dances in one category over seven rounds, each of them two minutes of dance. Sammy and I had all sorts of philosophies we used to take into every competition. I always felt dehydrated and stressed dancing at these kinds of events with Sammy, even without all the anguish I was feeling about what was happening between Corky and me.

It made for such a long, demanding day that I didn't really have any emotion left in me when, right at the end of the evening, they gave out all the marks and we learned that Sammy and I had won all five dances to become British Open to the World champions. We probably danced the best we'd ever danced in our lives, but to this day I couldn't tell you how I managed it. At first I was just relieved that after all that hard work, we'd finally achieved what we set out to do. I was also truly delighted to my bones to see my mother holding that trophy in her hands after all her years of hard work and sacrifice to help me fulfil my dream. But as we were presented with the award, part of me ached for the person who was missing from that day, and that person was Corky.

My bewildering double-life carried on. Throughout those crazy months after we won that title, Sammy and I were kept beyond busy competing, teaching, travelling, and enjoying a much higher profile now we had our much-coveted British Championship title under our belt. If I'd been busy in the years leading up to this, it was nothing compared with our schedule now.

During that time, Corky also made several trips to England, sometimes jumping on a plane from Texas just to spend a few hours with me. One time, I even managed to sneak away and visit him in Houston. It felt as though I finally had what I'd been longing for all those years – passion, attention, somebody showing me all the romantic interest I'd been craving, plus his big, laughing family who were all so warm and welcoming. I soaked up every experience, and I could never get enough.

Back in England, I introduced him to my mother and she recognised the connection between us was real and strong. She definitely wasn't happy about the situation, though, and she refused to condone our affair. She continued to do her best to warn Sammy, suggesting he took us both away on a holiday, but he just didn't seem to hear her.

To this day, when I hear the song 'Hello' by Lionel Richie, it takes me straight back to those days in my early twenties when Corky and I had just met. It was one of the songs on albums he'd post to me, and it was as though I was brainwashed by the music, by the flowers, by the romance of it all. He kept calling me, saying how determined he was that we would be together. Looking back, I wonder if the thrill of the chase was what inspired him to court me in this way, as he was very competitive in everything he did. But if he was getting a thrill from it all, I was getting lots of loving – the kind of attention I had sorely missed at home with Sammy. Looking back, it would be fair to say that Corky Ballas whisked me completely off my feet, and I had absolutely no idea what to do about it.

• • •

I stayed with Sammy for almost another year. That whole time, I was twisting and turning, trying to decide what to do with my life. Things had become very complicated, as my career with Sammy was going from strength to strength, all my dreams about dancing were starting to come true, just as Corky was putting more and more pressure on me to leave everything and be with him. Head or heart? Heart or head? I had absolutely no clue. All I knew was that my mind was all over the place, and my heart was heavy, knowing whichever I chose, I was going to have to give up a huge part of myself. I knew that I didn't want to hurt anybody, but it seemed inevitable. I felt paralysed, split in two, and could only believe that at some point I would receive some sort of sign as to what to do.

Things came to a head towards the end of 1983, during a teaching trip to Germany. Sammy and I were sitting in our hotel foyer, about to start our journey to our next job, six hours away. As usual, I was miles away with my thoughts, wondering what to do with my life, when some music started playing in the room. It was 'Hello' by Lionel Richie, and I took that as the sign I needed to finally tell Sammy what was going on.

I turned to my husband and I told him, 'I'm not in love with you anymore and I want to leave. I'm in love with Corky Ballas.'

If I'd hoped that Sammy had guessed and already knew something was going on, I was in for a nasty surprise. He hadn't even heard Corky's name pass my lips since we'd come home from Texas all those months before, but there were no flies on Sammy, and he knew immediately who I was talking about. He was beside himself with anger, the shit properly hit the fan, and everyone in our group got involved. We still had to make the six-hour trip to our next job, so we had to arrange to make the journey separately, which meant we needed to find an additional driver. It was all a huge drama, with Sammy refusing to speak to me until we got to the next town, where somehow we were able to put on a smile and step out on the dance floor and teach the lesson we'd been booked for. One thing both Sammy and I had in common: we were consummate professionals. Nobody noticed a thing.

Back in England, the next big dates on the calendar were the United Kingdom Championships followed closely by the Worlds, the latter being the only title Sammy and I had never won. By then, he'd obviously been thinking long and hard about everything, and he sat me down.

As usual, he had a plan: 'Give up your boyfriend, and I'll dance the World Championship with you. We can carry on as though nothing's happened.'

Around the same time, Corky got on the phone and he told me, 'You dance the World Championship and we're done. Give up your husband, or I won't be here for you anymore. I'm not waiting for you. You need to come and be with me now.'

I realise now that, if Corky had been more supportive of me, he could have said, 'Get that world title you've worked your whole life for, and we'll sort out everything afterwards.' Those titles are sacred in the industry, and winning them would have meant everything to me. Looking back now, I realise it sounds like I wanted to have my cake and eat it too, but neither man was giving in, and I understand why now. I should have made it about my time, my decision, but I didn't, I let Corky dictate the terms, probably because that was what I was used to.

By this point, I'd fallen in love with a man who showered me with attention, and knew exactly how to woo a woman. He was also a master salesman, and now he sold the idea of my brand new life to me: 'You won't have to work, I'll take care of you.'

After all my years of graft, this was honey to my ears. Corky had been around, he'd had loads of girlfriends, and he knew exactly how to offer me what I thought I needed. What I really needed was a break from all the pressure I felt I'd been under ever since I was 18 and started living and working with Sammy. Had my husband and I communicated better about what we needed from each other, we might have had a chance of repairing it all. Just as my mother used to urge Sammy to take me somewhere on holiday, she used to beg me, 'Tell Sammy how you really feel.' But neither of us knew how to express our feelings and the rot set in.

I was terrified and had no idea what to do. My mother advised me, 'Whatever happens, you get your World Championship. You've worked all your life for it.'

It was decision time, the moment to work out what I really wanted from my life. The idea of choosing a path that I knew was going to change my life forever was terrifying, so I tried to do my best to keep a cool head and look at my options: do I give up a loveless marriage that is still a successful partnership, and brings with it a golden future, world titles and the promise of many wonderful things? Or do I give up a passion like I've never known in my whole life, and may never know again?

No one was giving me any leeway, and it felt like the clock was ticking down while I made up my mind. Looking back, I really should have stayed and danced that last World Championship with Sammy. We were at the top of our game professionally and I'm sure that, by then, we would have won everything we went for ten times over. But I had Corky's words ringing in my ears and I was terrified I was about to lose him. I became so anxious, my body let me down and I developed a huge rash across my whole skin.

There was no easy answer. Whatever I chose, I knew I would be losing something precious. Finally, I thought, 'I love dancing, it's all I've ever known, but I can give it up. I can give up the one thing I love most in the world to be with this man. It's time to follow my heart.' However successful I'd been with Sammy and whatever prospects we had for our future, they couldn't compete with the passion between Corky and me. It was completely overwhelming, and ultimately made my decision for me.

I look back now and wonder again that I made the choice I did: to give up everything I'd worked for all my life, to move thousands of miles away from my mother to join a family I'd only met a handful of times, to share my life with a man I knew so little about, apart from a few romantic dates, a bunch of phone calls and some pretty flowers. All I knew was that I longed to be with him.

The last time I'd been forced to make a choice like that in my life was when Nigel had forced me to give him up if I went for the try-out with Sammy. On that occasion, I'd chosen dance over love, and it had broken my heart. I'd regretted it ever since, and I was determined not to make that mistake again.

So, with a heavy heart, I told Corky I'd be moving to Houston to be with him, and with an even heavier heart, I told Sammy I wouldn't be going to the World Championships with him.

Sammy did his best to persuade me to change my mind, but it was made up. I refused to go and we didn't even enter our names for a world title that we were absolute favourites to win. A lot of our rivals were shocked to hear we wouldn't be competing, and of course a lot of them blamed me when they heard why. I consoled myself that they were judging me without knowing what went on behind our closed doors.

As far as everyone else was concerned, Sammy and I were the Stopfords, an unbeatable team who did everything together, who got on very well as a pair, had a successful studio and seemed to have everything any dancing couple could ask for. You could understand their shock. I was shocked myself! I get that we were an unbeatable team, I get that we got to travel the world, I get that we lived in a beautiful home, that we were on the brink of winning this World Championship that was everybody's dream. It was what we all worked for night and day, and the idea of throwing it away when it was in the palm of your hand must have seemed unthinkable. Nobody really understood, and I only *thought* I knew what I doing. Years later, I realised I didn't really have any idea. I'd had no experience of such intense emotions before, so I had no way of looking at the bigger picture. I just had to give in to them.

And, really, that decision changed everybody's lives, because we were a shoo-in for those titles for many years to follow. If we'd won, the chances are we would have stayed at the top for a few years like so many other couples before and after us. Instead, with us being out, there was a big reshuffle in the rankings, and the next couple down who thought they'd have to wait, suddenly found themselves up top. Who did win after Sammy and I left? Donnie Burns and his partner Gaynor! Donnie wasn't even ranked second beneath us at that point, but suddenly all the rankings were up for grabs, and Donnie and Gaynor made the most of it. By splitting up, Sammy and I changed the course of dance history, as well as our own lives.

Months before, Sammy and I had already been booked to return to La Classique du Quebec, the very same dance event where life had taken such a dramatic turn for us both exactly one year before, so we decided to make this our very last event together. You couldn't make this up! From there, we arranged that Sammy would come home, while I would fly to Houston to start my new life with Corky.

You couldn't have asked for a more fitting venue for the very last time Sammy and I would ever perform together as a dance couple, going out at the very top of our industry. We both knew it was the end, but somehow we kept it together for one last dance. We won the championship, just as we had the year before, then we pulled ourselves together and prepared emotionally to step out one last time for our honour dance the following day.

Our last ever dance together was the Rumba, to the tune of 'Memory' from *Cats*, and it couldn't have been more mournful. I wore a very simple white chiffon dress. I didn't think anything flashy would be appropriate for such a solemn occasion for us both.

All our friends and other dancers were watching. Gossip had by now travelled through the industry that this was going to be our last dance together, and there wasn't anybody who didn't know about the romantic triangle that had developed between Sammy, Corky and myself. Everyone in the place knew what had been going on, and you could have heard a pin drop in the ballroom as we stepped out onto the dance floor together.

It was incredibly emotional. There wasn't a dry eye in the place, and I felt heartbroken myself. People couldn't believe I was leaving, and I couldn't actually believe it myself. In fact, I was panicking at the very thought of it. It felt very similar to when I split from Nigel all those years before, in that I had no idea what I was really doing, but that I was now set on a path I couldn't do anything about. With every dance step of our routine, I knew I was taking one more step away from everything I knew, and that I was giving up something indescribably precious.

I could hardly bear to look at Sammy's heartbroken face. I could only glimpse at him for a brief second and wonder what on earth I thought I was doing. What was I thinking? Where was I going? Routine or passion? The known or the unknown? Dance or love? Had I really made the right choice for myself?

Finally, with the last notes of the music still fading away, I took my leave. As we'd rehearsed so many times, I quite literally left Sammy standing on the dance floor, while I walked to the side, put on my huge fur coat and rode up the escalator. My taxi was waiting.

You've got to hand it to the non-stop Stopfords – right until we stopped, we knew how to put on a show.

And, just like that, I gave up the biggest dream of my life, to go and live on the other side of the world with a man I thought I loved with my whole heart, but who I only slowly realised I barely knew.

That's how I moved to America to be with Corky Ballas. I didn't know it at the time, but it turned out I'd managed to Rumba my way right out of the frying pan and into the fire.

CHAPTER 4
The Foxtrot

'The classic routine of Ballroom dancers, it requires smoothness and fluidity, combined with the release of the body swing that has to be perfectly timed to create harmony within the couple. Once mastered, it produces a romance of togetherness and artistry.'

Moving to the United States was one of the biggest decisions that I ever had to make, and I spent a year thinking about it. I was never confident that Corky and his family understood what I was giving up to move there, and it was certainly difficult in so many ways. Once I arrived and moved in with him on his family's estate, I spent ages on the phone to my loved ones back in England, my mother, my friends and, strange as it may seem, even Sammy, one of the people who still knew me best.

One day soon after I arrived, I was on the phone to my life-long friend Karen from my new home in Houston, Texas, catching up on all the news from England, when I found myself saying to her, casually as though it was the most normal thing in the world, 'Well, I must go. I'm waiting on a parakeet to match the colours of my drawing room.' We both burst out laughing at how surreal my life had become, surrounded by the trappings of wealth that didn't just feel unusual, but like a different planet from the one I'd left behind.

If I had to describe life in Texas in a word, it would be 'big' – vast, flat fields with huge roads crossing them everywhere, the motorways wider than anything I'd ever seen, with huge trucks belting along them.

The other word would be 'hot'. The very first time I walked out of the cool airport terminal when I arrived, I was hit with a blanket of hot air and, the whole time I was there, it never seemed to get any cooler. I'd spend all day every day in the flimsiest of sundresses and would still have to fan myself, while men would wander past, dressed in jeans, cowboy boots, huge buckled belts and of course great Stetson hats, seemingly oblivious to the stifling temperatures around them.

Every morning I did my best with my hair and makeup, but within a couple of hours, my mascara had run and my hair was frazzled, like I'd been dragged through a hedge – not that you'd know it from the huge smiles I was met with by everyone, everywhere. Every shop I went into, every restaurant or cafe, the assistant would be beaming at me, looking perfect themselves, and saying, 'You look beautiful – did you do something with your hair?' I'd look at them, wondering, 'Are you being serious?' but they always were!

The Ballas residence itself was a magnificent sight. The horse-shoe driveway where you'd pull up in your limousine to the front porch was just breathtaking, surrounded by beautiful trees and a swimming pool. It was already very impressive before you even went into the house.

Once you walked inside, everything was done up with the most immaculate taste, from the polished wood floors to the Mexican tiles in the bathrooms. Mrs Ballas, Corky's mother, had a wonderful sense of style and she made the home as perfect as she could for her family. There were maids and butlers to cater to your every need. At the click of Mrs Ballas's fingers, they came running.

Every evening, the maids would cook a most spectacular dinner, which they would serve at 7pm sharp on a huge revolving dining table, a 'lazy Susan'. They prepared enough dishes for the whole family, whole towers of fish, steak, piles and piles of vegetables, enough for a dozen people at least, whether or not the family even turned up! Whatever food was left over at the end of the night, the staff got to share between themselves.

Corky and his sister Nini were the only children still living at home – Nini was still at school – but the other three would often turn up and sit down at the table as well.

The trappings of wealth were everywhere. Mrs Ballas's flower bill alone was a staggering $10,000 a month. Everyone either had their own Mercedes, or got whisked around in the family's limousines. Plus, the family had their own helicopter company, so wherever anyone needed to go in Houston, they could just make a phone call. Where I'd always been used to using public transport, they were just as used to hitching a ride in a family helicopter or summoning a limousine to the front door. For the family, it was like catching a cab. For me, it felt almost decadent.

Although this constant display of wealth and success was extremely impressive to me, an outsider, I have to say that the attitude that came with it didn't always make me feel comfortable. My mother had brought me up to always be polite and treat everyone with the same good manners, but when I used to go out for lunch with Mrs Ballas, she could be off-hand with the waiting staff if they didn't do things right, and that really cut me to the core, particularly as my own mother had been a waitress. One day, she caught the look on my face and she said to me, 'Remember, Shirley, money talks and bullshit walks.'

Mrs Ballas was a wonderful woman in many ways and she dearly loved her family but, like so many other rich people, it was clear she felt a sense of entitlement to her wealth. That hurt me, as it made me think of my mother and everyone else I'd grown up with who were all blue-collar workers. For them, they'd started out with nothing and every pound note was a big deal. Mrs Ballas never realised, but I felt I had more in common with the wait-ress that day than I did with my future mother-in-law, as I found myself feeling protective of everyone I'd left behind.

I think it's fair to say my life had taken a bit of an unexpected turn, after I'd thrown all my chips in the air and rolled the dice back in Quebec.

Corky was born Mark Alexander Ballas, but was given the nickname Corky by his father as a baby, and somehow that name stuck. He never, ever went by Mark, and was known forever afterwards as Corky by everyone, from his family to the bellboys at his family's hotel, to everyone in the dance industry that he then entered.

This was the man for whom I'd left behind my family, my reliable husband, my love of dance, my profession, my whole life. I'd left everything I knew to move in with this man, and I'm not sure I even knew his first name was actually Mark until I saw our wedding certificate.

He was the fourth child of George and Maria Ballas. He had some Greek on his father's side, and Spanish, Greek and a touch of French on his mother's. Corky's parents had five children in total – all given nicknames by their father as Kukla, Bucky, Winkie, Corky and Nini – and I got to know them very well, as they all lived within a mile of Mrs Ballas's family home. The Ballas clan was undoubtedly an impressive family, full of fun and love of life. All big families have the potential for a bit of conflict sometimes, so it wasn't always plain sailing, but they formed a tight-knit family unit for the most part.

George Ballas, Corky's father, had already lived several impressive chapters of his life by the time I met him. Born the son of Greek immigrants to America, he'd enlisted in the US Air Force at the age of 17 and had gone on to serve in World War II, where he was a brave bombardier, responsible for aiming and releasing bombs from his aircraft. He worked his way up to 2nd Lt Officer of Special Investigation and he also served in the Korean War.

He was never a dancer himself, but he had a passion for dance. When he met his future wife, Maria Luisa Marulanda, he fell head over heels when he saw her in a studio in Laredo, Texas, dancing the Flamenco. She'd trained under the legendary Carmen Amaya and was always a delight to watch, even when I met her years later. Maria became George's first dance teacher, and there was an instant attraction between them.

One of Mr Ballas's jobs was working in the famous Fred Astaire dance chain that had 100 studios right across America, and also the Arthur Murray chain. These studios are immensely popular places where beginners go to learn to dance. He started off working for those chains and soon realised the potential for this massively expanding market in the dance industry.

After Mr and Mrs Ballas got married in 1952, George combined his business flair with Maria's talents and they opened their own dance studio in Houston called Dance City USA, the biggest dance studio in the world with more than 100 teachers on its payroll. The main hall covered 43,000 square feet and George once described it as 'a supermarket of dancing, with babes and booze and big bands all under one roof'. How could it fail? Sure enough, the numbers of dance enthusiasts making their way onto that dance floor were staggering. One legend who trained there was Patrick Swayze, starting his path to superstardom under that big roof.

How can I express the sheer scale of the thing? Well, in the UK, if we have a guest dance party in a studio, any member of the public can go along on one night of the week, say a Tuesday. But at Dance City USA, even with all their thousands of square feet, they had so many people turning up that they had to divide them up, have people whose surnames began with the letters A to D invited for the Monday, E to H on the Tuesday, and so on. Thousands of people were squeezing through those doors.

George remained integral to the business and had become a very high-profile figure in the American dance industry by the time he sold his studio in 1970. He had made a financial killing and moved his family into a beautiful home. They had already started to become quite wealthy just through his work in the dance industry, but it turned out he was only just getting started.

George and Maria's success with Dance City, along with buying and selling land, brought them a fortune, including a beautiful home in Crestbend, Houston, a grand mansion of a house sitting on

10 acres, surrounded by vast lawns and 300 trees. Well, it was those trees that inspired George, or rather the weeds that kept growing around those trees. He became obsessed with finding something to get rid of the weeds and keep his lovely trees undisturbed.

He was driving through an automatic car wash one day when he started watching the nylon bristles glide around his vehicle. He had one of those sudden light-bulb moments you hear about with great scientists. Nothing in his business life had prepared George for such a technical bit of wizardry, but he said it was like the lights just went on in a different part of his brain. Subconsciously, he must have been wrestling with the problem and now here he was, completely inspired! He went straight home and into his garage, where he set to work, punching some holes in a tiny popcorn can. He threaded the can with wire and an old bit of fishing line and bolted it to a rotating lawn edger. And bingo, he'd solved the problem!

Ever the entrepreneur, George took his idea to a bunch of corporations to develop, but not one of them was interested. Not to be downhearted, he went home and decided that he would sell his new invention, he'd just have to form a brand new company to do it, if he could only think of a name. And thus was the Weed Eater born.

Like all the best inventions, it was a simple solution to an everyday problem. He invested all his own money that he'd made from the dance studio into the business and got his own children helping out with orders and deliveries. Single-handedly, he turned his light-bulb moment in that car wash into $40 million-a-year empire. George Ballas was such an impressive man, with a mind that never rested, his focus always fixed, not on the financial destination or the riches involved, but on the journey he would take to get there.

Several years later, he sold the business for millions and millions of dollars, far more than he could ever have imagined when he was punching holes in a can in his garage. Mr Ballas never publicly revealed how much money he made on the deal, but, crucially, there were no continuing royalties included as part of the deal, something that would come back to bite him financially later on.

For a decade or so, it seemed like all George's ideas turned to gold, or rather to oil, which he quickly invested in, like the fine Texan businessman he was. Oil was priced at $30 a barrel back then, and the profits supported his dealings in a whole load of other areas, such as real estate, office development, oilrigs, even building a huge local hotel that they built and ran, plus their helicopter business.

It was all pretty glamorous stuff. But then, around 1980, the oil dropped to around $10 a barrel, Texas's economy tanked with it, real estate dropped to less than half its value overnight, and George's fortune was gone. He wasn't on his own, it happened to hundreds of rich businessmen in the area, but for the next decade it seemed like he couldn't catch a break. He fell out with his business partner, who built a rival hotel, and then a terrible fire broke out in the one George owned, with loads of casualties. It was just one catastrophe after another until, years later, the family ended up filing for bankruptcy to sort out their finances, a sad end for George, who'd achieved so much and made so many other people rich along the way. All the big houses and cars had to go, and they had to sell all their good deals to pay off their bad deals, so there was very little left.

I'm not sure Corky ever really got over the fact that the family had lost so much money, and that he himself had to start from scratch. George was a great man with a fine mind; he just made one financial boo-boo and it came back to haunt him, which meant the family had to adjust to a dramatic change in their fortunes.

They are all extremely fine people, and Corky's brother Bucky once explained it like this, 'You can take the money but you can't take the brain.' Sure enough, all his children had watched George operate as a canny businessman, and he passed on those skills, the brainpower and the tools, so they all went to earn good livings in lucrative fields. They might not have inherited the money that had previously been coming their way, but with the more important stuff, they were set for life. For me, it taught me something even more fundamental: never get too attached to anything, and never put all your eggs in one basket.

When I turned up in April 1984, fresh from my big exit from Sammy and the dance floor in Quebec, the tide was just on the turn in the family's fortune, but there was still plenty of money swimming around from where I was sitting. I might as well have been on a different planet from my life on the Leasowe estate.

Corky lived in a beautiful annex apartment on his parents' property, and I moved straight in there with him when I landed in Houston. As soon as I arrived, he announced that he wanted to completely redecorate it, telling me, 'The world is your oyster. Have whatever you want.' We ended up with thick peach carpets, which we never had to clean as all that got taken care of, while our bed sheets were changed every single day. I remember picking out some beautiful pale-grey curtains with big peach flowers on them, which must have been when I had that chat with my friend Karen on the phone about making sure I got a parakeet to match. Corky had a dressing room made for me with a mirror surrounded by light bulbs, like something out of a Hollywood movie. Every drawer was labelled and every shirt was hung up in order. Downstairs, we had beautiful furniture and a huge TV screen as though we were at the movies. The sofas were plush and thick, all the floors were polished wood, and everything dripped in comfort, wealth and luxury.

Corky had expensive tastes, but he wasn't alone in liking nice things. One thing I soon noticed about his whole family was that, for some reason, everybody's possessions were monogrammed, from the sheets and pillowcases on their beds to the back folds of their ties. Anywhere they could put their own silk-thread initials, they did. Any money that could be spent on personal luxury was spent. It was like walking into the glossy trappings of a five-star hotel every day of my life. It all felt quite intoxicating.

• • •

At the time I moved to Houston to be with Corky, he was running his own Pac-Man company, those machines we used to see everywhere. Later on, his father owned the West Chase Hilton, and offered Corky a job working there in the food and beverage department of the hotel. This time served Corky well, as he went on to become an outstanding cook. Although he liked the work, he equally enjoyed his position as the boss's son, which he thought gave him a bit of freedom and leeway when it came to actually turning up on time for work. His father wasn't having it, and kept reprimanding him, until eventually even he had had enough, and he gave Corky the sack. In his mother's eyes, though, her son couldn't put a foot wrong. From the time on her knee right through to his adult years, from my perspective, he was his mother's favourite, a little happy, cheeky, spoilt prince.

When I first met this handsome, dashing man, he had the confidence that all that family love and wealth would naturally bring, but in addition, he had his own unique gift of the gab and a way of charming the honey from the bees.

He'd been born into that beautiful family home, surrounded by luxury, and he'd grown up in the years when the family fortunes were always on the up and up. He dressed like someone who'd fallen out of the pages of GQ magazine, with beautifully-cut suits and perfect accessories. He had a taste for all the finer things in life, not just possessions, but dinners, holidays, the works.

But it wasn't just his looks and style that did it for me. Corky's warm personality was very appealing to me – he seemed like a dazzling figure that was larger than life. I'd always been focused on the world of dancing, which meant I'd never stopped working long enough to smell the flowers. Corky, on the other hand, had travelled, he could afford to go wherever he wanted, he could work whenever the mood took him, or he could choose to disappear off on holiday instead. All that life experience had given him a sense of sophistication, it meant that he could talk to anybody and was always sure of himself in any company or situation.

Plus, he was chatty and funny, with a great sense of humour that he no doubt got from his mum and dad. When it came to sharing jokes and having fun, I have to say, it felt the opposite to what I'd experienced in my life with Sammy, although, to be fair, Sammy was always consumed with building his business. He wasn't born with a silver spoon in his mouth as Corky had been, so the pair of them had very different priorities.

It meant when I got to Houston, Corky felt like a breath of fresh air, and I was drawn like a magnet to his lust for life and his laughter. It was something I'd never experienced, and I was falling deeper under the spell that he'd begun casting over me the year before. It was as though I'd spent my whole life up to that point working, swimming upstream, and then someone had invited me to stop for a while and let me gently paddle in some warm, shallow waters. What he had to offer me was just what I needed at that time in my life. At the beginning, life with Corky was a calm, quiet place in another world, far from the stress of the dance industry that I was used to. Little did I realise how this would change.

Part of Corky's huge appeal for me was his large family. George and Maria were wonderful, generous hosts, real jokers, and a good-looking, confident couple. Their whole brood together were, for the most part, a joy to be around, and from the very beginning, I felt it was my job to fit in with that family, and not the other way around.

Mrs Ballas was extremely family-orientated, the kind of mother who delighted in having everyone around her and loved planning events – I remember the Christmas plans would get mentioned come August and every year, there was a festive family photo-graph, with its numbers continually expanding as everyone in turn got married.

At first, I found things a little difficult with my future mother-in-law, as I think I was probably a bit intimidated by her confidence. She was great company but a real extrovert while I was still quite shy and finding my feet in my new situation and surroundings.

I remembered my mother's words, 'Straight spine, walk in, say your bit, don't take any shit,' so I did my best to follow that advice and it seemed for the most part to work for me. I saw there was a bit of a coolness between Maria and Bucky's wife Sharon, it had been a difficult relationship right from the time Sharon had first got engaged to Bucky. When I moved in, I felt Mrs Ballas and I also had a few difficulties; after all, we came from different countries, different lifestyles, different everything.

One day I sensed that the tension between the pair of us was beginning to grow, and I decided it was my responsibility to put it right before things went any further. I drove my car to the Westchase Hilton where I knew she was having lunch, and I waited for her in the car park. As she came out, I approached her and cut straight to the chase. I said, 'I know there's been tension between you and Bucky's wife. I don't want it to be the same if Corky and I are to be together. So we can make a real effort to get along, or this is going to be a much more difficult journey for me as well as you.'

She looked at me for a while, no doubt weighing it up that I'd actually mentioned the elephant in the room. Eventually, she said, 'I appreciate that. You and I are going to get on just fine.' From then on, she and I never had a problem.

Despite her tricky relationship with my future mother-in-law, Bucky's wife Sharon became one of my strongest, most trustworthy allies the whole time I lived in Houston. Many years after I moved back to London and even after Corky and I separated, she continued to be a great friend. In fact, once I got the job on *Strictly*, it was Sharon who lent me one of her beautiful jackets for the launch show and became a trusted sounding board for any problems that came my way in those challenging early months.

The first three months I lived in Houston, I didn't dance, I didn't teach – to be honest, I put my feet up for the first time in years. It felt very alien to me, although it seemed quite normal to everyone else.

Mrs Ballas took me in hand, bought me lovely shoes and hats, and invited me along with her to all the lunches and tea parties she attended, and she attended a lot!

I was able to meet lots of different people from all walks of life in a short amount of time. Maria showed me how to handle myself at all the different social events the family were involved in: setting tables, how to make nice conversation at a party, and how to write sincere thank-you letters afterwards.

I enjoyed all that lunching and socialising for the first six weeks or so, then one morning I woke up in a cold sweat, surprised by the realisation that I'd had enough of that lifestyle. All the hats, the pins, the sandwiches, the parties day in and day out were lovely for a while, but ultimately, they weren't the real me. I'd had the holiday I longed for, but I was ready to go back to work.

I said to myself, 'I just want to dance.'

I'd followed my heart to be with Corky, but if I'm honest, the novelty was starting to wear off for me. I had long felt I'd missed out on passion and romance, but Corky wanted to have so much passion, and so often, that in the end it became like washing my socks, when I'd have to 'lie back and think of England' – which I did because, by then, I was missing it so much. I know I said I wanted passion more than anything else in my life, but this was ridiculous. Note to self: be careful what you wish for.

Almost immediately after my arrival in Houston, there'd already been a little – how should I describe it? – difficulty between Corky and me, concerning a certain young lady who worked for Ballas Enterprises. Only a few weeks after I arrived, the telephone rang in our apartment. I picked up the phone downstairs, while he picked up the phone upstairs at the same time. Now I come to think of it, I'm sure I once saw a scene exactly like that in *Dallas*, where Sue Ellen Ewing was betrayed in just the same way by her husband, J.R. Anyway, let's just say I heard him talking to her in a way that I found not just inappropriate but deeply hurtful, as I'd given everything up to be with this man.

I didn't turn to the drink like Sue Ellen, instead I turned to my future father-in-law, George. In Houston, whenever I wanted wisdom and guidance about anything, he was the one person I always went to. To everyone, he was this larger-than-life figure, incredibly tall even without his big Texan hat, and he always impressed me with his straight talking and his practical, positive outlook on life. He was the first proper father figure I'd ever known, and I knew that, whatever the problem, I could trust him to give me the right advice.

Sure enough, he soon dealt with Corky's indiscretion in the customary old-fashioned Texan way. Did he take his son in hand and berate him for his deceptive ways? No, he just fired the secretary.

As far as George and Corky were concerned, that was the end of the matter, but for me, the first seed of doubt had been sown about my life in Houston.

I'd given up my home in the UK and my husband and my career just as I was about to become the world champion. From where I was sitting, I feared my reputation in the industry was in tatters, as everybody had swarmed around poor Sammy; I'd been cast as the villain in a big old drama because I'd gone and done a bunk. But I'd given it all up for love, or so I thought, and now here was my chosen one, doing the dirty on me. I was not exactly impressed, but can I truthfully say I was devastated? Was I properly in love with Corky? What do you know about love at 23, anyway? Probably a tiny bit more than you knew at 17, that's all I can say. What I did know for sure was that I missed dancing, and particularly competing. I found myself yearning for my previous life, confused and beating myself up for making the wrong decision.

I called Sammy. Funny as it may seem after all the pain we'd gone through, we'd stayed in contact following my move to Houston, and he'd even asked my opinion on who he should team up with next as a dance partner. I'd advised him to pick a girl called Barbara McColl, so that's what he did. That meant that when I phoned him that morning in tears, requesting to come back and pick up where we'd left off, he had to say, 'Shirley, I did what you suggested. I teamed up with Barbara and that's who I'm with now.'

He told me later he'd told his new partner Barbara about my request and she'd replied in two words, 'No chance.' This wasn't a surprise. Pairing up with Sammy had given her a wonderful opportunity to advance in the dance world, so it wasn't something she was about to give up. Just as Donnie Burns benefited from my leaving when I did, so too did Barbara and quite a few others. With my life-changing decision, I inadvertently changed the course of more than one career in the dance world.

I wanted my old life with Sammy, I wanted my 'Old Reliable' back at my side and, of course, our dancing, but he made it clear that that wasn't going to happen. There was no turning back for me. I'd chosen love over dance, and it was a mistake.

I called my mother and bawled my eyes out as I got everything that was bothering me off my chest. I realised I'd made a mistake and was terribly homesick. I wanted to come home to my familiar surroundings, and loving faces. My mother laid it out for me in no uncertain terms: 'Shirley, it's too late to go back to Sammy. You've made your bed. Now you, young lady, have to lie in it.'

These days, I look back on that whole time and I wonder, what on earth made me do it? I uprooted my whole life, everything I'd created and worked so hard for, to be with a man I didn't know at all when, if I'd been a bit more honest with myself back in the UK, I probably just needed a bloody holiday. I felt a helpless, hopeless sinking feeling at this point, and once again, I didn't know which way to turn. Should I stay? Should I go? I had a longing to be back on the dance floor, listening to the music, practising my steps, having a laugh with the other dancers. It was all I'd ever known. It was where I belonged.

Instead, here I was, stuck in Houston with a man I no longer had any trust in. I wasn't sure that Corky and I were in love now the initial passion had begun to wear off. It was becoming clear that we had very little in common apart from the dancing. He had become a little distant and cold with me, and it increasingly felt as though he didn't even like me as a person. I didn't know what he was thinking, but I knew I longed to go home to dance. That was a safe place for me.

Once again, I turned to George Ballas. As I shared all my thoughts and feelings, he immediately understood where I was coming from, and he helped me put a structure in place for me to get back to work. With his vast experience in the dance industry across the States, he knew there'd be a market for my skills as a teacher and I could afford to pitch myself at the top of the market. At the time, people were charging around $25 a lesson, and I might have been minded to even give a bit of a discount to get some students in the door and start making a name for myself. But George was having none of it, and he made me start my prices at $50 an hour. I was horrified, I thought nobody would turn up for that price, but sure enough, people started to flock in once they realised I was a professional champion, and George made sure I was ready to provide whatever they wanted. I taught all levels of dance – amateur, professional, pro-amateur – and all styles, American style, Ballroom dancing. If it moved, I taught it.

He also helped me develop my American way of thinking. My attitude needed to be a bit different to work in the States, compared with how I'd been used to training back in the UK. When I was learning as a young girl, my dance teachers had never really gone in for much praise; instead they criticised, found fault and offered multiple notes on how their students could improve their technique, their musicality, etc. In fact, the higher up you went, the stricter they became. So that was my mindset when I started teaching in the US, and it didn't land well with the students. I came across as too strict, too straight, too direct. The students came in smiling, but after an hour with me they left frowning, and I couldn't understand it.

George, who was a born salesman, explained to me, 'You have to blend criticism with praise, you have to be cool but you also have to be warm.' He asked me to give him a lesson, so he could see how I taught, and he quickly asked me to soften my style. It was too British, too direct. This new style of teaching was my introduction to the pro-amateur world of dancing, which pairs an amateur student with a professional dancer, just like you see on *Strictly*.

The amateur student needs far more encouragement than I was used to giving, but George gave me the skills to deal with the American society of dance. I had to learn how to give a private lesson that had the feel-good factor. They say, when in Rome, do as the Romans do. You don't need to reinvent the wheel. Just as Maria had guided me in the ways of Texan society life, so George guided me in the art of being a dance teacher in the US.

Both George and Maria taught me a lot about life and work, which I've carried with me to this very day, and for which I'll always be grateful to them. George also introduced me to the male-dominated industry of the country's dance, and showed me that you have to stand up for yourself as a woman in a man's world. He taught me how to run my business properly, and how to take care of my money – many grown-up tools for life. I felt blessed at least in this department. I was loved by both my future in-laws.

In return, I felt a great deal of love and respect for them, and that remained with me until the day they each died.

One of my most special memories of my mother-in-law was when, one day, she decided she was going to dance the Paso Doble for me. She put on her skirt, her fringe top, got out her castanets and Flamenco shoes and began to dance around the living room. I was absolutely mesmerised. She had arm work that I had never seen in a Paso Doble dancer, plus a self-awareness that was hypnotic to watch. She got so involved in the music that I could see she was transported into a different world through dance.

Things got a bit better for me once I was back in my safe place of the studio, and teaching dance. I had never asked for money from George and Maria the whole time I lived in Houston, I'd saved up enough by then to be able to stand on my own two feet, but the sheer fact that I was making an effort to make my own living only went down well with people as hardworking as they were.

Despite all my hours teaching, my urge to go back to competitive dancing became overwhelming. Although I realised there was to be no return to the UK for me, I had more sleepless nights wondering about everything I was missing out on from my old life.

The question was, where was I going to find myself a new dance partner? Someone I could give what Sammy had given to me, all the techniques, tools and training we needed to climb up the rankings and have a shot at making a major final again? Someone I could turn from a decent enough dancer into one of the world's best? Someone who had the same drive as me, the same passion for dance, the same self-belief when it came to chasing the dream?

There was only one person in my world who fitted the bill. The person I had in mind was 24 years old, a chef and a part-time pro-am dancer. Was I dreaming to think I could take somebody like that and get him into the final of any major championship? Was this even possible, let alone realistic? I was probably a bit crackers at this point. I felt I had no other options open to me, and I was so desperate I was prepared to try anything.

Thus, what began as a fool's dream would turn out to be the hardest journey of my entire life. It started when I said out loud for the first time one morning, 'I'm going to teach Corky to dance.'

CHAPTER 5
The Paso Doble

'The dance of the bullfight, where the female plays multiple roles, moving from the toreador's cape to a Flamenco dancer. It is ultra intense, extremely competitive but also sensual, as the couple battle for power and dominance.'

When I put the idea to Corky about trying to make it to a major dance final in the world, getting close to what Sammy and I had achieved, his eyes lit up. He already believed he was one of the world's best dancers, he just thought he hadn't yet been discovered, which I found quite strange but another sign of his bottomless confidence in himself.

Corky turned out be one of the most difficult students I ever taught. He was entitled, privileged and in no way used to taking direction. He always thought he knew best, when actually he knew nothing about my world. And when I say nothing, I mean nothing.

I tried to explain to him, 'We have to go back to the very beginning. I understand that you've danced at pro-amateur level and won the pro-amateur championships, but the world I'm about to take you into is a completely different place, and you have to be able to follow directions well.'

The thing about Corky was that money had given him an entry ticket to anything he'd set out to do in his life up until that point, and he didn't see why dancing should be any different. Sure enough, he had a lot of money, which meant we could afford lessons, we could invite good teachers to Houston, and we could fly here, there and everywhere ourselves, but it's fair to say that Corky was not a natural student, at least in the early days.

He'd grown up in a world of dance, where he saw other people making the hardest dance steps look effortless, but it never even occurred to him what might be involved, how it wouldn't just mean learning the technique of dance, but also everything about the industry and how it was run in the UK, the hub of Ballroom dancing at the time. He was clueless about all of that and just couldn't seem to come to grips with it in his mind. It would be like taking a good bus driver and telling them they needed to learn the ropes to drive a Formula One car in the Monaco Grand Prix. It took Corky a while to understand how far we needed to travel. I didn't realise at first, but I had definitely bitten off almost more than I could chew. It's safe to say that, from the beginning, I was probably desperate, and no one had any confidence in us as a team, certainly no one of any influence.

Once we agreed we'd do this together, I made several phone calls to England, when I told a few dance teachers that I'd part-nered up with Corky. They practically laughed in my face: 'You understand that you're coming from being the best female dancer in the world to starting at the bottom of the ladder again, with a man nobody's heard of, and he's a pro-amateur dancer.' What I was attempting to do was completely unheard of in those days, so I didn't exactly get any votes of confidence or offers of help.

People were happy to come to us for private lessons, which is different because teachers have to earn a living so they always agree to that, but I never felt from the beginning that anybody truly believed it was even a possibility for me to take someone from scratch and make them a British champion. I realised I was in this boat alone, paddling upstream yet again.

With Sammy, I had followed his direction from the outset, man leading woman. Now with Corky, I had to become the direction-giver. Back then, women didn't take the helm in dance partnerships, it was absolutely unheard of, and is still very, very unusual. For many years, from my perspective, it seemed Corky resented the fact that I was the one giving the directions. We could both be volatile and that made us good Latin dancers; we'd been known to slap and push each other around in rehearsals. As a young girl, I had always felt that Sammy was strong enough to lead us. Now, as a woman, was I strong enough to do the same thing in reverse, and take a man through the industry? Everyone I spoke to about it used to laugh and tell me, 'You're taking on the impossible. It will never happen. Why don't you just give up, go and enjoy your new life?'

To be fair to Corky, he had succeeded in his own world on his own set of skills – namely, a fit, strong body, hips that could swing for Texas, and a dazzling smile that made most observers forgive any technical limitations. He'd danced all his life, taking part in pageants, joining in with his parents' competitions, so he had a training background of sorts, plus his heart was always in it. However, so much more is required if you want to be a world champion. You have to learn the tools from the ground up if you want to become a world-class dancer and compete at the highest level, which was exactly what I wanted to do and what I had in mind for us. Corky didn't know what had hit him.

At the start of our partnership, there was no comparison between Corky and Sammy as dancers. Sammy and I had been natural partners from the very beginning. He was well qualified, a seasoned professional who had trained, like myself, all his life with a keen appreciation for the art of Ballroom dancing. Our combined skills made for perfection on the floor. It was strange because Sammy and I never had the real love affair and yet, we had all the right chemistry on the dance floor. With Corky, it was the complete opposite. We had all the passion of the real-life love affair and the romance, but we never found that same chemistry in our dancing.

Here I was, a British Champion paired with a pro–am dancer.. What on earth was I thinking? However, whatever Corky lacked in technical expertise, he definitely made up for with another quality – bottomless ambition!

Corky had aspirations to match mine, and he behaved as though it was only a matter of time before it came to pass. He already had that idea in his head, before I even started training him, and he always made it sound as though it was him doing me the favour. Right from the start of our partnership, he would say to me, 'Stick with me, baby, I'll take you places.' I used to think it was funny but I came to realise it was him putting on a brave front. People used to look at him like he was a Looney Tune. He said it once to Ron Gunn, a famous British tailor in our industry who used to make Corky's clothes, and Ron laughed out loud. But Corky didn't care, he'd answer Ron back or he'd crack a joke. Corky had an opinion about everything, including the way I was trying to teach him.

He made my life very difficult in the studio. Corky would shout and scream and cause all sorts of problems and tension between us, then the minute we left the studio, he could smile and joke as though nothing had happened. He could just drop it, but I found it much harder to do that. It took me a long time to get over his lack of respect for me.

Don't get me wrong, Corky had a lot of potential. He had the perfect body for a dancer, the right length of leg, the right length of arm, a tiny waist. He was already an experienced pro-am dancer, even if he was a bit what I'd call 'flash and trash'. He could do things with his body that were very impressive, he was both mentally and physically strong and he could move his body. I could tell straight away if someone had the goods, and Corky did, but did he have the brain?

When we went into the studio for our first lesson, I told him, 'We need to start right back at the beginning with the basics,' but he wouldn't hear of it. He wanted the choreography, he wanted the routines to have lots of 'flash and trash', he wanted to take any short cuts he could to create some razzle-dazzle. He used to say to me, 'Nobody's looking at those technical things, don't bother teaching me them.' He was a proud, self-believing man and handing his dancing over to me didn't sit easily at first. It was an uphill battle for both of us in different ways, and it would remain a challenge throughout our career.

I realised that Corky would be tested with a barrage of criticism once we set out to compete together. I was nervous about all the insults I knew he was going to get, hence my determination to teach him properly. What I had going in my favour was his determination. He wanted to get to the top and discover what it felt like to stand there and be the best in the world, as much as I wanted it for him. I think he soon realised that, if he wanted to be like Sammy or any other man at the top, he was going to have to give in and take instruction from somebody who had already made it and knew a lot more than he did.

Once he made up his mind and was ready to learn, he proved he had the ability to turn up first for practice, stay the longest in the room and be the one turning out the lights at the end of the day. His self-drive was second to none. It took us a while to adapt to our new regime but we got there in the end.

There's a lot of debate about what makes a great dancer, whether it's sheer talent or hard work that pays off the most. Am I naturally talented? I was fortunate to be born with some talent, a strong core and balance, but I was more fortunate to have the work ethic to make the best of what I had, and that was something Corky also developed. There are a lot of talented people in the dance industry who don't put the work in, and there are an equal number of people without that talent, but who are prepared to graft, and they'll always rise higher. I'd say Corky Ballas was a grafter. In time, he became 150 per cent dedicated to our professional partnership, as was I, even though it was like climbing a mountain with him, barefoot.

I was guiding Corky exactly the same way Sammy had guided me. I followed the same format that had worked so well with a man guiding a woman, wondering all the time whether that could work equally well even if it was a woman guiding a man. Could I be successful with Corky? Is it possible to start from scratch? I think the only people who believed it at the time were Corky and me, not a single other soul in the world.

Becoming a highly tuned dancing team involves a huge amount of effort and sacrifice. As well as all those hours in the studio – musicality, training, learning, teaching, arms, legs, feet, posture, neck, timing and more – you have to seek out the best teachers in the world and get on their books. You have to start building a team of experts around you, a group of people who believe in you and will support you. You have to decide who to put your faith in, who will lead you on the path you want to go. Of course we found teachers prepared to teach us, and we soon formed a network, but getting them to believe in us was a different story, and I never felt like any of them had any faith in our success.

Initially, I booked lessons with some teachers in the United States that Corky had previously trained with. I soon discovered there was the European way of learning, and there was the American way, and these two were worlds apart.

One of Corky's teachers was a man called Vernon Brock. He was training the US champions at the time, and that was his claim to fame. But from the moment we walked into his studio, it all felt very alien. He immediately had me doing high kicks, back bends and even rolling around on the floor, which in my world of dance was a complete no-no. I felt like I was cleaning the floor in my dress, and my high kicks couldn't even reach Corky's arm. Vernon didn't seem remotely bothered about the technical skills which I'd had drilled into me since my days with Margaret Redmond even though, to me, they were the backbone of any dance movement. Eventually, I said to him, 'Please, Mr Brock, this isn't the kind of choreography that I'm used to doing. I'm better if I just stand on my feet and you give me something technical.'

With that, he screamed at me, 'Listen here, young lady. Perhaps you were once the British champion, but you aren't anymore, and you've employed me to teach you. So get that in your head. You're starting off here like a pro-amateur team.

'When I give you a private lesson, you will give me the respect of doing what I've asked you to do.'

I was shocked at the time, but he taught me a valuable lesson that day: if you're paying for someone's opinion, you have a responsibility to listen to it.

I did my best for him. I jumped about like a blue-arsed fly. I tipped, I bent, I cocked my legs up; I rolled all over the floor and got dirty in my pretty dress as I tried to do exactly what he said. The results were disastrous. It was never going to run. I couldn't do it. I just wasn't that kind of dancer. As a teacher, you have to figure out what your student is good at and, in England, my teachers realised I suited basic choreography, and the more I stood on my own two feet, the happier I was. Vernon was all about creating far flashier choreography and routines and, for me, that was like trying to fit a square peg in a round hole. Years later, I came to love him, we came to have a great understanding and mutual respect, but we all realised there was no way Corky and I were going to succeed with Vernon's dance style.

Following that disaster, Corky said to me, 'Okay, Vernon was my teacher. Let's try with your teacher,' so I got straight on the phone to Nina Hunt who'd already played such a significant part in my life, and she agreed to come out to Houston and train us.

Several other teachers came from all over the world as well, including Alan and Hazel Fletcher, Robert Ritchie, Meryem

Pearson and Sammy Stopford, yes, *that* Sammy Stopford. If Sammy was on tour in the US, he'd call me and say, 'I'm passing through. Do you want me to come down and give you a lesson?' Sammy was happy to teach Corky and me, but I think deep down in his heart, he also wanted to check I was doing okay. Because he knew me so well, he could tell just from talking to me on the phone that I was miserable in my new life; he always had concerns about me being in Houston, about the way I was being taught, and whether I was truly happy. Even though we never discussed it, I knew Sammy had been devastated when I left; there was lot of sadness on both sides. You don't break up from a partnership that strong without great pain and sorrow, and I was immensely relieved that we'd been able to stay friends. I used to look forward to him coming, and it always made me feel more secure when I saw his face. There was a huge bond between us, something we shared that was just unbreakable.

Corky wasn't as respectful of these amazing dancers as I'd have liked him to be, and every teacher we invited in had conflict with him. He would sulk and show a lack of respect to them and to me. I was really embarrassed sometimes.

Alan Fletcher had been five times world champion and was an absolutely brilliant teacher. I should add that it didn't hurt that he looked like Robert Redford! He was alarmed by Corky's attitude, and the way he spoke to me in the studio, and he wouldn't tolerate his behaviour. Corky would say, 'All right, Jack,' and Alan would answer, 'My name is Alan Fletcher. My name is not Jack.' You could cut the atmosphere between them with a knife. Eventually, Alan told him, 'Change my air ticket, please. I'm on the next flight home if you don't change the way you speak to both Shirley and me. You need to learn how to take lessons, young man.' Corky's education was about more than dance at that point.

As Corky gradually learned the art of self-discipline and started to absorb all the lessons from myself and other teachers, we began to move slowly but surely up the ladder, until the day we decided to try our luck in competition. Finally, I was able to take a step back, look at Corky and think, 'I've moved this difficult pro-am student into a promising dancer and possibly – who knows? – a champion.'

When Corky and I first started to compete, it all felt a little bit strange for me, because even to compete in the United States, we had to come in at a very low level. I refused to let it bother me, as I thought, 'I'm learning valuable lessons starting again at the bottom.' It was all good practice for the day we would eventually head to England, which was already bubbling somewhere in my mind.

Corky and I soon started to get a little bit better, but it all came very gradually in comparison with that meteoric rise Sammy and I had enjoyed. I actually believed this was a great opportunity for me, as I was learning how to be a better teacher, and also gaining valuable insight into the industry. The majority of dancers have to start from scratch at the very bottom, but it was something I'd never done before. After about a year, we started to make the finals in the smaller competitions, and once we broke through these finals, we started to improve consistently. I discovered that gradual is always best – you learn a lot more that way.

For the first year we danced together, Corky and I still managed to balance all that training and competing with some fun and romance. It was a honeymoon period in our lives and I look back on it fondly. But, inevitably things change when you start to compete at a high level.

All my life, I have never liked to lose at anything. If I take on anything, whether it's becoming British champion or training a beginner, I want to do it to the best of my ability. So there's no doubt that, as the months went by, I became more and more focused on our dancing. Irony of ironies, I'd turned into a mini-Sammy Stopford without realising it! As a result of all this hard work, we pretty soon got into the top six pairs of the United States, and I felt it was only a matter of time before we became the US champions, or at least I convinced myself of that, because nobody else believed it. It was important that I kept the faith if we were to succeed.

The other aspect that altered the dynamic of our relationship was even more significant and life-changing for me. About a year and a half after my arrival in Houston, Corky asked me to marry him and I accepted his proposal. Once again I jumped into something without thinking; I don't think either of us was ready to settle down. I was never completely comfortable living in Houston, so I suppose I thought that getting married would bring me some security. For Corky's part, I think he realised that I'd given everything up for him and that it was the right thing to do. What are the right reasons to get married? I'm not sure we knew.

We decided to have a big wedding in September 1985, and Mrs Ballas couldn't have been happier as she set to work on all the finer details. We didn't like to mention we'd actually got married secretly in a registry office the previous month. As far as she was concerned, this was to be our big day and no expense was to be spared. The reception was to take place at the family's hotel, the Westchase Hilton, and we decided to get married at Second Baptist Church, where we both became Baptists.

Mrs Ballas did not disappoint when it came to putting on a show. Have you ever seen any pictures of those big over-the-top American weddings? Well, it was one of those – a huge fleet of cars, flowers everywhere you looked, six bridesmaids, six groomsmen, a beautiful dress and veil, the whole nine yards!

On my side of the family, Mr Ballas paid for my mother, her best friend Laura, Aunty Mavis and my brother David to come – four family members. Then I learned that Mrs Ballas had invited my father as a surprise! I know, you haven't heard about him for a while – well, me neither. Perhaps he had decided it was time for him to make amends, although I couldn't help but wonder why he decided to do it now. I was very shocked that my father had turned up, and he seemed disappointed that I wouldn't let him take me up the aisle – I insisted that was my brother's job.

Our worlds had been so far apart, with me raised in the UK, and Corky in the US, me from a poor family, and him from a rich one. We didn't really know one another at all well but, back in those days, we spent so much time in one another's company – living together, dancing together, travelling together – getting married just seemed the next step.

I didn't have the luxury of any independent thinking time. There were lots of questions that maybe we should have asked ourselves before we said, 'I do.'

Much later on, Corky accused me of being attracted to his money, but it wasn't the case, I was just basking in the warm bath of his passion for me. Meanwhile, I always knew he wanted dancing stardom, and with me he got a world champion who was experienced in the one thing he wanted to do. If he was completely honest, he probably couldn't believe his luck! He actually admitted to me much later, he was in love with my dancing, and that was his original attraction to me. He said, 'The problem with marrying your partner is you confuse the love of dance with the love of the person.' I was never really sure that Corky loved me.

Whatever the truth, we never asked ourselves any of those important questions, such as: 'Are we compatible?', 'Can we live together?', 'Do we respect each other?' Instead, we ploughed on and later found out all the answers the hard way.

• • •

Straight after our wedding, we went on honeymoon to Hawaii, where I was seriously ill. I thought I had some sort of infection, but Corky wouldn't hear of it, because he had this thing in his mind that I was constantly sick. I did my best to keep going, even when he announced that he wanted us to learn to scuba-dive.

I was very keen to keep my new husband happy on our honeymoon, so I tried to hide my nausea all the time we were bobbing about in the swimming pool, trying to get our PADI licences. My system failed me when it came to diving in the sea, and I was as sick as a dog, but Corky refused to let me go back to our hotel room. I felt ill the whole time we were away, and I could tell he was disappointed and angry with me.

As soon as we got back to Houston I went to the doctor, and it didn't even cross my mind what was really going on. I told the doctor all my symptoms, and then he gave me a blood test.

'Well, Shirley, you don't have an infection,' the doctor smiled. 'That's great,' I said. 'Do you think I just picked up a bug?'

'No, you didn't pick up a bug. You're going to have a baby.'

Shocked doesn't begin to describe how I felt. I couldn't begin to get my head around the fact that I was now pregnant. I was freshly married, and our dance career was just taking off in the United States. Corky and I had been tremendously careful because we were just starting out on our career, and I was actually on the pill but what can I say? I was overwhelmed by the news and started crying in the doctor's office.

When I got home, the first person I bumped into was my mother-in-law. I confided in her and she was delighted. When I told Corky, he took two steps back and appeared to be in deep shock. He said, 'But we're just getting somewhere in the dance world. What happened? Did you forget your pills?' He was not a happy camper.

Corky was still processing this surprising news when I picked up the phone to call my mother. She was the person I was most worried about telling, because I knew she wasn't convinced that my marriage was where it needed to be, nor that this would be a good environment for a new baby. I knew she wouldn't be thrilled, and sure enough, she made no bones about how she felt. Her immediate reaction was, 'Oh Shirley, you're not' – not because she didn't want me to have a baby, she was thrilled about that aspect of it, but because from day one, she'd never been convinced that my relationship with Corky was on solid enough ground or had strong enough foundations on which to build a family. In fact, she thought it was a big mess.

I was preoccupied with how I would be able to keep on training Corky even as I prepared to have a baby. I decided it would be a good idea for him to dance with his talented sister, Nini, and set about teaching her all our routines. Many times Corky didn't even show up for the lessons, so I ended up teaching and dancing with Nini, which meant I got some exercise, but it wasn't quite what I had in mind! Corky was MIA: missing in action.

If I'd felt vulnerable before I was pregnant, now I felt extremely exposed, and understood just how precarious the situation in which I found myself was. Here I was, newly married to a man I realised I didn't really know, and now we were finally getting somewhere in our dance career, I was about to change everything and have a baby. I felt very small and alone, thousands of miles away from the people who cared about me the most.

As with the arrival of most babies, for sure, our timing was definitely off. Those months sped by with my mind in a bit of a blur. We'd just started to improve our dancing results and then, bang, our little girl, or so I thought, was on her way. For a lot of the time, I suffered with morning sickness, but I didn't want to give myself time to rest, as I felt the pressure of keeping up our schedule as much as possible. Most people would have given up on their dancing dreams at this stage and not even bothered. We were right back on the first rung of the ladder.

Corky was always incredibly controlling about my appearance, remarking on things he thought I could improve, and the duration of my pregnancy was no exception. The whole time I was expecting, he became very concerned about the prospect of me putting on any weight. He said to me, 'Get too big and I'm out the door. I don't do fat, Shirley.'

He was also preoccupied with our training schedule, and he worked out that if I had our baby in May, we could be competing again in August, which would only give me a few weeks to get back in shape. For the umpteenth time in my life, I began to feel some pressure to keep my partner happy, while my doubts about Corky and his love for me began to grow.

I've suffered from weight issues all my life. I can easily pile on the pounds if I'm not careful, which is bad news for a dancer. Being pregnant, though, I decided this was the right time to eat what I wanted and stay healthy for my sake and that of my unborn child. I got a very specific craving for Shipley's doughnuts, which came 12 in a box, plus some milk to wash them down. This was a craving I had on a daily basis, and I gained my whole pregnancy weight allowance in the first three months, and Corky didn't attempt to hide his displeasure. He started monitoring everything I ate, then he secretly got hold of my doughnut box and hid a large black cockroach under the chocolate glazing. When I ate my next doughnut, the cockroach crackled in my mouth with its legs dangling on the outside. This made me vomit straight away.

No doubt he thought this 'creative' solution was to 'save me from myself' and that I'd ultimately thank him, but for anybody to want to do this to a pregnant woman is hard to believe. For my own husband to behave like this to me, the woman carrying his child, well … I don't have the words to describe how I felt at the time, or even to describe it now, all these years later. I can only say I recoil at the memory, and just hope nobody else ever has to go through the same experience.

As my pregnancy progressed, I went for three ultrasounds in total, and they all told me I was expecting a girl, and in my head I called her Elizabeth. I painted her room peach and had a baby shower for 150 women, where I gratefully received all kinds of pink teddies, toys and dresses.

Off I went to the women's hospital in Houston, which proved to be the height of luxury, and where I mistakenly treated the whole experience as a spa holiday. What I didn't realise was that every time I rang the bell, asked for a coffee or a sandwich, it was going on the bill. Mr Ballas had suggested I stay for a week and get some rest, and I took him at his word.

By the time I was ready to go home, I'd totted up a bill ten times the length of my body, thousands and thousands of dollars, which my father-in-law dutifully paid up. It's fair to say I learned a valuable lesson about hospitals in the private sector, hence my never-ending gratitude to the NHS back home.

I had a difficult labour. As well as my mother there to help me, the Ballas family visited, with Corky wanting to film the entire thing. I had my legs up around my neck, my mother holding a knee and Corky with a camera zoomed in on my private parts, which didn't feel very British. I started getting upset and Corky and I actually started shouting at each other, until my mother had had enough. She put her foot down and shouted, 'All cameras out,' which settled the matter. 'Out, out, out,' she said. 'I'll deal with my daughter.' The entire Ballas family were dismissed. Once again my mother stepped up.

In the middle of it all, on 24 May 1986, the moment came for my child's arrival into this world. There we were, all prepared for a little girl when out came a boy. Yet another shock!

Little Mark appeared and that's when my whole life changed in a second. I know everybody has their own story about the joy of a baby's arrival, but it's true that nothing can prepare you for it. He came out looking like an alien, all shrivelled up, and immediately I forever loved the mortal bones of him. Here was something that was all mine for the very first time, another person I was completely responsible for. I couldn't take my eyes off him, pledging to nurture him and love him always as best I could.

When it was time for us to come home, Corky didn't appear at the hospital to collect us. I didn't know where he was, and I wasn't able to get hold of him. In my head, I tried to make sense of it and cast as positive a light on it as I could. The traffic in Houston was always horrendous, it would definitely have taken an hour or more for him to get to the hospital. Plus, Mr Ballas had just paid my $30,000 hospital bill, and Corky himself had sent a stretch limousine and chauffeur for us, so I wasn't short of material comforts.

This was one of those occasions, though, when you learn the value of baubles, bangles and beads. I had all these luxuries around me, but it was the person, the interest and support that I craved. Corky knew I had my mother with me, and I deeply appreciated having her to lean on, but I missed dreadfully having my husband with me at that significant moment when I was bringing home our baby son. I assumed it was meant to be something we did together, but come the time, Corky had bigger priorities.

Mrs Ballas always had a take-charge attitude and, from the moment we got home, she insisted that I have a nurse to take care of Mark. She lived with us, slept on the couch and from that very first day, it was a battle of wills between the nurse, my mother, Mrs Ballas and myself as the mother of the baby. The blanket was on him, the blanket was off, it was the right time to feed him, it was the wrong time, the room was too hot, the room was too cold, he had the right clothes on, he had the wrong clothes on. He wasn't short of attention, that's for sure. I had all the usual pressures of being a new mother, trying to find my way with my new baby son, added to which I had all these voices in my ear, insisting on the best thing to do, and all contradicting each other.

Although I needed them, a part of me just wanted to be left on my own with my new baby, so we could work it out together, just the two of us. Although I didn't realise it at the time, I was also suffering from post-natal depression, which made me very tearful and exhausted, and gave me a lot of sleepless nights.

Corky remained very anxious that I get back in shape so we could get back to work. Mark was born at the end of May, and our next championship was due to take place in Florida in the August. Straight after that was the United States Closed Championships, which we'd set our hearts on winning, so that only gave me a few weeks to drop all the extra weight I'd put on during my pregnancy. Corky was on my tail, watching the scales, making me exercise to make sure I lost the weight – about 70 pounds in two and a half months, at the same time as going back to training intensely, plus learning to look after my newborn baby.

With all that going on, the few minutes when other people went off for lunch or dinner and my mother and I got to spend time with Mark on our own were my most precious. Mother and daughter together, enjoying my son, her grandson, gave me my calmest moments in amongst all the turmoil of what I knew people were expecting of me.

Corky and I had been running in first place just as I got pregnant, but when we returned to competition in Florida, we dropped to third, so we had some making up to do. From then on, we had just one month to get ready for the United States Championships, which for the very first time we won.

There was an awful lot of pressure on us both. Corky wanted to silence his critics once and for all, while I wanted to prove I could pull off what everyone had scoffed at, taking a brand new partner and training him to climb to the top of our industry. It was a tough event and it was just as well my mother was there to look after Mark, because from the moment we picked up that first US title, our feet really didn't touch the ground.

We went on to win that same US title many, many times. If winning so often was impressive for me after such a big break away from competition, training with a brand new partner AND having a baby, for Corky to do it was phenomenal. He'd done what he set out to do, the thing that nobody other than him had believed was possible when we began. To go from pro-amateur champion to United States professional champion was unheard of, and I'm not sure even today he realises how amazing and unlikely it was that he achieved it. We made history, we had become US champions in a very short space of time, and I like to think it gave a big poke to all our doubters from around the world.

With those US titles came a much busier schedule for us both – teaching, demonstrating, travelling to give lessons, travelling to take lessons. In England, you can drive up and down the country between venues in London, Blackpool and Manchester. In the US, the distances are much vaster, so we were flying all over the place, from Houston to California, over to Florida, back to New York, often for three days at a time, plus we started making annual tours to Japan. These trips made for huge chunks of time away from my newborn son, which plunged me into fresh waves of guilt and regret about leaving him behind. I wanted to do the work, but I also wanted desperately to be with him. Our lives became a massive juggling act of baby, packing, flying, unpacking, dancing, teaching, moving on, and I was trying to do the job as efficiently as possible so I could just get back to our baby.

I hated being away from Mark on those occasions we had to leave him behind. I used to sneak his pillow into my luggage so I could cuddle it whenever missing him became too much. I could at least hold my face to his pillow, inhale his unique baby scent, and that kept me going.

We were US champions over and over again, but I always had this niggling feeling that we were capable of more. I also began to wonder, not long after Mark was born, would we ever be able to hit the greatest heights if we stayed living in the States? Or did we need to move to Great Britain? Or should we just pack it all in and start being a 'normal' family? This was a decision we knew would affect all of us for the years ahead.

For the next four years, we employed British teachers to train us, and I tried to build our support network. To get to the top of the industry, you definitely have to have the right people around you, and that was difficult to create from thousands of miles away. I thought we needed to be nearer the centre of the infrastructure, living in the swing of things. I was just about to hit 30, and I wanted to give my career one last roll of the dice. I felt increasingly that with Mark to care for, I wanted to be near my own mother. Plus, as anybody who's been away from home for a long time will understand, sometimes you just want to get back to your roots.

I mentioned the idea to Corky, but he wasn't in the least bit interested and he had a point. We were US champions, our diaries were full, we were travelling all over the place and we had this wonderful new baby. We'd had terrible problems with a maid who'd been mistreating Mark, and when my mother heard about that, she made the executive decision that, instead of us having to move, she'd come and stay with us in the States. Just like that, she became Mark's chief babysitter, so that was a huge weight off my mind.

By then, we'd moved away from the Ballas family home into our own home in Katy, a city just outside Houston, but I still longed to move to London. The house was enormous but the area was horribly quiet and my mother said it was like a morgue during the day when everyone was off at work, and it didn't really feel like home for any of us.

When Mark was a baby boy, I sat down again with Corky to have the same discussion about whether we should move to the UK. I realised I was suggesting something that would require an enormous effort – selling everything off, leaving all that we'd known, finding a new place to live, uprooting our family and finding a school for Mark – but I was ready. By then, we'd been US champions several times and I think Corky was also beginning to wonder if we should try to do better, even if that meant living in Europe. My husband's ambition finally caught up with my longing to go home. So we decided to sell up and make the move to England, something that absolutely horrified Mrs Ballas.

I didn't know how us moving back to London would be perceived by other people in the dance industry, and nor did I care. I think the perception was that I'd thrown away my career by choice and I'd done a bunk at the height of my career with Sammy. I believed people thought I just wasn't good enough with Corky. As we thought more about making a big move to England, friends told me people in the industry were gossiping: 'Why are they moving?', 'They're never going to make the final', 'They should be content with what they've got.'

That had been spelled out to me in no uncertain terms during a chat I had with a teacher on one of my very first visits back to the UK. 'Shirley,' she began, in that pretend-kind way lots of people speak, 'you made the decision to leave years ago, so why don't you go away, have a family, enjoy your life? Because there's no way you'll be accepted back here in Britain. You'll be a wallflower.'

Well, anyone who's ever met me will know that her words would only make me do the very opposite of the advice she gave. I am many things, but I am not, and never will be, a wallflower. On the contrary, it was this kind of attitude towards me that kept propelling me forward. The more obstacles that people put in my way, the more determined I was to go round them and keep moving on. I needed to learn more about my industry. I needed to learn about human ego, and what it would take to get this average couple into a UK final. I became even more determined.

Moving back to the UK in 1990 meant Corky and I went through a dramatic change in our lifestyle. Gone were the limousines, the helicopters, the acres of lawn and all the sunshine we'd been used to back in Texas. It was a case of riches to rags, and yet another restart for me. The Ballas family's fortunes were on the wane by then, which meant George Ballas wasn't able to help us fund our big move. The lack of financial support was fine by me, I was used to that, but for the first time in his life, Corky was on his own.

Of all the houses in all the world, or in London at least, how did we end up walking into a three-storey house right opposite Sammy Stopford's home in London, and buying it? Well, as I said, for several years, Sammy had stayed in touch with me in the States, with our paths crossing many times. When I mentioned Corky and I were thinking of moving back to the UK, he knew of some new houses being built in the Docklands. He advised, 'If you move into it, great. Otherwise you can always rent it out. Either way, it's a great investment.' We put a deposit down on one of the houses Sammy had mentioned, but it wasn't going to be ready for about a year after Corky and I first moved back.

Instead, we rented a one-bed terraced property in Mitcham, south London, not far from where I'd lived above The Nest restaurant all those years before, when I'd first moved to London from Yorkshire. Just like my first room above the restaurant, this was filthy too, with bugs growing in the carpet, a million miles from all that luxury we'd known in Houston, but we did our best to clean it up and added a fresh coat of paint to all the walls. I had no problem adapting to our new surroundings, I was just glad to be back in London.

We'd already put our deposit down on the house in the Docklands, but we struggled to sell our house in the US, which meant we had hardly any money and needed to work. This was where Mick Stylianos and his wife Lorna Lee gave us a huge opportunity.

Mick and Lorna had been in my life for years, competing against Sammy and me back in the day. They still owned the Top of the Stairs Dance Studio in Norbury, that glamorous place I used to gaze out on from my window above The Nest. Now here I was inside that very same studio, gazing back out at my old room where I'd lived more than a decade before. Mick was still teaching in the studio, and I started to go there every day and sit watching him and his wife teach. If any couples came in looking for lessons, Mick would say, 'We're booked but you can have a lesson with Shirley.' He had great confidence and faith in my teaching ability, and at first he didn't even charge me any floor fee, because he wanted to help me get myself sorted. That was a massive boost for me; it helped us build our business again in the UK, and I'll never forget Mick and Lorna's kind gesture. Not only that, they lent Corky and me some money to get our first car, a Ford Fiesta. They were beyond generous.

Coming back to London I had a lot to prove, more to myself than anyone else. Corky and I both had our demons. I was starting again from scratch, crawling my way back up the UK rankings, having dropped from the top to the very bottom. Meanwhile, Corky had seen his lifestyle change overnight. His parents had lost their huge fortune, and now here he was living in London with me in a tiny two-up, two-down. He had been a very materialistic person in the early days, but it was fair to say he adapted to his new environment without too much complaint. He was a tough charac-ter, and I've never in my life met anyone more resilient. If someone ever said to him, 'You can't do this, you won't do this, you're crap,' he'd find a way to make it happen. It was all fuel to the fire, and he matched me in having something to prove.

I didn't ever get the feeling people were interested in our return to the UK, and of those who were, many didn't try to hide their disdain for Corky with his brash American showman ways. One woman during a private lesson told him to his face, 'You're nothing but a fart in a paper bag.' But Corky, being Corky, just smiled at her and said, 'All right, well why don't you come over and teach this fart in a paper bag how to dance? Come on, baby, you can do it.' And just like that, he won her over. It didn't matter who thought he was crap, he thought he was great, and that is a major part of winning at whatever you do. If you have no self-belief and you have to rely on other people to tell you you're any good, you're fucked, basically. I learned that from Corky.

We had several teachers throughout our time living in England. I liked them all and got great guidance from them, but there was always this thought in my head that, no matter how much money we spent or how many lessons we had, no one really believed in us or took us seriously. However, one man proved the exception to this rule, and he was to change our course in dance.

Around the same time as our move to the UK, I had travelled to Japan for work. I was on a bus travelling between one huge city and another, when I sat next to a man called Ruud Vermeij. We started chatting and ended up talking for the entire six-hour journey. He was an actual professor, and he was telling me all about his theories on dance. I thought to myself straight away, 'I would love to take some lessons with this man.' I could tell he had brand new concepts and intellectually based ideas that I was sure could inspire us. By the time I got off the bus, I was feeling very excited by the prospect of working with him.

The Professor had been a competitive dancer himself but had never made it into the top six or been a champion of the world. However, he was a self-educated man in the art of dance. He became the first ever instructor in the world to obtain a doctoral degree in ballroom dancing. He had degrees in music and dance studies, but he also studied psychotherapy and counselling. To him, the mind was as important as anything the body experienced, and his broad outlook became key to what Corky and I managed to achieve.

When we first went along for lessons with Ruud, it gave the rest of the industry yet another reason to mock us. 'Why on earth would Corky and Shirley go to Vermeij? He's never made it. What does he know?' But the Professor had been responsible for the success of amateur world champions Louis van Amstel and Julie Fryer. Knowing the results he'd had and with his theories, I became hell-bent on having lessons with him to further my education in different areas of dance, other than just foot and leg technique.

Now, of course, he's celebrated as one of the world's greatest teachers and coaches. He's had many champions who have passed through his studio, with students and teachers across the industry hanging on his every word, but when I first came across him, people weren't so ready to accept his teachings. I, on the other hand, wanted to try something new, and I was desperately looking for somebody who would put no boundaries on us, who had faith that 'if you believe, you achieve'. I needed somebody who would invest in us and guide us, and I found that person in Ruud Vermeij.

What I've realised more and more over the years is that a teacher has to give much more than a lesson full of technical expertise. The most important quality they have to offer is hope. Plus, there's a whole philosophy to dance, which a lot of students try to avoid because it's too demanding, but if you give yourself over to it, it can be very enriching.

Don't ever think dance is just about where you place your feet. Succeeding in the world of dance competition needs a lot more skills than this. You have to work out all the politics, the people, the dynamics, and it takes time and a huge effort. You have to follow all the possible avenues, and it won't just land in your lap; you have to figure it out. The meteoric rise I enjoyed when I entered professional competition with Sammy Stopford was amazing and I learned a lot from him and that whole period, but my true education in my industry came when I was struggling with Corky. Going back to the very bottom and working my way back up the ladder was without doubt the hardest thing I have ever done, but the rewards were immense, and the lessons remain lifelong.

Our house in the Docklands was eventually finished, so my mother, Mark, Corky and I all prepared to move into our new home. That meant we were now living opposite Sammy and his partner Barbara, with his kitchen overlooking our bedroom!

Whenever Corky and I headed out to practice in the morning, Sammy would often spot us. He used to hang out his window and shout at us, 'You keep going to practice. I'm still going to beat your arse.' And then he'd shut the window again. It wasn't long before I got my own back, though. I knew Sammy was trying to watch his weight, so whenever I spotted him from my window heading for a snack, I'd get on the phone and shout down the line, 'You stay away from that fridge.'

Once we moved in, there formed quite a strange dynamic between the two couples. We weren't anywhere near the top of the rankings while they were second in the world, so we represented no threat, and they became extremely helpful to my family. There were many times when my mother couldn't get Mark to school in Dulwich, so Barbara would drive him there in the mornings. Barbara and I would confer every day, and sometimes she'd even interrupt her private lessons and run into the school in her high heels to pick up my son. All Mark's friends would ask him, 'Who is that?' He'd just answer, 'That's my Aunty Barbara.' There was always someone different picking up Mark from school, so he was quite used to it.

After the first year of living in the UK, we started to break through into the top 48, what you might call the tail end of the table. Corky knew everyone still thought he was crap, but if all the criticism got to him, he never once let it show, in public at least. In front of everyone else, he kept a big smile on his face and seemed to be able to take it all on the chin. In private, however, he increasingly took his frustrations out on me, and I would lash out in response, leading to constant tensions between us.

On the other hand, that same sense of competitiveness causing us to battle constantly with one another meant that when we did stop fighting long enough to compete, we became a formidable partnership, well-matched in our determination not to be beaten.

One time, we walked out onto the floor at the British Championships, and under his breath, I could hear him saying, 'Ching, ching, ching.' I muttered, 'What are you doing? What are you saying? Concentrate, Corky.' I was getting quite agitated because I was such a serious person when it came to dance. He whispered, 'I'm putting on my tin suit. Bullets won't penetrate this. Everyone can laugh at me, everyone can say I'm crap, but the bullets stop here.'

He would protect himself by creating armour around himself, and if anybody critiqued him, he would visualise the bullets flying off. As time progressed, our dancing got better and better, and I think Corky's strength of mind was a key factor to our success.

He had charisma, energy and more stamina for the whole final than anyone. He could do 100 dances in a row and still be standing, still be kicking in that final Jive, which later on went to serve us well. But more importantly, Corky had this unique strength and backbone, so that no matter what barbs people threw at him, they bounced off and it was that quality that helped seal our success.

We were very popular wherever we danced. We did shows all over the world, and Corky's humour and sense of style made him a natural showman. What I brought was my experience. Did we have the magic? With Sammy, it had been natural, but with Corky, it wasn't an easy gift. We found it over the years, as Ruud Vermeij helped us find a strong chemistry on the competition floor. I came to discover that this kind of chemistry could actually be taught.

The Professor continued to be instrumental, not only in our dance but also in our private life. He had the philosophy that you had to be prepared months before any competition. He made sure that we were focused on the right things, not just on our bodies and how physically fit we were, not only on our practice but also on our strength of mind. What Corky lacked in body rhythm, he made up for with his speedy feet, so the Professor made us concentrate on our strengths like that, not our weakness, which gave us a lot of confidence in what we were able to do well. After all my years of taking lessons from different teachers, the Professor's positive atti-tude came as a breath of fresh air.

At the UK Championships in 1993, Donnie Burns, who was at that time still an active competitor, interviewed us on camera. All those years before, me leaving the country had enabled him to move up the rankings a lot more quickly than he would have done otherwise. He wasn't just a dancer, but one of the men at the top of the industry. Corky and I had had a few run-ins with Donnie by then, and we knew he didn't particularly care for us.

During the interview, he asked me to describe my strengths. In a really squeaky voice, I said immediately, 'I have a very good partner, we're able to work together and he gives me the confidence I need and vice versa.' When Donnie asked me to describe my weaknesses, I took some pleasure in being one of the few people to ever answer Donnie Burns back. I replied, 'I don't have any.'

Corky was a bit more reflective of his evolution, saying, 'I think definitely a more sincere approach to becoming the dance, and not being the dancer Corky Ballas.' This over-privileged Houston boy had come a long way.

We moved to London in 1990. After all the sacrifices we'd made and all the upheaval for our family, it took us another five years to finally reach the pinnacle of the industry. Every couple in the top 12 was fantastic, but from the time we arrived in London, we decided we couldn't sit around and wait for them to retire, we had to beat them. It was the same philosophy Sammy and I had adopted, not waiting for dead men's shoes. It was one of the most difficult but rewarding times of our career.

Corky and I climbed up the ladder slowly but surely, until in 1995 we found ourselves back at my old stomping ground, the Winter Gardens in Blackpool, for the Open to the World British Championships, the title that I'd first won with Sammy in 1983. Physically, Corky and I were the fittest we'd ever been and we'd also finessed our mental states working with Vermeij. By then, we were spending four hours every day with our coach and then a further four hours practising by ourselves. We'd spend even more time on the treadmills or exercise bikes, and followed diets religiously together. There was also by then an increasing tension between us personally, but somehow we kept it together for what we were trying to achieve.

We were exceptionally well prepared in 1995, and only one couple stood in our way: Sammy Stopford and Barbara McColl. They were the number-one couple at that time, long-time reigning champions, and now they had Sammy's ex-wife snapping at their heels. It had taken me a long time from 1983 to get to this position, where we slotted in right behind my ex-husband and his partner. It had been a long and painful journey that Corky and I had both believed in, when nobody else did. I always had that one single goal driving me: would it ever be possible for us to get that British title? They say you sink or swim by your decisions. Well, I'd certainly sunk with my decision to leave Sammy for Corky, but now here I was back at Blackpool, and prepared to swim again.

Corky and I had the night of our lives, from the floor spacing we chose to use, to our grooming and the way we presented ourselves. For this event, I'd chosen a plain black dress, with no stones or any accessories, to go with my short dark hair. I wanted to be as understated as possible and let the dancing speak for itself, which it did. It felt like we had a bright light following us round that evening. Through every round we went from strength to strength. Our stamina was amazing, every step fell perfectly into place, and every single thing seemed to go right on that day. I was finally back in my comfort zone, and knew it was my time.

The results were announced. We won the Cha-Cha-Cha, then we won the Samba, then Sammy and Barbara won the Rumba, then we won both the Paso Doble and the Jive. We'd done it. We were Open to the World British champions. I'd done it once before aged 23 with Sammy; now I managed it again aged 35 with Corky. I believe to this day, I'm still the only female who's ever won it with two different partners. When it finally sunk in that we'd won, I was overwhelmed with relief and joy. I just sat down and cried. It had been a very long journey from that 14-year-old girl who'd first left home to this 35-year-old woman who'd, against all the odds, taken a pro-am dancer and made him into a British champion. It felt as though, finally, the pressure had been lifted and we would get the respect from the industry that we craved.

To his eternal credit, Sammy was the first one to walk out onto the floor and applaud us, and later, he was the first to send flowers of congratulation. He had a true sporting spirit, which you don't often see in today's dancing. I caught a glimpse of him as the results were called out. I looked at him, and he looked at me. He knew it all – how much I'd struggled, pretty much my whole life, for everything I'd got. If I'd stayed with Sammy all those years before, we'd have easily held the record ourselves. We were unbeatable, 'unstoppable'. Instead, I'd made the choice to leave and I'd lived with it, even though it meant I had to take a much, much harder journey back.

Sammy knew it all, and I think, in his own way, he respected it. There's always been a unique connection between Sammy and me – it's not always been an easy one, at times it's been downright difficult. There have been times that people have tried to split up our friendship and pull us apart, but somehow through all this we have managed to remain cordial and respectful towards each other, and Sammy showed his sporting colours that night on the dance floor when Corky and I beat him to win our first British title.

• • •

We were lucky enough to win the same title again the following year, 1996, and at that point, Corky and I were ready to call it a day and retire from competitive dance. We'd achieved everything we had set out to do. For myself, I'd silenced all the doubters and it was finally time for me to become a full-time wife and mother.

By now, we had been teaching and demonstrating, travelling all over the world for over a decade. As well as our British titles, we were undefeated for ten years as US International Latin champions. Whatever the point we wanted to make to all our critics and doubters, we felt we'd made it. So did we retreat quietly from the scene, and settle down to raise our son, walk into the sunset and enjoy a happy, serene marriage? Well, what do you think?

Instead we got busier than ever, teaching, demonstrating and generally keeping the show on the road. Corky was a dynamic, inspirational choreographer, great at cutting music and putting numbers together. I had a lot of respect for his skills, and he was inspiring for our students. He always had a great energy and gave 100 per cent in his private lessons, while I remained as hot as ever on the technical side.

On the personal side, however, the cracks that had appeared in our marriage even before we'd left Houston had now become huge, gaping fractures, which neither of us chose to look at too closely. These days, I have some sympathy for Corky. He'd watched his family experience a dramatic downfall in their fortunes, he'd moved to a tiny tin-pot house in London away from his family and friends; he knew the whole dance industry was against him and wanted him to fail, and somehow he'd kept smiling, apart from when he was taking it out on me, which was a lot of the time.

That might explain, but it doesn't excuse, the way he spoke to me, the shouting and the insults. Corky would get a lot of bad write-ups and negative reviews, and because I didn't seem to get the criticism he did, he started to sneer at me, 'You think you're so infallible.'

He constantly lashed out at me, using the most offensive possible words he could for a woman on a regular basis, calling me 'a low-life, mother-fucking c**t'. He would say to me, 'Queen Athena, goddess of dance, that's what you think you are.' He frequently swore at me, and if I tried to call him out on it, he'd sneer at me and say, 'Well, that's just the way I speak, so you'd better get used to it.'

These days, I only have to hear someone use the C-word to be triggered straight back to that time in my life, when I was constantly hearing it thrown at me. When I used to get upset, I was always told, 'It's just a word, it doesn't mean anything,' but to me it did and I couldn't bear it.

Corky was a man who liked perfection in a female, a slender wife with the perfect body and no human flaws. From the beginning of our relationship, his determination to perfect me picked away at my confidence – 'Does everybody in England have teeth like that?' he would ask me. 'Go and get them fixed.' So keen was I to make him happy that on the day I married him, I had a mouth full of braces.

When I look back now, I realise that, with all the pressure we put ourselves under, something had to give, and we didn't take the time to invest in our marriage. The whole time we lived in the UK – the financial pressures, frequently moving house, all the things we had to do to become champions, it all came at a cost. The biggest sacrifice was being absent from our son, and the biggest cost was the toll it took on our relationship.

We'd always had a volatile relationship, we were already squabbling before Mark came along, which is why my mother had expressed her concerns, but by the time we retired, we were properly at each other's throats, and it was just a bad scene all round.

On the occasions when we did voice our disagreements, things could get horribly out of hand. Many times, we had horrible slanging matches, which resulted in me being locked either in my room, or sometimes outside the house.

It would have been a lot worse if my mother hadn't been living with us. She didn't have to say anything, she's quiet and meek on the outside, but she has quite a presence, and Corky and I were definitely both better behaved than if she hadn't been there. Just as she had with Sammy, she kept telling us both to take time to focus on ourselves and our marriage, but we just never seemed to find the space in our schedules.

My mother had given up her own life to help raise our son, she did our cooking, our ironing, everything she could to make our lives easier so we could concentrate on pursuing our goal of becoming British champions. Corky and I both knew that the only reason we were able to win in 1995 was because we had so much help from her, and for that I will always be extremely grateful. I used to feel that Corky also appreciated her, until I read a devastating article that he later wrote when I got my job on *Strictly*.

More importantly, she had a sixth sense for when a row was brewing, and a maternal instinct to scoop up Mark and get him out of the way before things properly blew up, turning up the TV while Corky and I were slinging abuse at each other. This meant Mark was kept away from the worst of it, thank goodness.

All the time we were competing there was just something off in the connection between us. For my part, I could probably have been more patient with him, but I knew we were on a short time-line if we were to do well. From him, though, I never felt I received the respect I deserved. After we retired, I thought to myself, 'Okay, let's give this a proper go.'

I think both Corky and I were starting to feel increasingly unhappy, but I didn't feel I had a choice. I'd made a life with this man, I didn't want a second failed marriage to my name, and I definitely didn't want Mark growing up without a father as I had, so I thought I'd better stick it out and make the best of it. Corky seemed just as resolute on improving our relationship, and on many occasions over the years we made huge efforts to go to counselling sessions together and did our best to follow all their different advice.

Despite our determination to make it work, there were arguments between us every single day. A normal journey to a private lesson or an exhibition soon became a nightmare as anything we talked about descended into a bitter battle of wills and I began to feel increasingly uncomfortable in his presence. It got to the point where I developed a nervous rash of hives, where I scratched my skin until it was red raw and it would bleed. Also, I started feeling like I always needed to go the loo. I couldn't hold in my pee, which my doctor told me was a sign of acute anxiety. On our trips abroad, my friend Karen noticed I was often run down with illnesses such as ear infections, but we put it down to the fact that I was trying to do too many things at once, and being pulled in different directions. I didn't really know how to say that I felt I was having one long, never-ending panic attack, from one day to the next. How do you begin to explain this? I began to go on medication for anxiety, because life started to feel too hard for me to get through day to day.

From the day I met him, Corky was always immensely popular with the ladies, a good-looking man who loved women and the art of seduction, the chase of it all. To be tied to one woman was always difficult for him and now we were having such a tough time, he started to disappear for hours of the day. Increasingly, there began to be rumours about other women, which I tried to ignore, but the threat of it always ate away at me. He increasingly started making excuses for not coming home. There was one woman in particular he knew, a promising young dancer who had caught his eye. He told me he couldn't come home because he was 'fixing her light bulbs'. Well, word got out and Corky's excuse became a running joke in our industry as a euphemism for bad behaviour – funny now, humiliating at the time.

Corky and I had by now established ourselves as coaches and trainers to some of the best dancers in the world, so we had earned front-row seats at the British National Dance Championships, where the Rising Star final was about to take place. I was walking along the back row with my son, when the woman in question sidled up to me, clearly the worse for a drink or two, and said, 'You and I need to talk.' I tried to duck it, saying I had nothing to say to her, but she refused to budge. Suddenly, it seemed as if everything went into slow motion as I turned round to face her, just as she said, 'You need to get used to the fact that I fucked your husband.'

I can remember I was standing there in a beautiful evening dress. The ballroom was packed and everyone was looking at us, probably keenly aware of what was going on. There was a little white angel on one of my shoulders, and a little red angel on the other one. The white angel told me, 'Keep walking,' while the red angel said, 'Sock her in the gob.' So that's what I did.

I punched her and she rolled away. I'm not proud. All I could hear around me were people whispering, 'Is that Shirley Ballas?' Needless to say, I did not return to my front-row seat. I left the ballroom without watching the Rising Star final, totally embarrassed by my behaviour. I was mortified that I'd hit this girl, but enough was enough. I was humiliated, and it was one thing too many. When I got home, though, Corky brushed off the whole episode as something meaningless, and I found myself similarly carrying on as though nothing had happened. What on earth was the matter with me?

At first, bizarrely, despite all the rows, we were somehow able to walk onto the dance floor and perform as harmoniously and electrically together as we ever had. I couldn't make that same switch from fighting to laughing, so increasingly, I distanced myself from him and buried myself in work. I think my passion for dance rescued me from the worst of it, but then I think dance has probably rescued me from most things in my life.

Life became like a treadmill – working, looking after Mark, making sure my mum was happy, trying to keep Corky happy.

Should I have spent more time with my husband and tended to his every need? Possibly, except whenever we did spend any time together, it would only be a few minutes before the fur started flying again. The writing was on the wall for a long time, even though I remained in complete denial – I just didn't want another failed marriage.

Finally, though, even I had to admit defeat. We'd spent Christmas in Texas with his family and were leaving that day to head back to England. I was sitting on the stairs when Corky came out of his office, and I asked him, 'Would you like to go back to bed for a cuddle?' He said, 'No, you need to get yourself dressed, I need to talk to you.'

He took me into the kitchen and announced, 'You need to know I've been having an affair.' I stood in the kitchen, feeling shocked and bewildered.

For several years, I had suspected this very thing. I'd voiced my concerns to Corky, but he had accused me of going out of my mind, told me I was stupid to even think it, that I was making a big deal out of nothing. He made me question my own sanity to the point where I sought counselling for what I thought were increasingly paranoid thoughts and fears. I felt like I was in a constant state of confusion, anxiety and suspicion. When I eventually found out the truth, I was actually less upset by the affair than by the way it had made me feel all that time I had guessed it was going on. As much as it hurt me, it was almost a relief to find out that I wasn't going mad and that my instincts had been right.

The woman in question was a student of mine, and showed great promise. Later, I found out that Corky hadn't wanted to admit the affair to me but her partner had found out and given him an ultimatum: 'You have 24 hours to tell your wife, or I will.' That was why Corky had sat me down that night, not because he felt bad but because he had no choice. He told me it had been going on for six months but he was sorry and wanted us to try again. Later, she told me that it had actually been going on for three and a half years. She had no problem sharing with me every last sexual detail of the affair she had been conducting with my husband behind my back all that time.

I was completely devastated as I packed my bags and cried all the way home to England. We'd built a family, a home, a business, the stakes were really high for both of us, and I was fearful for the future. But was I really that shocked? If I'm honest, I think I was more hurt by the woman's betrayal than by Corky's as she'd been my student, someone I considered a friend.

It was at that time that I started spiralling proper into significant depression. It was a very confusing time. Corky and I took turns wanting to leave, wanting to stay, like a ping-pong ball going back and forth.

As Corky's parents became a bit frailer over in Houston, he started to spend more and more time there, taking care of them. In fact, the sweetest thing he ever did for me came after we had spent a long time apart. I went back to Texas to visit his parents in their new home, and he showed me the apartment upstairs that he'd built for himself to be near them. That's when he told me, 'You know, we could start again. We could have holidays, we could make time, it could work.' It was very tempting to go back, but I wasn't ready. And then later when I thought I might be, he wasn't.

It just wasn't meant to be. We both learned the lessons we'd always needed to learn, but sadly too late in the day.

In 2007, the emotional flame between us finally went out with a whimper not a bang, but with a divorce as nasty as you would expect from two people who had been arguing for 20 years, and I felt he made the whole thing far more difficult than it needed to have been.

For me, a lot of my fears for the future centred on money. Throughout my marriage, Corky had been the banker of the household, he had insisted on taking care of all our accounts, so I didn't have any idea about all of that, I just went to work. That was an important lesson for me, and for anyone reading this. Take care of your own money, and make sure you always have some savings for your own rainy day, because you never know when it may come. I had to learn to take care of myself, but it was going to take a while.

During those tough times, I leaned a lot on my dear friend Terri Martin. We had been close with Terri's family since we moved to the UK. Her daughters, Georgie, Jerry Lee and Rae, were very close with Mark growing up, and Rae was even a dance partner of Mark's at one point. Terri is one of my oldest and dearest friends, and her support really got me through those dark days.

Corky helped both of his parents through long illnesses, sorted out their care, paid all their bills and did everything they needed. Looking after them really brought out the best in him, a side I hadn't seen in a long time. I was reminded of the hardworking person I'd met over 20 years before, the one who'd changed my world so dramatically.

By the end, whenever I looked at Corky, I felt equally sorry for both him and myself – sorry for the way people had treated him, for the way he'd had to leave his home, and for the way all the promise in our relationship had been extinguished along the way.

Throughout my life, I'd achieved everything I'd ever wanted through sheer hard work and determination, but our marriage I had to admit was beyond me, the one thing that couldn't be saved by sheer determination, no matter what we tried. When I thought of all that fun we'd had at the beginning of our relationship, it was like looking at a film of two completely different people. In his eyes, I definitely think I failed him as a wife, but equally, he let me down as a husband.

I'm grateful to have had him play such a big part of my life, I'm grateful that his family is my family, and that he's the father of my son. I learned a lot from him in the long time we spent together. I always thought I had to be the rock for Corky, the one to show him the tricks of the dance world, but actually he was the rock for me on several levels. I always got nervous about dancing with him, about people criticising him, but actually I didn't need to worry about him at all – he had a fuck-you attitude and he inspired the same in me. I learned to let negative energy and criticism flow through me and turn it into fuel.

It was time for me to find my own tin suit.

CHAPTER 6
The Waltz

'The matriarch of the Ballroom dances.
It has a unique rise, fall and rotation,
requiring a strong usage of feet and ankles.
When applied correctly, this gives the dance
an ethereal magnificence.'

Whatever Corky and I put each other through during those many, tumultuous years, we can always congratulate each other that we got one thing absolutely right between us – our beautiful son Mark – although I know we can't take most of the credit for how he turned out, as my mother and brother were a huge part of his life throughout his childhood right up until he was 21.

Nobody else in our industry had babies at the time I was competing, especially ones they carried around with them while they travelled all over the world on tours, exhibitions and competitions.

I've always wanted to be that person who, if someone tells me, 'You can't,' I want to show them, 'I can.' Having a baby wasn't going to stop me, it just gave me something else to prove. We took him everywhere with us, carting him all over the world, there wasn't a country he didn't visit, while we juggled demonstrating, teaching and all the time looking after this gorgeous little boy.

Corky and I were trendsetters in that regard, we broke the mould and it certainly took some organising, but fortunately Mark seemed to take everything in his stride. He really was a happy chappy.

From when he was six months old, following our careers meant we had to leave Mark behind with carers and childminders. It never sat well with me leaving him and I took him whenever and wherever I could.

You always want to believe your children are safe at home. Mark was born a very happy child and settled well with being left with other people, except for this one particular lady. He would scream bloody murder whenever I had to leave him in the house with her. As he was approaching 16 months by then, when he put his body against the back door and screamed, I just thought it was because he missed me and didn't want me to leave, but as a young, new mother, I never really took the time to find out what was behind it. It was only when it came to my attention through a different babysitter that poor Mark had bruises on his little body, that I realised to my horror he must have either been hit or hurt in some way.

This particular carer looked after Mark 24/7 and also kept an immaculate home. It was only years later when I looked back on the episode that I wondered, 'How do you keep such a spotless home with a baby? What did she do with the baby all day while she was doing the cleaning?'

I was beside myself with guilt that somebody had abused my son and I hadn't picked up on it because of the hustle and bustle of my busy professional life, running around everywhere.

I rushed to call my mother and told her I had decided to retire from dancing. When I shared the circumstances of my decision with her, she was beside herself at the thought of her grandson being left with anybody who didn't treat him well. We shared that concern for him, and she offered to do everything she could, including coming to stay with us so we could continue to work, knowing Mark was safe. It meant she gave up her own life to help raise our child, while Corky and I were off travelling the world.

From the age of 18 months until he was 21 years old, my son only ever had two babysitters and they were my mother and Mrs Ballas. It was a huge change of lifestyle for my mother. She'd never had to drive much the whole time she lived in Wallasey, but you definitely need a car to get around in Houston – there's no easy access and very little public transport – so in her mid-fifties, my mother had to learn to drive on the other side of the road!

She was there for Mark's chickenpox, his measles, every bump and scrape, which is why I say I can't take all the credit for the man he's become. A lot was down to my mother, and she got it right. Her calm presence definitely gave Mark a lot of security. She had the patience of Job, and was strict with him when she needed to be, spoiled him rotten when she felt he deserved it. They went everywhere together, she never left his side and she succeeded in creating a very happy environment for him, both in America and the UK. I think Mark learned his toughness and his resilience from his grandmother, also his kindness, calmness and loyalty. He still calls her his very hardcore Scouser nanny!

My mother used to spend several months of the year in the States and then take Mark back to the UK. This worked out well when we later moved to London while he was still a little boy, as he was already used to all things English, so he wasn't thrown at all.

My brother David played a big part in Mark's upbringing, too, teaching him many of the important things in life. David took him fishing and for other excursions like bike rides and trips to the beach. On one occasion when he was still little, Mark had beautiful, long curly hair. I went to Japan for an extended trip and when I got home, I discovered David had cut off all his beautiful curls, due to my brother's conviction that he wanted Mark to toughen up and blend in a little more with the housing estate where he was staying. Needless to say, I was emotionally distraught. It had taken me months and months to grow all those beautiful curls, and now they were gone!

Being raised on the housing estate, David was a tough guy on the outside, but really, he was quite a softie on the inside, and it was his softie side that always came out with Mark. Both my mother and brother were there as often as they could be throughout his childhood. Mark was a very adaptable child, and I suppose really he didn't know any different. He was either with Corky and me in person, or speaking to us on the phone wherever we were in the world, two or three times a day. Unfortunately for us, there was no FaceTime back then, so I couldn't see his little face. After three months of being away – and it could be that long when we went off to teach in Japan – you can only imagine how that felt. In total, Corky and I missed five Christmases with our son while he was still very young, because we were away working. I guess one consolation was that I knew he was safe and happy with his grandmother and his uncle, but the times apart still seemed very long.

Without realising it, I was following in the footsteps of my own mother and her frequent absences during my childhood. She was never there, but it was so she could earn enough money to look after my brother and myself. I did the same with Mark, following the exact same pattern as my mother, never being there for all those tiny moments. Now, I'm convinced I should have changed that pattern and stayed home a lot more.

At the time I rationalised that I was doing it all for the money, to provide a secure future for him, just as my mother had done for me, but if I'm honest, it was really to fulfil my own ambitions. Since my childhood, I'd always propelled myself forward, fuelled by my father's absence, and by those girls at school and my mum's friends who said I'd never amount to anything. I'd started my career driven beyond anything to make something of myself and now, even though I was a parent with responsibilities, I didn't have it in me to change direction or even put the brakes on.

That meant that while I was trying to be the best mother I could possibly be, and while my love for my son knew no bounds, I can see now I put my ambition first, above everything, and it's something I'll always regret. I've got pictures of him crying with chickenpox all over his body, and where was I? Far away, working. If I could go back in time, I would have done anything not to miss those five Christmases. I'd always been determined not to fail at anything I did and the irony is, through all that effort, I failed at the most important thing of all: being the mother I would have liked to be.

Fortunately, I have a son who understands why I did what I did, and also he's turned out incredibly well, but I still feel enormous guilt and regret for the times I wasn't there and I've certainly tried to make up for that in the years since. I know he felt secure and loved, and he also realised it was our work that was supporting our lifestyle. He never complained. When I asked him later if he ever thought he'd missed out on anything during his child-hood, he said, 'Don't worry about it, Mum. Ordinary would have been boring.'

Certainly, as he grew up in that world of constant change, I believe it helped him gain a broad outlook on life. Mixing with so many people of different nationalities has served him well as he's become older. He became a fantastic travel companion at a young age, and still is to this day.

Whenever we toured Japan, we longed to have Mark with us. As soon as he finished his school term, my mother would drive him to the airport, where they'd pop a little tag around his neck and put him on a flight to Tokyo, and someone else would collect him at the other end. He was only five at the time – transatlantic flying at five, can you imagine? – and he loved it. When he got to Japan, he couldn't speak a word of the language, but that didn't seem to faze Mark. Instead, he learned to communicate with gestures and body language, and could somehow manage to talk with his body to anyone.

Mark definitely enjoyed being part of our performing world, which he considered his 'normal'. He always wanted to dress up himself, whether he was in a Spider-Man outfit or Batman outfit. By the age of five, he could even cue our music! He always had a great ear, and when we first moved to England, my mother started taking him on Saturday mornings to train at the Italia Conti Academy of Theatre Arts – ballet, jazz, tap, acting, singing, you name it, he did it.

When he got to 11, it was our hope that he'd start going to the nearby school, Dulwich College. However, Mark had other ideas.

He told us, 'I'm not a briefcase kid' and said he wanted to go to the Italia Conti school full-time. Performing was in his whole being.

When Corky had been a little boy himself, it had always been his dream to go on the stage, and he had many opportunities with his great voice and acting skills. Unfortunately for him, his mother didn't want him to do it, so he never got to pursue that dream. When Mark made his choice aged 11, Corky and I were both delighted that he'd chosen that route. While I wanted Mark to follow his heart, I was a little bit concerned about whether he'd be able to complete his academic education, and I found myself with exactly the same dilemma as my mother had had for me all those years before. What to do for the best when your child has a dream?

From a very early age, Mark was into his music, all types of music – Flamenco, Nirvana, Gypsy Kings, just to name a few. Corky would often sit with Mark, singing and playing guitar with him. One of the fondest pictures in my mind from that time is being at Mrs Ballas's house for Christmas, when Mark and Corky would play guitar, and Maria would get up and dance for us, clicking her castanets and wearing her fabulous Flamenco shoes. What wonderful memories for all of us!

Another picture comes to mind. When Corky and I officially retired from competitions, the whole hall was standing and applauding us. By now, Mark was aged ten, and it was at that exact moment he turned to me and said, 'I want to compete, Mummy.' I said, 'Oh no, you don't, Mark.' He replied calmly, 'Oh yes, I do.'

It was the end of an era for Corky and me, but it was just the beginning of one for Mark. I was a bit surprised because by that age, he was already showing great promise as a musician, but as well as all his training at Italia Conti, he'd also been having baby Ballroom classes with a professional teacher on Saturday mornings, and it had clearly got under his skin. I made all the right noises about enquiring whether it was what he really wanted to do – did he know what was involved, all of that – but secretly, I was delighted. The apple did not fall far from the tree.

If I'm really honest, deep down I believe that possibly Mark was drawn to the social side of dancing more than anything else and he wasn't particularly good when he started. When he found a partner called Vikki Larman, she wasn't impressed with his standard, so I offered a package of training and travel, which her mother thought would be beneficial to her. This meant Vikki got brilliant training, and in return, Mark got to dance with the world's best juvenile girl. Within six months, with their talent and capacity for learning, they were winning every single title in the Under 12s, including British and International championships.

Despite all that success, I'm convinced Mark's true passion was always music. Once he was enrolled full-time at the Italia Conti school, he got the chance to do everything, singing, drama, acting and dance. But I know his dream was always to have a career in music, Broadway, the West End stage, or film – and later in his life he got to fulfill many of those dreams.

• • •

Years later, I would travel over and back to New York to see him perform on Broadway in the musical *Jersey Boys*, and there's a line from that show that has always stayed with me: 'Everyone remembers it how they need to, right?' I choose to remember as many things as I can in my life as a positive experience.

They're very successful now, but when I first met Derek and Julianne Hough, they were two little blonde, blue-eyed children in a dance class in Utah. The dance studio was called Center Stage Performing Arts, and it was one of the most sought-after in the world.

Corky and I used to go there to teach three or four times every year, and we used to love it, because there was so much talent in the room. I remember every child being extremely gifted.

I recall watching Julianne performing the Cha-Cha-Cha when she was very young. There was something special about the way she moved, with a maturity exceptional for a child of her age. She came over to me while I was teaching a class, and I painted a little cross on her forehead with my finger. I told her, 'You have the X factor, young lady.' She asked, 'What is that, Mrs Ballas?' I replied, 'I don't know, darling, but whatever it is, you have it.'

One year we made the trip to Utah, and we noticed that both Derek and Julianne were missing from our class. When I enquired where they were, I was told that their parents were going through a divorce and they weren't dancing at the moment. I was also informed that Derek was getting up to all sorts of mischief. There were five children in their family, and I remember hoping Derek and Julianne would go back to dance, as I could see they both really enjoyed it. I didn't want them falling between the cracks, and Corky enquired as to whether we could get in touch with the children just to say hello.

We weren't able to talk to them that time, but the following year when we returned to Utah for our annual trip to the studio,

Derek appeared once again in the classes. At the end of one lesson, he walked up to us and said, 'If only I could move to London. It would be my dream. I would love to learn like Mark, and get amazing training.'

When we returned home, we had a discussion with Mark, who had formed a friendship with Derek over the years. We told Mark what Derek had said, and outlined to him life would be quite different if Derek came, that it could be challenging for Mark, who was used to life as an only child. Mark, however, said he never really enjoyed being on his own, he embraced the thought of having a brother, just as we were keen to give Derek the opportunity that he so clearly wished for. Later, I often wondered how it was for Mark, sharing his life, his parents' attention, the family finances, his home. But no matter how he felt, he never once complained and just got on with sharing everything.

We met up with Derek's dad, Bruce, and over a brief conversation with him, it was decided that Derek could come over for a few months to train in England, as there appeared to be difficulties with his parents' divorce.

Later, Derek shared with Corky and me that he had been desperate to leave behind his life in Utah, especially his school life, where he was horribly bullied. He'd had to change schools constantly because he kept getting into all sorts of trouble, and he couldn't seem to fit in anywhere. I think his dance lessons had become a bit of a refuge, and so the idea of moving to London and training with the best teachers in the world appealed to him, not only from a dance perspective but also as a means of finding a permanent sanctuary far away from those bullies that were making his life tough.

Derek was 12 when he moved to London, and I watched him blossom fast within the framework of a schedule and a regime. These weren't things he'd always had in his life, and initially he found it heavy going to adapt. However, later he came to appreciate that it was exactly what he'd needed to progress as he did. I think it was a very painful decision for Bruce to let Derek go that far from home, and he contributed financially to put him into the Italia Conti school; Corky and I also did whatever we could to help him. Derek really came to life there, flourishing in both his academic studies and in Ballroom and Latin.

In the dance world, it's completely normal for families to take in other children from abroad, in order to help them further their careers and partnerships up and running. It's like having exchange students to stay, with everyone pitching in. Years later as an adult, Derek defended the decision as well, saying in an interview, 'People will say, "How could your parents let you go off to do that?" I think it's great that they saw an amazing opportunity. That is the reason we are here today.' Today, Corky and I are both proud of Derek and happy that we had a part in guiding him through his education, through the Ballroom and Latin world, as well as the stage world, for ten important years of his life.

Almost as soon as Derek started school in London, he began to become extremely focused and driven, something soon noticed by both his father and his younger sister Julianne back home. It was presented to Corky and me that Julianne too would like to come to England. What we thought would be a three-month stay ended up lasting for about five and a half years. She was ten when she arrived, fifteen and a half when she left.

I found at the beginning that it was a little bit harder for Julianne to settle, but after a short space of time, she assured us that she didn't want to return to Utah. She wanted the same opportunities as her brother. Julianne was, from a very young age, the most competitive child I ever came across.

For his whole life, Mark had been on a rigid schedule, so was completely relaxed following a tight schedule but, at the beginning, it was more difficult for Derek and Julianne to adapt to this different way of living. However, they soon settled into their new life, and seemed to enjoy living in our beautiful home, going to an amazing school, and sticking to a proper schedule that they both told me they'd been missing. They seemed very happy and purposeful in their new surroundings.

All three children had formidable work ethics when it came to dance, although academically it was a different story. There was a lot of competition in the house, and I found Mark, Derek and Julianne, without even being pushed, all strived to be the very best.

With Julianne by now also attending the renowned Italia Conti Academy the children's scheduling became increasingly demanding. Mark was doing well at the time with his dance partner Vikki, but it was becoming a bit of a military exercise, trying to juggle all the different dance lessons for each of the three children, as well as my own teaching schedule. Corky and I both still had to work full-time to support the lifestyles of three actively competitive children, so it made sense for Mark to partner up with Julianne. It meant they were able to share classes and make the logistics just that little bit easier.

Getting all three children to school on time was a feat in itself – getting them out of bed, fed and off to the train station, picking them back up at the end of the day, then sorting out their extra activities. We even splashed out and paid one of Derek and Julianne's old jazz teachers from the US to fly over and teach them, so they had a familiar face in their new surroundings, and could keep up their high level of jazz. We had many people helping us out in the home, so the children could focus 100 per cent on their trade. Corky and I put our heart and soul into these three children, and spread our cash to make sure we treated them all the same.

As the children became settled, you could see that dance was in their bones. They got to travel all over the world together as a group, competing in Europe, and doing just as well in the theatre world. The trio became known as the 'Ballas Brat Pack' – week after week, we'd walk into a different ballroom somewhere in the world for them to compete, and you'd hear a collective groan as we walked in – 'Oh, they're here again' – which was understandable, because they seemed to win everything they entered from a young age. Mark and Julianne won all the Under 14 titles, while Derek would triumph in the Under 16s. Then when Derek went up to the youth category, Mark and Julianne would take over from him and start winning in the Under 16s, and that's how it went on, Derek leading the pack with Mark and Julianne following close behind and winning all the same championships.

Mark and Julianne danced together for five years in total while Derek had several partners throughout his career, and between them they won every trophy it was possible to win in the junior divisions. I put everything I could into teaching them the fundamentals of Latin American dancing, while Corky would inspire them with his own unique brand of showmanship. Between us we educated them on choreography and technique, as well as good manners and how to become polite and kind human beings.

Financially, it became quite draining to keep three children in private school, and to keep them in dance lessons, both Ballroom and Latin. It wasn't just Corky and me raising them; it took an army of dance teachers and other people stepping up, and to all those people who helped the children find their way, I can only express my gratitude. They know who they are.

Derek and Julianne's parents were not in a position to help further, and Corky and I were really feeling the stretch, until one of my own students, a businessman called Lester Smith, very kindly stepped in and provided some extra funding every year. With the help of Lester and his wife Sue, we were able to keep Julianne in her ballet and singing lessons, as well as her beautiful dresses by Elaine Gornall – the best dressmaker in the business. Two other incredibly generous people at that time, John Kimmons and Carrie Chiang, also helped support Derek and Julianne through those years, and for that I was very grateful.

Personally, I found raising somebody else's children quite difficult. There were all the usual conflicts between adults and young children trying to get their own way. If I knew they were testing their boundaries, I had to tell them off, knowing all the time I was responsible for their welfare, their careers and helping them along the way, constantly aware that I wasn't their real mother and trying to do the best I could.

Because they were both Mormon, I'd made a promise to their father Bruce that I would do my very best to take both Derek and Julianne to Mormon Church every Sunday. This meant that, every week, wherever we were in the country, we would find the local service, sometimes in a church or sometimes in a school hall. I learned quite a lot about the religion myself, as I'd be sitting there listening to stories about their church's leader, Joseph Smith, while these two children would be curled up fast asleep on my shoulder. I did my best to adhere to the rules for two Mormon children. Bruce sent me the Book of Mormon to read, and educated me on the required dress, special days of the week and other restrictions so that I could be equipped to help them in their studies as Mormon children.

This could be challenging because all the junior competitions ran on a Sunday, which for Mormons is a day of rest, so I had to navigate my way between Bruce's world of the church, and my world of dance. I did my very best to follow all the different rules and respect the children's Mormon culture.

I tried to encourage both children to call home as often as possible, and catch up with their parents. It was often complicated, because their parents were going through a bitter divorce, but I did my best to get them to communicate. With this, I had the help of their mother Marianne's new partner, Aaron Nelson. He would give me advice on how to help the children, and without him, it would have been a lot more difficult. Sometimes, if I wasn't sure what path to take between the wishes of Bruce and Marianne, I'd pick up the phone to Aaron and between us we'd work it out.

Because I had left home and been through exactly the same thing myself aged 14, I know it must have been difficult for the children at some points, that they missed their parents, and that it wasn't easy for their family back in America either. Fortunately, Bruce was in a financial position to come over to the UK once or twice a year, and the children got to go back there too during summer holidays. During these visits, Bruce would always ask them to stay, but Derek and Julianne's urge to dance and compete meant they always asked to come back to London to be with us.

I'm sure both the children, and Julianne in particular, felt homesick for their family in Utah. I made sure to ask her regularly if she ever wanted to go home, and that if she wanted to return, we'd help her. I wanted to make sure she knew that nobody was forcing her to stay in England, but she always looked me straight in the eye and replied, 'I don't want to go home. I want to stay here,' so she did.

Through all the ups and downs of their family lives, the children always remained focused on eating, sleeping, guitar and vocal lessons, as well as band practice and, of course, dance. Mark, Derek and Julianne's success was phenomenal – world titles, British titles, everything they went after. With that came job offers of demonstrations, which they all found a lot of fun, and in between was the everyday stuff – school, eating, sleeping, jazz and ballet lessons.

I kept them all so occupied they didn't really have a chance to sit down and reflect on their lives. That was something my mother-in-law Mrs Ballas had advised. She told me, 'Shirley, you've taken on someone else's children. The best thing you can do is keep everyone really busy.' I took her advice and did my best to run a tight, purposeful ship, and we never seemed to catch our breaths. Before we knew it, six busy, bumpy but glorious years had whirled by, and the children's attitudes towards what they wanted from life started to change.

Julianne wanted to go home to the US and have what she called a 'normal life', as she put it, in high school. At that point, her mother Marianne was staying with us in London as well, and I found it very helpful to have another adult living with us. In fact, she'd settled so happily in the UK she didn't want to leave, even though her daughter did!

When Julianne announced her decision, it brought home to me what a huge sacrifice my own mother had made for me, letting me move out of home and supporting me through thick and thin, all those years before when I moved in with Nigel and his parents, aged 14. Now here was Julianne, aged 15, moving on with her life. I was sad at the time about the choice she made not to finish school in the UK, but when I look back now, I realise she made absolutely the best decision for herself.

Once she returned home, she would call me often and it seemed she had it all sorted out in her head. Things didn't always go according to her plan, but I tried always to be there for her, sending little care packages over to the US whenever she needed a little bit of help and encouragement.

My long-time dream for Mark and his partner, Julianne, was that one day they would win the Under-21 British Open to the World Latin American Dance Championships, but she decided she wanted to go home. Mark wasn't sure he even wanted to continue dancing – but, as fate would have it, he met a prospective new partner called Daria from Russia and had to make up his mind whether to continue or give up. With only a few months of extremely hard work and long days in the studio, Mark and Daria managed to win the Under-21 British Open to the World title.

With another partner called Yulia Musikhina, Mark went on to win many more titles. She came to live with us, too, for about three years, and became a very good friend of mine as well.

I was training him throughout that time, which kind of worked. I was dedicated to him, but very tough. I've always been able to switch between the personal and the professional side with my students, and Mark was no exception. If he had a bad day performing, I'd tell him. I tried to encourage him, but also be realistic. He got incredible results, which was why it was a bit of a shock to me when, one day, he announced that he was sacking me as his teacher.

Yes, really! He sat me down one afternoon in the studio. It was when he was sitting at the top of the rankings and everything was going well, but he told me, 'I can't do this anymore. It's too intense.'

I was a bit shocked at the time, but Mark has always been old beyond his years, and wise like his grandmother. He realised that our time together should be fun, not just comprised of all this training and discipline – we were supposed to be living together at home, not in a military boot camp – and so he gave me the boot! When he did that, he soon started losing in competitions and falling down the rankings, but he told me he didn't care, he'd rather have a good relationship with me, and he'd rather have the ultimate mother than the ultimate dance teacher.

Derek meanwhile made the choice to stay in London and study for his degree in theatre. Both he and Mark started working in the West End, and up and down the country. They seemed to love being on the stage as much as the dance floor. Then they both received an opportunity to appear on *Dancing with the Stars* in the United States. Corky had actually sent all their information to the *Strictly Come Dancing* team in the UK, but we never heard back from them. Instead, it was the producers on the American version of the show who invited them to join.

Early in 2007, both boys came in, sat me down and told me, 'We've decided we don't want to do the competitive dancing any more. We want to go out into the big wide world and see what opportunities we can get, starting with *Dancing with the Stars*.'

Mark was a little bit reluctant at the time, as he'd also received some offers to appear onstage in the UK, but a lifelong friend Darvina Plante reminded him it was a once-in-a-lifetime opportunity. She told him, 'The West End will always be here, Mark.' So in the end he decided to go. At the time, he said he'd only do a season or two – famous last words.

Within a week, Derek and Mark were on their way to California where, fortunately for them, Corky sprang into action and got an apartment sorted out for them. By the time they got to LA, they had a two-bed, two-bath apartment all ready for them to move into.

Before I knew it, all the birds had flown the nest and I was completely alone for the first time in many years in my home. Their departure left an aching space that it took me a long time to come to terms with.

Even though it broke my heart saying goodbye, the move back to the States was a great opportunity for the boys. The best part of that whole period in my life was watching the children grow and go on to be successful in their own right. During their time on *Dancing with the Stars*, all three went on to win it several times. Derek and Julianne went on to have many brilliant successes throughout their careers, as did Mark. Mark was the final actor to play Frankie Valli in the musical *Jersey Boys*, and closed the 11-year run of this iconic show in front of Frankie Valli himself. Frankie and Bob Gaudio hand-picked Mark for the role. Mark later went on to perform the same role at the Ahmanson Theatre in Los Angeles, and the legendary Muni Theatre in St Louis, a venue that seats 11,000 people. Frankie and Bob also invited Mark to personally induct them into the New Jersey Hall of Fame.

I remember when Mark was still small, Corky bought a picture of the New York theatre scene and hung it on our wall. There was a little yellow taxi in the corner with Mark's name inscribed on the licence plate, and Corky said, 'One day, that'll be our son, he'll be on Broadway.' Twenty years later, he was.

I remember being there with the family on the opening night of *Jersey Boys*, and I think I was more nervous for Mark than Mark was for himself, and then something happened that made me even happier. All the theatre staff wanted to talk to me about Mark. They said, 'Can we just say something about your son? He's the absolute gentleman, he recognises everybody, talks to everybody, includes everybody, the whole crew from wardrobe to the doorman. He's extremely kind. It's been a pleasure to get to know him.' It was exactly what I'm sure every mother likes to hear.

For me, if you looked up the word 'loyal' in the dictionary, you'd see Mark's face staring back at you, and I promise I'm not just saying that as his biased mother; it's how I've seen him treat people all his life. I know he would never do anything to hurt anybody. His talent speaks for itself, but I'm most proud of the kind, caring person he has always been and continues to be.

Mark's number one passion has always been his music. An accomplished singer-songwriter and guitarist, he has studied many styles since the age of ten, including flamenco, rock, blues and folk. He has written and recorded his own music for years, and has toured many times across the United States, playing in venues including bars, clubs, theatres and several arenas, most recently with his and his wife's band, Alexander Jean.

Mark and his wife met at a casual music night at the home of a mutual friend. Mark arrived just before his performance slot, and was instantly intrigued by the voice that was on before him. The room was very crowded, making it impossible for him to see the face of the soulful singer, who seemed to have the whole room hypnotised into silence as she sang from her gut. Her name was BC Jean, a successful singer-songwriter, best known for writing one of the most influential songs of her generation – 'If I were a Boy' – which happens to be one of Beyoncé's bestselling singles in the UK.

After BC's last song, Mark went to set up. As they traded their places, he could not believe that powerful, raspy voice could come out of such a young, beautiful, small package. She sat down front and centre as Mark put on a show, using his eyes to flirt with the talented blonde in the front row. Before he went home that night, he eventually gained the courage to sit down next to her, properly introduce himself, and ask for her number. They dated for a year and half before writing their first song together, which led to them officially joining forces musically. Using their middle names, they created their indie band Alexander Jean, and they've topped the singer-songwriter charts since 2015. Mark and BC got married at the end of 2016, and I couldn't be happier that she is the woman by my son's side.

CHAPTER 7

No Music, No Dance, Just Silence and Stillness

For a good part of my life, I've struggled with anxiety. When people have asked me, 'Are you happy?' I'd often reply, 'What is happy?'

I struggle a lot with the weight of the past, particularly events connected to my brother. It's easy for me to go to a place where I feel anxious, where it feels like black clouds have gathered above me. It can feel like my heart is heavy inside my chest, even sometimes as though I'm about to have a heart attack. The panic is terrifying, but the loneliness is worse. I wouldn't wish it on anyone.

Over the years, I've had medication for this, but in some ways I've discovered the medication can often make me feel worse. My mind goes foggy, I start to move really slowly, and the anxiety remains within me, anyway.

The tools that I try to help myself with are deep breathing, reading aspirational quotes and reading up on inspirational people. I try to focus on positive things and of course always try to stay busy. If I sit still for too long, I find my mind goes round and round with things in my head like a tornado, until my brain gets exhausted and I can't sleep. Depression is definitely something that has run through my family, and of course my brother David struggled with spells of this illness throughout his life.

David, my mother and I were one tight unit for the first 14 years of my life. As a child, I was often the one crying, so my mother would push my pram to the bottom of the garden so she could get a minute's peace, while David was her angel, sleeping all day and constantly smiling. He was a beautiful little boy, at his happiest when at my mother's side. He was extremely close to her, very clingy and sweet, but he definitely had to toughen up when we moved to the housing estate, just to survive.

In fact, growing up in such a place forced us both to toughen up from a very young age. Not only did David develop the tools he needed to look after himself on the estate, but he also started looking out for all those around him who he felt were being picked on. I think many things happened on that estate that my mother and I were not privy to, which made life a testing existence for a sensitive soul like him.

David's exterior shell had to become tougher and tougher. I always knew him more as a gentle giant, but you'd never guess by looking at him sometimes, with his big bovver boots, direct gaze and towering frame. He was definitely a figure of strength and authority on the housing estate, both for himself and for many others.

With my mother having to go out to work while I was a child, my brother often became my primary caregiver. As I said earlier, if he spotted me hanging out on the streets, he'd make no bones about sending me home. Sometimes I was lucky and spotted him first, and I'd start running home in the opposite direction so he couldn't catch me to tell me off. With no dad there, David behaved like a father figure. He wouldn't let me hang out on the estate, and when I did, other people would say, 'That's Kola's sister', so I never really experienced much antagonism because of him. At the time I always thought he wanted to spoil my fun, but later on I realised just how protective he felt towards me.

Despite his very warm and loving nature, David had a very serious side. Sometimes he was moody, and I realise looking back that even then he might have been experiencing waves of anxiety and depression. I found it very easy to wind him up, dancing in front of the TV while he was trying to watch it and making too much noise by crunching my cornflakes, and I found the simplest thing could set him off. With my mother's frequent absences, more often than not, it was just him and me in the flat, and David ruled the roost.

David watched my back, but he was also watching out for my career. When I left home at 14 to start out on my dancing dream, he encouraged me all the way. He knew I wanted to dance from a young age, and he always said, 'Don't you give up on your dreams. Don't listen to anybody who says you can't do it. Go out and make something of yourself.' He didn't have a jealous bone in his body. To me, he was never anything but encouraging.

It was almost as though he wanted more for me than he ever did for himself. When it came to his own career, he seemed content to do a bit of this, a bit of that. He was a cheeky chappie, a jack of all trades who liked turning his hand to different things. Whatever he did, he did extremely well – whether it was tile-laying, painting or even just going to the gym, he would get completely absorbed in the process and always pull it off. He was a total perfectionist like myself and much brighter than me at school; he just didn't apply himself in the same way.

As a young man, he announced he wanted to be a chef, so my mother saved up for ages, bought him a motor bike, gave him all the proper knives and everything he needed, encouraged him in every way possible and sent him to catering college. He was always proud of everything that he made there, even if it did come home on his motorbike all bashed up in a thousand pieces. The problem was that, for one reason or another, David never stuck at anything for long, even though whatever he tried, he did to his very best.

My brother was working on and off doing different jobs when he met a lady called Eileen and they went on to have a beautiful baby girl. They never lived together – David lived at home with my mother, where he raised his daughter, Mary, and in later years he devoted the majority of his time to looking after her, as well as my son Mark.

My brother and I always had a deal that if anything ever happened to me, he'd take care of Mark, and, in return I'd take care of Mary if anything happened to him. As Mark grew up, David was already fulfilling his part of the deal, and the pair of them enjoyed a wonderfully strong bond. By this time in my life, I was doing quite well and I loved being able to help financially with David and his daughter. I tried to be there for him in the way he'd always been there for me. As brother and sister, we had an equal amount of drive in us, just in very different directions – mine was to succeed professionally, while his was to be the best father and uncle possible.

Eileen had two sons, David and Philip, from a previous marriage, and my brother also took them to his heart as if they were his own, looking after them and raising them alongside Mary.

Performing the Rumba with Corky in The Netherlands, early 1990s. Our career was on the up here and we started placing in all the major finals.

The winning number and a winning team! My second Open to the World British Latin American Dance Championship win, having won previously with Sammy in 1983.

A lovely snap of my mum and my brother, David, as a young man.
They lived together for many years and were extremely close.

David used to take care of Mark
along with my mum when I travelled
the world.

David in happier times, with his
daughter, Mary, on her first day at
Kingsmead School. Tragically, Mary
went on to lose both parents at a very
young age.

Mark, Julianne and Derek
celebrating the boys' birthdays,
May 1999.

Taking in someone else's
children is not always easy,
but we worked hard to make
them feel truly part of our
family. Our Christmas card
pictures got bigger and bigger.

David with Mark and Julianne, after their victory at the under-16 British Junior Dance Championship in Blackpool. He passed away shortly after.

Mark picked up his first guitar age three. It's always been clear that his biggest passion in life is his music.

Mark, Derek and Julianne notched up ten wins between them on *Dancing with the Stars*. Here they are after celebrating win number five.

With Ruud Vermeij: a fabulous teacher and the first ever instructor in the world to obtain a doctoral degree in Ballroom dancing.

A demonstration on Rumba with Riccardo Cocchi. We had passion, on and off the floor. Demonstrating with him was one of the highlights of my career.

With Yegor, I learned to laugh like I
had never laughed before in my life.

Denise Weavers took me in all those
years ago, after my split with Nigel,
and has been a dear friend ever since.

One of my favourite ever students.
Teaching Tom Cruise the Salsa –
oh what a mover!

Nigel Lythgoe and I dated for a short
time, but became firm friends after. This
is one of my favourite photos with him.

All aboard with my favourite ladies – my mum, Audrey, and friend, Terri, helping me get over my breakup with Yegor on a cruise. My face says it all, really!

I've been very blessed in my friendships. Here I am, all glammed up with my dear friend Karen Hilton.

With Lorna Lee. Lorna and her husband, Mick, have been in my life for years. I'm so grateful for the help they gave me when building my teaching business in the UK.

I have spent several years living with these two boys, Alan and Nathan. They are my gay gaggle and I am their princess. Alan was the first person to christen me the Queen of Latin.

We've had our ups and downs over the years, but, as I've grown older, I've learned to forgive. Here is a recent photo of me with my very handsome father.

There is no better feeling than dancing with my son. Beautiful feet from both of us here! (Photo by Jerod Harris/Getty Images)

One of the proudest moments of my life was watching my son walk down the aisle with his gorgeous wife, BC Jean. (Photos by London Light Photography)

Mark's success on the stage has been phenomenal – especially when it comes to his roles on Broadway. Here he is with Frankie Valli, who hand-picked him for his role in *Jersey Boys*, and giving it his all in a promo shot for *Kinky Boots* – in which he played the lead, Charlie Price.

(*Jersey Boys* photos by Jessica Fallon Gordon; *Kinky Boots* photo by Matthew Murphy)

A truly talented performer and singer–songwriter, Mark has been playing guitar and writing music nearly all of his life.

With Sharon and Bucky Ballas. Sharon was one of my most trustworthy allies when we lived in Houston and remains so to this day. She lent me a stunning jacket for one of my first appearences on *Strictly*.

My first *Strictly* show, 2017. Not bad, considering I hadn't put on a latin dress or a pair of dancing shoes since 1996! (Photo by Guy Levy/BBC)

Lights, camera, action! With my fellow judges Craig Revel Horwood, Darcey
Bussell and Bruno Tonioli, at the *Strictly* launch show in 2017. (Photo by Guy Levy/BBC)

Motsi's debut – I'm no longer the new kid on the block. I was so delighted when
Motsi joined us on *Strictly*. She is supremely talented and a joy to work with.

(Photo by Mike Marsland/WireImage)

On top of the world! Reaching the summit of Kilimanjaro with the brilliant team from Comic Relief. (L-R) Alexander Armstrong, Osi Umenyiora, me, Anita Rani, Jade Thirlwall, Ed Balls, Leigh-Anne Pinnock, Dani Dyer and Dan Walker.

(Photo by Chris Jackson - Handout/Getty Images)

Cooking breakfast for the entire team with the lovely Dani Dyer. The altitude didn't help make my food taste any better … (Photo by Chris Jackson/Getty Images for Comic Relief)

Full-on glam for the 2019 BAFTAs.
(Photo by Karwai Tang/WireImage)

With the lovely Camilla, Duchess
of Cornwall, and Craig Revel
Horwood at a tea dance to
highlight the benefits of older
people staying active. Buckingham
Palace, November 2017. (Photo by
Gareth Fuller - WPA Pool/Getty Images)

Where I get all my poise and glamour
from – my gorgeous mother, Audrey.

The moment I started to fall in love
with Daniel Taylor. One of the first
photographs we ever had taken together
at a Christmas party.

Me and Danny with our gorgous dog, Charlie.
I've finally entered the happiest chapter of my life.

Whenever I was at home in the UK, at four o'clock every afternoon, I would call him. He'd be on his way home with Mary, and I'd be on my way home with Mark. The pair of us would chat for ten minutes or so – about the children, what we'd been up to, what we were having for dinner, all the daily little details of life. We had a very strong bond. We were in two separate worlds, but I always thought he was pretty happy where he was.

I don't really know what went wrong for David in the last part of his life. I knew that he'd once written a letter threatening suicide, which of course I realise now was his cry for help. At the time, I called him and tried to talk to him about it, but somehow it just got brushed aside and swept under the rug.

My brother was having waves of unhappiness, punctuated by short periods when it seemed as though everything was fine again. I hadn't lived on that housing estate since I was 14, but I know that his life there wasn't always easy. Twenty years ago, we didn't really understand problems with mental health the way we do now, and even if we had guessed he was suffering, I'm not sure we would have found the language we needed to discuss it. Instead everyone skirted around the subject, both for his protection and our peace of mind.

These days, we're all a lot more sensitive to the mental health of people we care about, particularly men, who haven't been used to talking about it, and we're more alert to the signs. At the time, I didn't really take his problems too seriously and I didn't see the signs. I wouldn't have known what to look for and, if you're not equipped for it, you can miss them. I would talk to him about his mental health, but he would poo-poo my concern and change the subject. If I asked him what he'd been up to and how he was feeling, he would quickly move the subject on to Mary and something funny she'd done. He seemed happier doing that, so I let him.

In the last year of his life, David increasingly suffered with a lot of anxiety and went in and out of depression, going through great highs and then equal lows. When he was ill, for several months my mother stayed with him and she found it quite a struggle. She held him in her arms while he cried, night after night. He wouldn't eat, and would tell her he thought his life wasn't worth living. David would describe how he felt he was in a black hole that he was struggling to get out of. We all hoped fervently it would pass.

He was very sad that his relationship with Eileen appeared to have ended. She had her own problems by then, including struggles with alcohol and depression, so it was a pretty bleak scene all round. He wanted her to be in his life and was miserable that she wasn't. I'm not sure that was at the root of his problems, although he seemed to think it was. He became more and more unpredictable and fixated on his wish to be reunited with Eileen. At one point, he ran away with a knife, someone on the estate raised the alarm and suddenly there were police helicopters out looking for him. My mother and I talked about it, but she always reassured me, 'I've got a handle on it', no doubt not wanting to alarm me, a couple of hundred miles away. Things had definitely got worse for David by then, although I had no idea how desperate he really was.

Communication has not always been the easiest of things for my mother; she's the absolute opposite of me and keeps her business close to her heart. She would never be one to say, 'Oh my god, this happened,' or 'Oh Shirley, you need to come down.' She's not that person. She's always been a strong character and just always dealt with whatever was thrown her way – even when, much later, she was diagnosed with cancer, she kept an optimistic, practical frame of mind. Whenever there's been a problem in the family, she's far more likely to say, 'We can deal with it. You keep on with what you're doing.' So that's what I did. I never really realised how bad things had got, and that's something I still have to live with.

Where David had previously experienced all those highs and lows, gradually, his depression took over. He lost a lot of weight, and my mother couldn't persuade him to eat anything at all. She took him to the doctor's, where they gave him some pills, but we were never really given any direction about how we could best look after him. The doctors seemed to be of the mind, 'Just give him a pill and that should solve all the problems,' but those tablets didn't seem to be doing anything for David.

My mother decided to take him to hospital but, as they pulled up in the car outside, my brother spotted some people on the steps and recognised them as friends from the housing estate. Having always been known as 'tough Kola' around there, he feared that it would make him look weak if he was seen going into the hospital to ask for help.

David was a private person, just like my mother, and he didn't want anyone knowing his business. He certainly didn't want anyone knowing he was sick. As he became increasingly unwell, he became more and more nervous of people on the estate becoming aware of his fragility, and that would stress him out. Many things began to trigger him, but that was one of the biggest catalysts.

On that fateful day outside the hospital, when he was in such critical need of professional help and should probably have been sectioned, he made my mother turn the car round and drive him home.

• • •

In December 2003, I was in London with Mark, while my mother was up north with David. Mark had been invited to perform at St Paul's Church in Covent Garden. It was a big deal for him, he'd been given a solo at his school's carol concert, so I thought it'd be fun to have as much of our family there as possible. I called both my mother and brother and invited them to come along and support Mark. David wouldn't hear of it, he had no wish to come, while my mother was reluctant. She said, 'Shirley, I really don't think I should leave him at the moment.' She was worried about David being left on his own, but me, not understanding the full depth of my brother's problems at that time, I was determined she should come to London. She was very reluctant to leave him, but I became quite insistent, telling her, 'He'll be fine for one night, Mother, come on, it'll do you good.' I even spoke to David about it, and he agreed, telling her, 'Go on, I'll be fine, don't you worry.'

By this time, my mother had been staying with my brother for about eight weeks, going without sleep all that time as she struggled to take care of him, plus she was going out of her mind with worry. I thought she needed a break, just one night off, a few hours with Mark and me away from all that stress. Of course, ever since that weekend, she has never stopped blaming herself for leaving David, but it was me who pushed her to make the trip.

After she finally relented and travelled down to London, we went to the concert together and had a lovely evening. As soon as we got home, I tried to call David straight away but I couldn't get through. I had a sinking feeling inside, right to the depths of my tummy, as I started to imagine all sorts of awful things.

To this day, I'm quite clingy and I need to hear from the ones I love quite frequently, even if it's just one word to let me know they're okay. Travelling around the world for work, I used to be quite relaxed about all that, but now, if I don't hear from someone as soon as I try to get hold of them, an overwhelming fear takes over me, and I'm pretty sure this dates from that terrible weekend when I couldn't get hold of David.

With my brother not answering, I called Eileen and asked her if she could possibly go round and check on him. It was late in the evening by now, almost midnight, but she agreed to go round with her elder son, David. I didn't hear anything else from her, so I decided to go to bed and try again first thing in the morning.

That night after his concert, Mark had asked me if he could stay out at a friend's house. I reluctantly agreed, as I always preferred it if Mark's friends came to us, and I didn't particularly like it if he or Derek, who was still living with us, stayed at other people's houses. Mark was 17 by then, and it was one of the first times he'd stayed over with friends.

I didn't sleep well – as every mother will know, you never do when your children are out and about, and you only really fall asleep properly once you hear the key in the door. At six o'clock in the morning, the doorbell rang, and Derek went to see who it was. He called me and said, 'I think you need to come down. The police are here.' With Mark still unaccounted for, my heart was in my mouth as I went down. Even now, I can picture the scene as though it happened yesterday. Derek was at the door, I was halfway down the stairs, and my mother had come out of her room too to see what all the commotion was about, so she was standing just behind me.

Everything at that point started happening in slow motion. As the police officers stepped inside, Derek moved aside and they looked up at us on the stairs. I felt sick with dread. Then one of them said, 'Mrs Rich?' So, with my heart heavy with what I realised was the implication, I slowly moved aside and instead it was my mother who had to step forward.

It was her son, not mine, they'd come to talk about, to break the saddest of news, the most life-changing, soul-destroying news any mother will ever have to hear. As gently as they could, they said just a few words that changed all our lives forever. I'll never forget it. It was surreal, confusing and overwhelming. My mother, Derek and I were all left standing there – silent and stunned as the first great waves of shock started to hit us.

I'll always wonder what went on that day at my mum's house in Liverpool, once she had left for London. Later, we discovered David had filled up his fridge with groceries and even some fresh milk, so it didn't appear that he had woken up in the morning feeling as though he was going to take his own life. I always ask myself whether he tried to call someone to invite them round and they couldn't make it. Had he tried to contact Eileen? Had he tried to contact a friend? Was anybody mean to him? I'll never know. After he died, I read all the notes on his medication and there in the small print, it said, 'May accelerate thoughts of suicide.' Nobody had warned us about that and we didn't realise it ourselves. For whatever reason, by the evening, he'd left his back door unlocked, he'd moved his car to a different spot, and he'd hanged himself on the stairs in my mother's house. He was 44.

How low do you have to be? What goes through your mind? It must have been sheer desperation. That big dark black hole David had told us about had somehow got the better of him. Everybody's experience of despair is so unique, so personal, that I can't even begin to guess. My heart bled for my brother and everything he went through that night. It still does.

All those poor people who've themselves been through anything similar with a loved one will need no telling about the kind of day we had. For anyone else, it's probably almost impossible for me to describe – the chaos, the hundreds of phone calls, not knowing what to do or even to think through all the tears, your adrenaline pumping away as you try to do a hundred things at once, having to tell yourself what's happened over and over again even while the other part of your brain bats it away and refuses to believe it's true – and underneath all that, slowly absorbing that stony-cold realisation that nothing will ever be the same again. What can I say? It was simply devastating – the darkest day of my life.

The day the police came to our house in the early morning, I will always remember was a Friday. After the devastating news, I wasn't sure what to do or who to call. With Corky by now living back in the United States, the first person I could get hold of was my ex-husband, Sammy. He came round immediately, saw what a state my mother and I were in and volunteered to drive us up to Liverpool. What should have been a four-hour drive felt more like 24 hours, because the traffic was bad. I couldn't get hold of the coroner or anybody else because it was the weekend. Once we finally arrived, well, if receiving that knock at the door was a shock, walking into my mother's house was numbing.

David's cigarette butts were still in the ashtray, all his clothes were there; we found his groceries in the fridge, his fresh milk and even a half-drunk cup of tea. The whole thing was surreal, and I just walked around waiting for the true reality to hit me. I was dazed and unable to come to terms with any of it.

During the dark days that followed, the only thing that kept me going was knowing I had to stay strong for my mother. I didn't want to let anything out because I felt responsible for sorting things out and getting a grip on this awful situation. It was terrible for me to see my mother in such a state, and I didn't want to increase her burden by adding my sadness to hers, so we both suffered in terrible silence, often reduced to sitting in the front room, staring at each other, tears running down our faces, saying nothing, because there were no words.

We had to wait out the whole weekend before we could visit the funeral parlour or even get hold of the coroner. It was the darkest, longest weekend in my whole life, still trying to make sense of why a 44-year-old man would take his own life on that one day that my mother had decided to go to London to watch her grandson. There was simply no explanation I could find.

I went round to talk to David's former partner, Eileen, who was still suffering from the total shock of going to the house with her son and finding his body. Both of Eileen's sons, David and Philip, had only ever known my brother David as their father, and they too were traumatised. Everyone was reeling. Nobody seemed to be able to take in the fact of my brother's death; instead, we just ended up having the same conversations over and over again, going round in circles, asking all the same questions but not getting any real answers, not solving anything but finding words easier, somehow, than the silence.

I called Corky in America and he wanted to be with his family in the UK, so he immediately set off to travel all the way from Houston. Everybody was beside themselves and it was left to me to try to deal with all the practical arrangements, as David's funeral needed to be planned and questions answered. When we eventually visited the funeral parlour for the awful opportunity to say goodbye, everyone in the family came, including my mother, Mark, Derek and Corky, but I decided not to take Mary. I didn't want her to see her father in his coffin, and thank goodness I made that decision. To see this big, strong character I'd known all my life, lying there so helpless and so hopeless, it was more than I could bear. I'm so grateful that I chose not to take her that day, and that she could remember instead the feisty father who had raised her.

David was extremely proud of his daughter, particularly through her schooling years. He used to take her to school and pick her up daily; she was the centre of his world. There was a big oak tree on the edge of the school grounds, and after he died, her teachers told me there hadn't been a single day when David wasn't standing by that tree, waiting for Mary to come out so he could walk her home. He was never late dropping her off in the morning, never late picking her up in the afternoon. The teachers said he always stood in the same spot under this big oak. Very movingly, they said even after his death they were convinced they could still see him in that same spot. As I said, he was a jack of all trades, a master of none – except being a dad. He knew exactly what he wanted to do when it came to that, and Mary was extremely lucky to have him. She was ten when she lost her father.

In planning David's funeral, I didn't really know where to start, and neither did anybody else. We worked through the list of booking the church and the cars, inviting the guests, while my mother sat still and silent. It seemed that, for the first time in my life, my mother had no idea what to do, and it was up to me to take charge of a very difficult and dark situation.

Mark wanted to write a song for his uncle about his life, about being raised by him, and I knew this would make a touching tribute for David, although I worried whether Mark would find the strength to get through it in the church.

During the dark days that followed, one thing kept me going – my determination to give my brother the proper send-off he deserved. He had so many great photographs, so in the end I got a big strip of wallpaper and stuck on as many of them as I could fit. That helped keep me busy.

I went through all the photographs he'd taken throughout his life, and it was a great comfort for me to discover that, as well as working hard, he had had some wonderful times. He might not have ever had a big flashy job or loads of money to throw around, but he knew how to have fun with his friends, and make other people happy. These photographs told a story in themselves. In his free time when he wasn't working, he'd be off fishing in France with his friends, Phil and Sally. Through the photographs, I real- ised he'd seen many different places in Europe, tried lots of different things and enjoyed a great many happy experiences in his life. That was a great source of comfort to me.

The dreaded day came for us to make our final farewells and bury my brother. I went outside the front door as the hearse pulled up, and there was a throng of people all along our street and up our driveway. It was astonishing to say the least. All the guys on their motorcycles, tipping their helmets as my mother walked past, friends I hadn't seen since I was a child. All here to pay their last respects to my brother.

When we got to the church where I'd expected that perhaps 50 people might turn up, I was again overwhelmed. It looked as though 500 people had come along to say their goodbyes. You couldn't move inside and the crowd spilled out from the church into its surrounding grounds. I don't think my brother ever knew how loved he was, and I hope he was looking down that day to see how many people attended to pay their respects to a man who had gone through all the trauma of bullying and abuse that he had, and yet had done so much for so many on that Leasowe estate. To know that he was so loved was beautiful, and I felt it even more for my mother than I did for myself.

Inside the church, I remember sitting looking out at the sea of faces, preparing to stand up and pay tribute to my brother. It was the hardest thing I'd ever had to do in my life. As I went up, Mark whispered to me, 'Don't cry, Mum. Try to be strong for all of us and for Nanny.' I remember my voice breaking several times, but I knew I had to get through it because right in front of me were my mother, Mark, Derek and Corky and I knew they were all suffering too.

I gave my speech, which included how terribly sad it was to lose my brother but also the different aspects of his life, all the fun times I remembered having with him, all the great memories, how he'd helped raise Mark and what a beautiful job he'd done with his daughter. I tried to thank as many people as I could who had passed through David's life. I wanted people to know the man that I knew and how much he meant to me as a brother. I really tried to do him justice, and I hope he was looking down on me and that he was happy.

Then it was Mark's turn to get up to sing with Derek and Corky, but pretty soon he broke down and started sobbing, and the whole church fell silent while he tried to regain his composure. The song that he'd written for David's life was a touching tribute, and there wasn't a dry eye in the house by the time he'd finished. You could hear other people weeping as he walked back to his seat, clearly exhausted.

David has left a huge gap in our family, and the traumatic manner of his passing still takes its toll on us even now, nearly two decades later. I lost my brother, my best friend, the person I spoke to every day, the protector of my mother and myself.

Over the years, my mother and I have had a lot of counselling for this loss, and our therapist has always done his best to make us feel that we shouldn't take so much responsibility for what happened. Inevitably, though, you do. To this day, I can honestly say that we blame ourselves. If we'd known more about mental health, if we'd known more about the pills he was taking, if we'd known more about how he felt, if my mother had decided not to come to London that day, if I hadn't picked up the phone and insisted on her coming ... if ... if ... if ... all these ifs. It all runs through your mind as you wonder, was there something, anything, we could have done to save him?

Nobody has ever blamed anybody else for what happened. Instead my mother blames herself for not being there that day, and I blame myself for convincing her to come to London. As bad as my mother has always felt, I've felt equally terrible and responsible – for being wrapped up in my own life, not seeing the problems, not spotting the signs. The counsellor explained to us that if somebody is intent on that course of action, nothing we could have said or done would have changed anything. But, deep down, I'm convinced that if I'd seen how seriously ill he was, had I been educated on mental health, I could have done something. It's possible for people to get over this illness if they get the help they need. I could have made sure my brother did. We could have reached out together to specialists. Then, perhaps, he would still be around today.

David's daughter Mary has always been part of my life since the day she was born, and I can truthfully say she's never given me a spot of bother. She's always been a child that never once asked for anything, and I've always wanted to be there for her and give her any possible thing she might need. I felt for my niece because she suffered tremendously; David was her lifeline, it was apparent for all to see how much they loved each other. It broke my heart to see her aged ten with her heart shattered into so many pieces.

After Mary lost her dad, it was decided she should move to London and be with me. I sent her to a private school in the city but she couldn't settle. She wanted to move back up to the north of England and be closer to where her father was buried. I told her,

'I'll support you in any choice you make on one condition, and that is that you don't move back to the housing estate.'

It wasn't that I ever wanted to separate her from her mother. It was more that, by this time, Eileen hadn't been well for a long time, and I knew she didn't have the means to look after her daughter. Mary always had the potential of being able to do something special with her life, and she has.

Instead, I sent her to St David's College, a boarding school in Wales, where she flourished in her studies. Following her father's death, Mary became intent on doing a job that meant she could help people in one way or another. Sure enough, now she works as a healthcare scientist in a laboratory – in fact, her proper job title is Senior Healthcare Technical Officer in Histocompatibility and Immunogenetics. It's beyond me exactly what she does but I know it's very important, and she's completely dedicated to her job. What makes her even more impressive is that she's achieved all of this, working to help others, while suffering herself with severe Crohn's disease. She never lets this stop her chasing her goals, and I couldn't be more proud of her.

On top of all that she's polite and gorgeous, but I can't take the credit for how she's turned out. It's all down to those ten first important years she spent with David. He doted on her, she was everything to him.

You never, ever get over the suicide of someone you love, and I think it will always be a weight on my shoulders and those of my mother. It's not something we'll ever be able to put down. After I left home at 14 and during those years I was off travelling the world, the bond between my mother and brother became incredibly strong. They were closer than close, and I knew his death would be catastrophic for her. That's why, ever since we lost him, I've tried to have her with me as much as possible. I try to make my mother laugh every day, I call her several times throughout the day just to make sure she's okay, as I used to do for my brother. That four o'clock phone call to him is probably the thing I still miss the most.

It's a cliché because it's true, that it takes something so awful and devastating to give you a proper perspective on what's important in this life. I was always intent on making my circumstances better, on being successful in my profession, on getting to the top of my industry. I was on a steam train, aiming for the top. In my industry, everybody seems to be so focused on who's earning this, who's winning that, it's a dog-eat-dog world and it becomes hard to get off the train, or the hamster wheel, as my son puts it. The two weeks I spent up north sorting out my brother's belongings changed all that for me. I'd taken only a tiny backpack with me and had just the clothes I stood in, but nobody cared, least of all me. A ballgown was never going to bring back David.

People ask me now, 'Where do you live?' and my truthful answer is, 'Wherever I hang my hat.' Whether I'm in a tiny room somewhere or at my mum's house up north, it doesn't matter to me. I don't need a fancy place, it's just not important. Material things are no longer important to me. Family and friends mean the world.

When it came to my attention that my brother was ill, I should have dropped everything I was doing and gone up with my mother, talked to my brother face to face, seen for myself the extent of his problems and stayed by his side. Now, if any member of my family has an issue, I'll drop everything in a New York minute to be with them, and everything else just has to go on the back burner. I will never say to anybody I care about, 'Sorry, I can't do that,' because my loved ones must always come first. In a way, it's made my life much simpler and it's put my priorities in order.

What's really important to you in life? This is the question you have to ask. Making sure your loved ones are okay, keeping them close whatever it takes, being the first one to pick up the phone after an argument, making sure you're being the best version of yourself you can possibly be as a role model, helping people with their dreams, inspiring them to believe that anything's possible. And when people are feeling fragile, you have to see the signs and make room for them, listen to them properly, open your mind up to what is really going on in their life.

I used to concentrate on my own part in trying to cheer my brother up, I used to say to him, 'Come on, David, you'll get over this,' because I was uneducated in what he really needed. I should have made it all about him and what he was feeling. You cannot tell people how to feel. You might think you know what's going on, but you aren't the person in their shoes, and these are some of the reasons I take the blame. He was in a dark black hole and I couldn't help him out of it. It will haunt me until the day I die. It's been 17 years now since we lost him, and not a day goes by when he isn't in our thoughts.

CHAPTER 8

The Jive

'The dance which asks, who has the strongest stamina? The freshest look with changes of speed and fluidity. When you have to do it as the fifth dance, after seven rounds, three minutes a dance, it becomes an endurance test.'

Things changed massively for me in the first years of this century, testing me in ways I wasn't prepared for. Corky was still there at the beginning, but within a few years he had chosen to leave for good and was making a new life for himself back in the United States.

In a short space of time, lots of other unforeseen things occurred. Corky left, then Julianne and her mother Marianne went home. I had a lot of money stolen from me by my cleaner, and that left me very uneasy and untrusting about letting anyone new into my home. And then David died. He had been my greatest protector, and without him I felt very vulnerable, exposed and found myself going into a very dark corner of my mind.

It was as though all the pillars that had kept my house standing up were falling down one by one, and everything seemed to come down in a crash around Christmas. Nearly two decades have passed since that oppressive time in my life, but even now, December is not a month I ever embrace. I always feel that if anything is going to go wrong, it will invariably happen at Christmas. It's a shame because I realise everyone else is gearing up for a festive time, and it makes me feel quite alone with my fears.

Even without my deep, long-lasting grief for my brother, it wasn't easy for me to see all these people leaving my home. Rationally, I knew they were only getting on with their lives, basing themselves in a different place, and our connections didn't need to change, but another part of me felt as though they were all leaving my life for good.

There was no doubt, the on-off, long drawn-out parting between Corky and myself made for a hard breakup. He was the father of my child and I'd been with him for over 20 years. Whatever missiles we'd flung at each other during that time, it was the most significant relationship in my life up until that point. Now, without a dance partner, about to be divorced for the second time, I started looking back at all the failures in my life. Failed relationship with Nigel. Failed marriages with Sammy and Corky. I beat myself up into believing I was just one big loser, and it seemed some people close to me and in the industry had no problem making me feel bad and reminding me of all the disasters. Sometimes they said it as a joke, but to me it didn't seem funny.

I've always been married to my work. Whenever I have any downtime, my mind races at a thousand miles an hour. I'm not a relaxed person at the best of times, and I've always tried to deal with that by dancing and then dancing some more, staying busy and occupied. Travelling around from country to country always suited my personality, filling page after page of my diary with notes, appointments and tasks so that you can hardly see any blank space. Derek used to become so fascinated with my diary, he once asked if he could take a photograph of it, because it was so packed with bookings and other appointments, it was virtually illegible.

He'd say, 'Only you can read that, Shirley.' So moving at high speed has never been a challenge for me; it's when I've had to stop for any length of time that the rot sets in, and the video cassette starts playing over and over in my mind.

All those people close to me moving on at the same time was obviously a change in circumstance that was going to take some getting used to, but for me it went deeper than that, no doubt stemming from my father walking out on us all those years before. My mum would occasionally ask me, 'Does it bother you about your dad?' and of course I would always say, 'No, of course not,' because I never wanted to hurt her feelings. But does it really? Well, I wonder. It must have an effect on you, how you're treated as a child by someone you instinctively put a lot of trust in. To this day, when people leave, it cuts me to the bone in a way I've never been able to rationalise properly. In my head, I know I have nothing to worry about, but somewhere deeper down, I have a problem believing they'll ever come back.

Looking back, I realise I was very co-dependent, needing people around me all the time. There had always been someone strong and loud sharing my space, initially my mother and David, then Nigel, then Sammy, then Corky. In recent years, there had been the children, Mark, Derek and Julianne, filling the house with their laughter, noise and mess. Then Julianne and Derek's mum Marianne had come and lived with us for six or seven months, and that was an absolute hoot, having another woman my age to gossip with and help look after the children. The children had all their friends coming and going as well, so our house was like a proper circus.

Now everything had gone quiet, and here I was, a woman in her late forties, living by herself for the first time. I found it incredibly hard, and I was constantly tired and anxious. I booked as much work as I could to hide the fact of how lonely I was. My days were still packed, rushing from one lesson to another, but coming home and putting my key in the front door was when I started feeling unhappy about being on my own, and sorry for myself. I didn't have the energy to cook anything, Instead, I'd just come in, put my bags down and have the same food from the fridge night after night. I didn't even bother to turn on the TV, I would just sit on the floor of the corner of my office, crying uncontrollably, asking myself over and over again where I'd messed up and made all the wrong decisions, and questioning whether I'd ever have anyone to share my life with again. Who'd want a woman in her late forties, especially someone who'd made as many mistakes as I had? My career was still going well, but when it came to my home life, I felt as though every decision I'd made was wrong, and there was no way of putting it right. I beat myself up about the past and feared for the future.

I started sinking like a stone, going to a very bleak place in my mind, and I wondered if it was that same dark hole my brother had often talked about. At night, I would have visions of myself falling, and wake up with night sweats. Eventually the doctor I was seeing quite regularly prescribed me antidepressants, and the next thing I knew, I was taking all sorts of things, pills to help me sleep, more pills to keep me going through the day; I was like a baby's rattle with everything I was taking. That went on for quite a while, until one day I decided to share with my mother the difficulties I was struggling with. She told me straight, 'You've been looking after a lot of people for a very long time. It's time you looked after yourself.' I made the decision to come off all the medication I was taking and get a grip on myself.

I will never forget those dark days and even now, those feelings can still haunt me occasionally. It's why I do whatever I can to support mental health campaigns. I feel an incredible sympathy whenever I hear of anyone else suffering from something similar to what I went through. It always irks me when people say, either about me or someone else, 'Oh, she'll be fine. She's really strong.' Looking at me from the outside, I was still highly functioning, still teaching, still judging, a woman with no worries on her plate. They would never have guessed what was going on in my mind behind the wall I put up against the world. What people often don't understand is, for many sufferers of this kind of anxiety, that tough wall is just a coat of armour; it's never the full story. We're all a lot more fragile than we appear.

Throughout my career, I'd always been able to make my own money and stand on my own two feet financially, but during my marriage to Corky, he had made it clear it wasn't my business to deal with any of our paperwork. He wanted that job for himself, and so for the 20 years of our marriage he did it all. That meant that when he left, I had to learn to do it all myself, and I found it a very steep learning curve.

Despite all my years of hard work and all the success that we'd had, I didn't come out of that marriage at all well off financially, and it felt as though I was starting again from scratch. Fortunately, I was lucky enough to have someone on my side that I could trust with my last coin: my old boyfriend, Nigel Tiffany.

Nigel and I had lost contact following my dramatic departure from his life ahead of my try-out with Sammy Stopford. He remained very upset for several years afterwards and stayed out of my way at any events where our paths crossed. Then he got busy with his business career, at which he did incredibly well, I moved to America, and our lives went on very different paths, until I moved back to London in 1990 and we reconnected. Years later, I walked into a ballroom and spotted Sammy, Corky and Nigel all sitting together, having a drink. It's a strange world we live in. Some things, you just couldn't make it up.

When Corky left, Nigel stepped back into my life, both as my friend and financial adviser. He helped me understand things like mortgages and investments, and for the first time in my life, I was in complete control of my money.

Nigel once revealed to me just how hurt he'd been at the time I went off with Sammy after that fateful try-out in south London, all those years before. He did concede, though, 'You made the right decision when you chose to dance with Sammy.' Nigel was always Ballroom, I was Latin, we wanted different things, it was as simple as that.

I described earlier how dancing with Nigel had felt like falling into the arms of a Rolls-Royce. Now I told him the same thing, and he was equally nice in return. He said if he was a Rolls-Royce, I was a car that was still in the process of being built, but when I got on the road, he knew I would be a Ferrari: 'There were still bits being added, but you were always going to be brilliant in the future.' I'm lucky to have him as my friend to this day.

As I've said, during our marriage, Corky and I were blessed with a beautiful lifestyle. I remember once chatting with my friend Karen on an aeroplane coming home from Japan, telling her how we wanted to find a nice home. She happened to be flicking through an issue of *Country Life* magazine, and right then and there on the page, she spotted a lovely house in south London, which seemed to have everything I'd just been describing to her. Well, guess what, that's the one we ended up buying!

Corky and I soon made enquiries, an offer was made and, before we knew it, we were living in the house of our dreams, which became our home for the next decade or so.

The house had its own name, but Corky decided that he would rename it 'Live With Passion', and you could say we did, in good times and bad. It was a beautiful home, even when I was creaking around in it by myself. Corky was long gone but we still had financial dealings to sort out as part of our separation, and then out of the blue, he told me he wanted to sell up.

I had no choice in the matter when it came to selling and he also insisted on having half the furniture. The saddest part for me was watching his team wheel out the piano that the boys used to practise on. Watching that little bit of history disappear from my life freshly broke my heart.

We were halfway through a very difficult, drawn-out divorce, and although I knew it was the right time for a new chapter for me in fresh surroundings, and it would be good for my mental health, it was still a wrench to leave the home where so many significant events in my life had taken place – where we had spent so much of our married life, and where Mark, Derek and Julianne had all grown up.

There was another house that Karen had seen in the area. She was always on the lookout! I thought it might be way above my budget, but my mother came down to visit and I told her about it. The estate agent couldn't arrange a visit for some reason, so we thought we'd go and see if anyone was there. A man opened the door and invited us in for a coffee. We ended up having a good chat and he offered me a great deal, plus a few more weeks to come up with the finances. It was still above my budget, but I took a deep breath and put down the deposit. This would be the very first house I had ever bought by myself, an enormous step for me.

Guess who I ended up selling my old family home to? Karen and Marcus! Thankfully, they quickly changed its name again. And guess who my new neighbours were? Sammy and Barbara! I guess some things never change.

. . .

It wasn't long, though, before I was packing my suitcases again and, in 2007, I moved back to America. At the time, I rationalised that it would give my career a fresh boost by having a new base, but if I'm honest, after Mark, Derek and Julianne went back to the United States, I was miserable living in London by myself as my whole life for the last decade had been running around with the children and training them, which I found all very exciting. Only a few months after Mark and Derek moved to the US, I basically packed up, rented out my house and followed them to LA. It wasn't so much the apple not falling far from the tree as much as the tree upping sticks and following the apple. I couldn't imagine me being in London while my son was in the United States. Fortunately, Mark was happy about me being in LA with him, and it turned out to be one of the best things I ever did.

It meant I got to stay near my son and blow a lot of the London cobwebs away. I'd like to say I got to enjoy the warm LA sun on my face, but in fact I was often inside the studio for long hours every day, so I didn't actually catch much sunshine. As the children's work on *Dancing with the Stars* took off, I often visited the studios and the producers took to consulting me on which dancing couples they should invite on, what kind of routines to introduce to the show, all sorts of things. I was in a position to advise them on styles and trends that were constantly evolving in the dance industry, and I enjoyed doing it. I was always sending information about my students to different shows across the world, and I like to think I've helped a lot of dancers further their careers in all the corners of the globe where these TV shows are so popular.

I even started appearing on the *Dancing with the Stars* spin-off show, *AfterBuzz* – like a US version of *It Takes Two* – and giving my opinion as an experienced dancer on all the performances. One season, they decided to make a feature about a dance industry icon, and I was flattered and thrilled when I discovered they'd chosen me.

Before I knew it, my days were packed, what with my long hours teaching and running to and from *Dancing with the Stars* to see how the children were doing. This also gave me more than my share of dazzling A-list celebrity encounters. Basketball legend Kobe Bryant was in the audience one evening, and Mark introduced me to him. Everyone was flocking around him, a massive superstar even by Hollywood standards. Another evening, Henry Winkler turned up, so of course I got my picture with 'The Fonz'.

One of the nicest people I've ever had the good fortune to come across was Donny Osmond. He was one of the contestants on the ninth season of *Dancing with the Stars*, which he went on to win with his partner, Kym Johnson. I kept bumping into him backstage, we got chatting and ended up becoming buddies, always sending each other pictures of our families. While I was living in LA, it became a regular weekend treat to go and see him perform his residency at the Flamingo Las Vegas.

Probably the most unexpected superstar encounter I've ever had came when I was booked for what I thought was a regular private lesson with a new client – except when I got to the studio, it turned out to be Tom Cruise. He wanted to learn some salsa steps as a surprise present for his then wife, Katie Holmes. Because his wife was tall, I took my friend Alan with me, so he could play 'Katie' while I got to play 'Tom'. I've always been a massive fan of Tom Cruise, so I had to concentrate hard on not being completely awestruck as I was dancing in his arms. At the end of the lesson, he gave me a massive hug and said he'd enjoyed every minute of it. Considering he's a man who's used to climbing on top of skyscrapers and throwing himself out of aeroplanes, he was surprisingly nervous about taking his first Ballroom steps, but I can say that, just like everything else he sets his mind to, he was a dedicated student, a natural dancer, and of course, the most charming, polite person you could ever wish to meet.

The hardest part of that whole era in my life, post-divorce from Corky, was learning not to be so dependent on other people, to enjoy my own company, to live by myself and enjoy filling the space. However, I should perhaps mention that I was not entirely on my own.

Quite soon after I arrived in LA, I was introduced to Nigel Lythgoe, a man I was surprised I hadn't met earlier in my life. Just like me, he came all the way from Wallasey and, just like me, he had dedicated his life to dance and it had rewarded him with a wonderful career. Funnily enough, our paths had never once crossed in all those years before I met him in LA at a function. We went out for dinner and ended up having a brief love affair. It was great fun while it lasted, going out in his Rolls-Royce, dining in restaurants facing the Pacific Ocean and comparing our journeys all the way from the Wirral to Malibu. Ultimately, it wasn't meant to be, but we stayed friends. He is such a warm and charming man.

There were several other charming gentlemen in my life, two of whom definitely deserve a mention, for bringing a lot of happiness and laughter into my life where there had been angst and heartache for far too long a time. Between them, they taught me two important lessons – one, that if I'd thought my heart had been broken for good, well, guess what, it turned out it could be mended, and two, as every woman and possibly man reading this will know, there's no fool like an old fool, especially when it comes to love.

Riccardo Cocchi came into my life as one of my students. He was an unbelievably talented dancer in the amateur ranks, but more importantly, he was also charming, attentive, elegant, sophisticated and, most significantly of all, a gentleman. I think after everything I'd been through, he felt like the human embodiment of a cool glass of lemonade in the sun. We were together for several years, living part of the time in the US, and part of the time in

London, as well as travelling a lot together, teaching and occasionally performing. One of my great memories was going with him to visit his family in Italy, where I was introduced to his two huge, hairy Chow Chow dogs. He had a remarkable family unit – always important to me – and they were very attentive and caring. If they even noticed the age gap between Riccardo and me, they never said anything.

Over the years, as his coach, my ambition for Riccardo knew no bounds, so I embraced the opportunity for him to dance with a new partner – Yulia Zagoruychenko. They enjoyed a meteoric rise and I realised they'd be travelling the world and spending all their time together. It was inevitable what was going to happen. Just as I predicted, they ended up falling in love and becoming ten times world champions. I was devastated at the time, but when I look back, of course I'm happy to see such a talented couple do so well in their career. For the time I was with him, though, it was a relief to feel normal again.

I was then on my own for a while before I met another gentleman, Yegor Novikov, also a very talented dancer and one of my best ever students. I was sharing a house by then with my best friend Alan Grundy in LA, so when Yegor needed a place to stay, he moved in with us.

I should tell you about Alan at this point, as he's been so important to me for so many years. Alan first came into my life when he was nine years old. He was from Liverpool and I taught him as a juvenile, I taught him as a junior, I taught him as a youth and I watched him become the amateur Open to the World British champion.

THE JIVE

He was the very first person to give me the nickname, 'Queen of Latin', after all my titles with Sammy, Corky and the success I achieved with my students. He said it wasn't just because I was a good dancer, but because of my passion for what I did for a living. He was about 18 when he first called me that. He's 40 now and he still does. Sometimes, these days he'll call me 'the Madonna of Ballroom dancing'. Whatever, I'll take it.

Alan and I lost touch for a few years when he went to work as a dance director on the cruise ships, but he turned up in my life in LA, just as I was getting over the whole Riccardo business. Alan appeared exactly when I needed him most. He moved in with me and it was like having a brother in the house again. I used to tell him frequently, 'You really are the perfect boyfriend, Alan, just without the sex.'

Alan used to take care of my house in London while the children were growing up and he was very involved in their lives, picking them up from school in his little yellow Mini. When he moved into my home in Los Angeles, it was like having a husband again, only Alan was gay. I guess you could have called him my gusband!

Alan's wonderful partner, Nathan, also moved in with us, and we became like the three musketeers. Nathan was particularly nurturing. He would run my bath, turn down my bed, prepare my meals and even rub my feet. Alan looked after my hair, make-up and styling, and helped me keep on top of household bills. We did everything together. We laughed until we cried, watched movies and had a good old gossip. Looking back, those were some of the happiest years of my life. I always thought that if I found a husband who was a combination of the two of them, I'd be doing very well indeed.

Yegor and I started out as great friends, and then it gradually turned into something more special. With Yegor, I learned to laugh like I had never laughed before in my life. We consistently made each other burst into happy hysterics, and I was always extremely relaxed around him.

We also shared a tremendous drive to make the best of ourselves. Yegor came from Russia and had two disabled parents. They all lived in a tiny apartment and it was clear he intended to work as hard as possible so that he would be in a position to help his parents. Well, that was something I could relate to. He was extremely kind, caring and protective of his parents, who I got to know and became very fond of. There was quite an age gap between Yegor and me, and some of my friends, including my own son, made no bones about pointing this out to me, something I happily ignored.

The years between us only became a problem when it became evident that Yegor, like Riccardo before him, hadn't really lived his life yet, and that he wasn't at the point where he was ready to make a commitment.

I think we both always knew it would never go the distance. During the good times, we used to agree to 'just go from day to day and see how it goes'. During the bad times, his infidelity raised its ugly head. Once was forgivable, twice became a deal-breaker, and it was clear the trust had broken down between us. However, we had a lot of fun while it lasted which, again, was roughly five years. I'm grateful for the time I spent with him, that we remain friends, and that he has continued to be an important, loyal person in my life.

• • •

Romance, family, friendship, work, I'm grateful to say I've had them all in abundance. However, the one thing I've really had to struggle with over the past several years within my industry is intimidation from the men at the top.

Don't get me wrong, I appreciate that I've been incredibly fortunate and successful, and for the longest time, work was my salvation when all the other things in my life were falling apart around me. If I'm honest, though, I've never found the Latin and Ballroom worlds the easiest to operate in.

I would say it's not really a 'sharing' industry, and everybody tends to take care of and watch out for themselves. I've always done my best to share my work when I've had an excessive amount, but there have been times when I've felt it's not been reciprocated. There are exceptions – like Mick Stylianos, who helped me when I returned to the UK with Corky – but that kind of generosity is rare, and I guess I can understand why. Probably like every other industry, the dance industry is incredibly competitive, with teachers chasing the best students, because that's their livelihood. As well as keeping hold of their own couples, every teacher is spending just as much time also looking for new ones. It's slim pickings and competition is intense.

I've always been confident about what I can offer to my students. I've been dancing since I was seven years old, and I've spent my whole life working my way up through the ranks, as well as teaching and creating world champions. It warms my heart to see my students achieve such huge success on the global stage, but it seems as though that hasn't always gone down well with everyone. From the moment I set out on my own, things seemed to become more and more difficult. The more successful I became as a female in that world, the more it seemed the men at the top wanted to put me down. I can say now that, despite all my hard work and success, for many years I felt like a bullied woman within my industry.

That may sound dramatic, but it's a cut-throat, dog-eat-dog business, and if you don't have the right people on your side, it can be a very lonely place.

Most of the top females are married, so they come as part of a team and always have support. It's a case of strength in numbers but, when I was on my own, I always felt like one person up against a group. The dance industry, contrary to what anybody might say, is definitely full of politics; it has been male-dominated for as long as I can remember, and those men at the top just didn't seem to like me doing well. Whether it was because I was a woman, working by myself, or whether it was just a personal thing against me, I'll never really know.

All those years before, after Sammy and I separated, our departure from the competitive scene gave Donnie Burns the room he needed for his big break and he went on to become several-times world champion. From there, he went on to become president of the World Dance Council, which gave him a position of unmatched influence and power over the whole industry.

With all his achievements, it's impossible not to have respect for Donnie Burns as a dancer. But as the leader of such an important professional body, he and I do not see eye to eye.

Back when I was friendly with Donnie, I witnessed how political the industry was and how important it was to stay on good terms with people. I felt uncomfortable at times with what

I perceived to be harsh treatment of those who did not meet the exacting standards or messed up relationships, and sure enough, my own turn eventually came.

The dance world is like a minefield where you have to be careful where you tread. As my relationships with senior figures in the dance industry soured, I lost a lot of students. Soon, I was forced to sit back and wonder just what the problem was between these men at the top and myself. Was it because I didn't do exactly what I was told? Was it because I didn't toe the line, because I didn't always agree with what was said? Was it because my friend Alan's nickname for me – 'Queen of Latin' – had caught on and become a bit of a calling card for me in the dance world? I guess we'll never know.

It might have suited all those men at the top for me to pick up my ball and go home, but that was never in my character. Believe in what you're doing and keep moving forward. You're in control of your own destiny. Don't leave it in the hands of someone else. As rocky as those waters are, you have to keep swimming upstream, believe in your value and keep going.

What exactly did I do? Well, when they throw you a lemon, you make lemonade.

Donnie Burns once said to me, 'It doesn't matter how many people try to put you down, Shirley, you're a total survivor. You always get back up and keep going.' However he meant it, I took that as a compliment because it was the truth. Whenever I've had to restructure my work and change course, I've always been able to do it.

I've been very fortunate in my career in that I'm able to teach all levels. I chose at a young age to be qualified in all the technical aspects of dance, which means I can take anybody who comes in the door and show them how to dance.

Now with the men at the top intimidating professionals into leaving me, this is what I did – I taught everybody, from beginner-child to advanced student to pro-amateur dancing, which is the kind of partnership you see on *Strictly*. It's so popular, there are competitions all around the world and it's really big business, no doubt boosted in recent years by a certain dancing show that gets shown everywhere and inspires people of all generations to put on their dancing shoes.

In many ways teaching these couples at all the different levels was a breath of fresh air after the gladiatorial nature of some of the teaching that went on at the highest levels of the industry. Some of those teachers made it their business to create a type of intim-idating atmosphere, and even seemed to go out of their way to humiliate young dancers for their own entertainment. That never sat well with me. Everyone is trying to do his or her best, and nobody deserves to be treated like cannon fodder.

I've been guilty of giving a bad lesson myself, of bringing my negative energy into the studio if I've been personally upset, going through a breakup or something, until one day a student taught me a valuable lesson. I was working with a couple from Dallas called Rangel and Veronica, and giving some feedback that I thought was really direct and passionate. Rangel took me by the hand and walked me out of the studio. He didn't want to say it in front of his partner, but he told me, 'Shirley, you're obviously not having a great day and I just want you to know that your energy is not helping us. We're getting nervous. I know you mean well, and I say this with love, but … you are not coming across well.'

I will always appreciate the actions of Rangel that day. I'd let myself become preoccupied, I'd lost focus and he put my train back on the track that day with his kind gesture. He probably has no idea, but that conversation made a huge difference to my career. If he happens to read this book, maybe he'll realise.

I believe we all have a responsibility as a teacher to give 100 per cent of ourselves to our students, whatever level they're at. Maybe they won't become the world champions but their result is just as important as the person at the top of the rankings.

Everyone wants to learn, and it was a real joy for me helping enthusiastic students improve dramatically beyond anything they themselves thought possible. Some dancers want to be world champions, others just want to have fun. As long as each of these leaves the studio better dancers than when they walked in, then I've done my job.

• • •

Some of the happiest days of my career were spent in LA, teaching all day then going along to *Dancing with the Stars*. They were a wonderful mixture of hard work, great people, glitz and glamour, but at some point, as with all things, you start to wonder: what's next?

On the face of it, with my expansion into pro-amateur and social dancing, plus my prosperous connections in the world of TV, my career looked secure. However, I was getting that niggle, so familiar to me at various crossroads in my life. I was working incredibly long days, but I knew at the back of my mind that I wasn't going to be able to keep up all those hours indefinitely.

As I've mentioned before, Mark always calls the dance calendar a hamster wheel with one event after another. In November, it's all about getting ready for the British National Dance Championships, then in January, it's time to start preparing for the UK Championships. By March, you're already thinking about Blackpool and then as soon as you've come back from the Winter Gardens, it's time to start thinking about the Albert Hall. Don't get me wrong, I love it all, but at some point in your life you have to take your nerves in both your hands and prepare to jump off that wheel and do something different, otherwise you'll get to the end of your career and realise you never did anything else in your life but bounce from competition to competition.

I was also starting to feel more and more pressure from my industry. All my hours in the studio, the months I spent travelling across the world to judge competitions, even the connections and friends I had made through *Dancing with the Stars*, I didn't feel could insulate me from the negativity that I perceived to be directed at me from certain people. In fact, all the positive attention the children and I got from our links with such a huge TV show only seemed to draw fresh fire from the same people in my industry that I had done my best to avoid for so many years.

I got the feeling that certain people were trying to interfere with my work. I'd watched other people's careers be derailed left, right and centre, and I didn't want to be the next one under the bus. So whenever I took a breather, I tried to look at the big picture, and work out what I should do next before, once again, I ran out of track. By the autumn of 2016, I was really beginning to wonder what I might do, and if I had anything left in me for yet another personal transformation, for one more spin of the wheel.

CHAPTER 9
The Samba

'A unique dance with multiple rhythms that must be used. Technically, unlike the other dances that tend to have a constant rhythm, it requires changes of speed, dexterity and attitude. Emotionally, it is a happy, party dance, encouraging lots of participants to mix and mingle. Full of intricate timings and choreography, it requires a real team effort all the way through.'

Mark and I were driving along in LA, chatting away about everything as we always did, when my son suddenly mentioned a piece of gossip he'd heard on the dance industry grapevine.

'Apparently, Len is thinking of giving it up in Great Britain. I think you should go for the job. There's no one better.'

Of course I knew exactly what he was talking about. *Strictly Come Dancing* – one of the UK's biggest TV shows since it started in 2004, single-handedly responsible for the surge of interest in ballroom dancing that has transformed my industry over the last few years, and is still drawing in millions of viewers on Saturday evenings every year.

The ballroom dance industry is a small, intimate world. Everybody hears everything, whatever country they're in, whether they're performing, judging or teaching, and no one more so than my son.

'Don't be silly, Mark,' I replied immediately in the car that day. 'No one's going to take a 57-year-old woman with barely any TV experience for a job of that magnitude.'

Mark just shrugged and we changed the subject. I pretty much forgot about it after that, although it might have remained somewhere in my subconscious, tucked away at the back of my mind.

I'd known the show's long-time head judge Len Goodman almost all my adult life, because we lived in Dulwich, and he lived just over the river. He'd trained my ex-husband Corky and me sporadically during our career, and he'd often popped over for dinner. Len's always been a great supporter of mine, he was one of my best adjudicators and he's always flown the Shirley flag and been a big fan of my dancing, long before he got the job that turned him into a household name.

I'd watched *Strictly* and then *Dancing with the Stars* turn Len into a massive TV star and celebrity on both sides of the Atlantic. He was a man with a keen eye for dance and a real expert in his own field. Like everyone else around at that time, I'd heard the rumblings that he was thinking of stepping down, and now here was my son telling me I should go for the role myself.

Don't get me wrong, after so many years teaching, performing and working in the industry, I never had any doubts about my skills as a dance judge. And I was a massive fan of *Strictly Come Dancing* and had been involved at a distance for years, training many of the past and present dancers that appeared on the show, both on the original British version and its many international spin-offs all over the world.

It was the 'TV' bit of 'TV dance judge' that stopped me in my tracks. As I explained to Mark, I had never been a TV person. I just wasn't equipped to do it. But he made his case in pretty strong terms when he brought it up again later.

'You've followed me on the US show for years. You've seen it all and you know how everything works. You know exactly what's going on. You know all the dancers. Your life is dance. Your world is dance. Your heart belongs on this show.'

The fact that it was my son saying, 'You must go, you must try' persuaded me that this just might be an opportunity for me, plus I didn't want to be a hypocrite. Throughout Mark's life, I'd always told him to go for everything 100 per cent and I didn't want it to appear that I would say that to him and then not try for something myself. So I decided that if the opportunity ever came up, I would give it a go.

In October 2016, halfway through Len's final series, I was teaching in England, prior to the International Championships, when I called the *Strictly* producers to see if there was any space for one of my couples to get on the show. For years, I'd been sending the production team information about potential dancers, so this was nothing new. If a couple ever expressed an interest to me in appearing, I always did my best to see if there might be any opportunity for them to get on the show.

That October, the producers and I arranged to meet for a coffee to discuss my latest couple. They came to my studio and sat watching while I finished my lesson. Then off we went for a coffee, where I relished this opportunity to meet these women who clearly had their hearts invested in the show.

A few days later, I received an email asking me, 'Would you like to come in and have an interview for the role of a judge on *Strictly*?'

It was that casual. Sometimes the best things in life just find you. I was shocked by their invitation and chose not to share it with anybody. At my own expense and with no agent or anybody else to advise me, I returned to London in early 2017 and decided I would just embrace the opportunity to have an audition.

It was clear that a lot of people were also going for this job. One evening when I was judging at the United Kingdom Championships, I sat down at a dinner table, where people were speaking of little else. It seemed that everyone knew someone who had either got the job or was going for it, and all sorts of rumours were flying around. There was clearly a lot of interest. It made me realise I was best off keeping quiet. I said to myself, 'As long as I don't say anything, nobody will be any the wiser.'

I flew from LA to London for this audition and travelled straight to the TV studio, never believing in my own mind that I would be qualified, because there were so many aspects of TV that I knew nothing about, plus I knew nobody had ever heard of me, and I assumed the producers would be seeking a household name to replace Len.

When I came over for the interview, I was suffering with a bad back. For a long time, I'd suffered with sciatica, and it was feeling particularly painful at the time. The lady in the makeup department suggested I put an ice pack on my lumbar region. I was sitting in my jeans and by the time she'd finished doing all my hair and makeup, I stood up to discover the ice pack had melted all down me. I had a big wet patch on my jeans. Fortunately, the makeup lady didn't panic at all. She said, 'Put your dress on, take your jeans off, we'll put them in the dryer for you.' I even had to take off my panties as they were wet through too. Imagine that – no underwear for my *Strictly* audition! Fortunately, it was a black dress so you couldn't tell, LOL.

I went down to the studio feeling relatively calm. Because in my own mind I didn't think I'd ever get the job, I was able to tell myself I had nothing to lose, and the audition might turn out to be a useful experience.

This was my first ever meeting with Craig Revel Horwood, who sat there all ready to do his bit. I'd never met him before but his face was instantly familiar from TV. Now up close and personal, he seemed larger than life, very at ease with himself, unlike me. It was clear he knew his stuff.

Although I felt pretty calm, I found the first audition to be quite overwhelming. It was in a freezing-cold room in the middle of winter, with lots of people around us, doing a host of different jobs that I didn't understand at the time. It was hard to get to grips with how the system behind the desk operated and work out which of the multiple cameras I should look into. Plus, the whole time I had this bad back that I was desperately trying not to focus on, so it was safe to say I probably wasn't the most relaxed. It gave me an appreciation of how difficult TV can be, especially if you're a novice who knows nothing about it.

After the audition, which personally I didn't feel had gone very well, I went home that night and chatted with Mark, who gave me some fresh advice: 'When you do an audition like that, Mum, you have to be yourself. You have to be real, be who you are. Don't be intimidated. You know your material. You've trained all your life for this.'

If I'm honest now, I think I was more self-conscious about my working-class roots than I'd let on. I was thinking, 'I'm just this kid from a housing estate. How am I going to fit in with all of them?'

Fortunately for me, I have a very optimistic, glass-half-full son, who was able to point out the positives.

'British viewers love down-to-earth people who never pretend to be anything other than who they are. You are blue collar, so don't try to hide it. Embrace it.

'It's a show that's all glitz and glamour, and you're bringing something different. You're saying, "This is how I did it." You've been on a long road, you've literally bent over backwards to get to where you are, you've had a massive struggle and that's inspiring for viewers, especially ones who share similar struggles. You can help people believe that they can achieve.'

I was scheduled to fly home to LA the very next day, but that same evening, the show's executive producer Louise Rainbow called me and asked, 'How do you think it went?' I decided to be honest, and admitted I didn't think it had gone very well. She replied, 'If you can change your flight, you're welcome to come back into the studio and let's have another go.'

I quickly changed my flight back home to the US and headed back to the BBC. I had Mark's words ringing in my ears, 'Just be yourself.'

This time, I was wearing just a casual jumper and jeans, much more like myself. I felt a lot more relaxed, not in pain and not so tired after my journey from the US. The studio was much warmer and there were a lot less people around – just Louise and a couple of camera crew. This was a different scenario altogether.

I found myself feeling far more relaxed, happy to be quite funny, and the audition, almost needless to say, went 100 per cent better than the day before. I felt I was able to express myself properly, and for that I was extremely grateful. They thanked me politely and, as I walked out, I reminded myself there were literally dozens of people lining up for this job, all of them more experienced in TV than me. I truly was the novice, but in that second audition, I knew I had given my very best, and that was all I could hope to do.

A month later, I was back in the United States. I'd put everything to do with *Strictly* out of my mind and was teaching in the studio when my phone rang. The name came up as Louise Rainbow, so I took a deep breath and answered it. Instantly, she said, 'Hello, Shirley. We would like to offer you the job.'

For the first time in my life, I actually fell to my knees. I didn't know what to say, I had no idea they'd want someone like me and I had no idea how much I'd wanted it until that moment. After a few seconds, I realised Louise was still on the phone, while I remained on the floor, feeling extremely emotional. I could hear her asking, 'Are you okay, Shirley?' And just like that, I got one of the biggest jobs on British television.

• • •

The first person I FaceTimed was Mark. I pressed the button to call him, he picked up immediately, took one look at my face and said, 'Don't say it, Mum. You got the job, didn't you?' He knows me so well. He didn't even sound surprised. The next two people I shared it with were Derek and Julianne. Julianne seemed ecstatic for me and immediately sent me the biggest bouquet of flowers. When I told my mother, all she could think about was the fact that this job meant her daughter was coming home to the UK. Everyone in my trusted circle was deeply happy for me.

Then the challenge became to keep the news under wraps until the BBC decided they were ready to announce their selection. It was terrifying walking around with that big secret, so, to keep myself busy, I sat down to watch all the previous series, every single show. I wanted to see how different people operated, what worked and what didn't. I've always been over-studious. I'd spent years sitting with Mark, Derek and Julianne, watching every move they made on *Dancing with the Stars*, making notes, giving advice. In all those years, I never missed one of their shows and I loved every moment. Up until this moment, though, everything I had done was to make other people shine. Now, suddenly, it was all about me, and I found that a very strange experience.

On top of all of that, I had a lot of other duties to fulfil, because I was still in the States teaching. It was important to me not to get too overexcited, and it felt crucial to keep my own job going as well. I never take a new project for granted, even something as dazzling as *Strictly*. At my age, and having worked in this industry for over 40 years, I know I could work for you today and you'd be really happy with me, and then next week someone could say, 'I'm sorry, you don't fit the job.'

I would like to think I have always kept my feet firmly on the ground, but I have to say the excitement of getting this job meant I did struggle to keep a lid on it. I had watched the children go from strength to strength on *Dancing with the Stars*, and I'd even seen Corky join their ranks and be successful. I'd always been the one in the background, watching them, applauding them. Now it seemed I was about to get an opportunity to do something I was truly passionate about.

I was planning to keep quiet until the public announcement, but there was a leak in the papers before I even officially accepted the job. Of course, there are a lot of people involved in the process, plus all the others wandering around the BBC who might have spotted me going in for the interview. Suddenly everyone in the media was scrambling to find out, 'Who's this woman?' especially as no one beyond the dance world had ever heard of me up to this point.

As excited as I was by this unexpected turn in my career, I found it a confusing time in some ways, with all the extra attention I started receiving. Many people I hadn't heard from in years took the opportunity to contact me, which was all quite unsettling, and it was definitely a time when I found out who my real friends were.

Soon after I got my job on *Strictly*, a so-called 'friend' said to my friend Karen, 'She may have paparazzi following her. All she needs now is a Mercedes and a tunnel.'

Karen's son Henry was with them and he asked, 'What does that mean?'

Karen, horrified, had to explain to him, 'That's how Princess Diana died, it was a terrible tragedy.'

When this was relayed back to me, I was completely shocked. It felt very hurtful and spiteful, with its implication that I was behaving as though I'd got above myself, whereas I knew I'd been keeping very quiet and trying to adjust to my new role.

Because I knew it was so far from the truth, for once I tackled this person on their tasteless comment. All they had to say in reply was, 'Oh come on, Shirley, you need to develop a sense of humour.'

I came back to London in the early summer, in good time for the official press launch. I also received media training from the BBC. The lady despatched to look after me must have thought

I'd find it a struggle, as she seemed pleasantly surprised by how well I coped.

I felt embraced by the whole BBC team. It was like a cloak around me for protection, and the whole *Strictly* team couldn't have done any more to make my life easier. And at the centre of it all was Louise Rainbow, who I realised really early on was taking a huge gamble on me by picking somebody that nobody had heard of. She was rolling the dice, and I was determined not to let her down, nor anybody else at the BBC. That was my priority, to make the team of Louise, Jo Wallace and Sarah James proud of me, to do the best job I possibly could.

For the official press announcement, the other judges were asked what they thought of my arrival. I didn't know Darcey Bussell at all, we hadn't even met each other at that point, but she spoke admiringly about my dancing credentials, as did Craig Revel Horwood, who I had met for the first time at my audition. He called my appointment 'fantastic news'.

I had first met Bruno Tonioli ten years before, when he was a judge on *Dancing with the Stars* when the children were on the show, so I knew him and was very comfortable with him. It reassured me when I learned that I would be sitting next to him on the panel. He has fabulous spirit and I couldn't say enough good things about that man. He's the type to hold your hand and give you a cuddle, and he laughs all the time. When he was asked about me, Bruno was really warm, saying he'd known me for years, reminding people what a good dancer and trainer I was. It was just the encouragement I needed.

At the launch, one of the BBC bosses, Charlotte Moore, confirmed to the press that 'Len's are big shoes to fill'. As if I needed any reminding! No pressure. But I knew that was her way of telling people, 'This is a big deal. Please give her a chance.'

I was perfectly aware that I was stepping into some big dancing shoes. Len Goodman had been there since the beginning, he was the king of the ballroom and he'd proven himself over the years to be the consummate showman. He was perfect for that role on the show, and when he decided to leave, I'm sure he not only left a big gap on the judging panel but also in the homes of people who'd taken him to their hearts through all those years. It was crucial for the show that the producers got his choice of replacement just right, there was a lot riding on it.

I knew Louise had faith in me – she'd seen me teach, she'd seen me judge, she knew I not only had the knowledge but also the passion for the show. With Louise, I felt I could bank on the fact that she was such a straight talker, and that she'd tell me what worked and what didn't. We have that in common. We both work hard and talk straight. Like me, she was a people person and always wanted to see others doing well. She never seemed to get flustered despite the responsibility of such a huge show sitting on her shoulders. Like me, she was a woman who had got to the top of her industry, and very quickly, she became somebody I looked up to and learned a lot from. It was really important to me that, as a woman, I got to fill that fourth chair. As I've explained, I feel like I've been struggling to stay on top in a male-dominated industry for too long, so it was significant in a very good way that I got to balance out that panel.

I had told myself that I would wake up every day with the eyes of a newborn baby – 'stay positive' – bat away any fears that threatened to overwhelm me, and try to always see the cup as half-full. The press were incredibly supportive from the beginning, so it came as a nasty shock the first time I realised the lengths to which somebody would go to sell their story on me.

It was in September, the week before my first live show, and still nobody really knew who I was. I had gone up north as it was my mother's 80th birthday, and it was the first time in her life she'd ever had a big party. I'd organised the whole thing for her, a big sit-down dinner in a local hotel for a hundred people, an enormous cake, music, you name it. We were all ready for this special birthday party and extremely excited for her – and then the day before her special day, one particular article came out in the press, written by my ex-husband.

By this time I had got myself a publicist. Normally, when an article comes out in a newspaper, my understanding is that you get a heads-up beforehand. In this case, we got no notice in advance. To this day, I'm not really sure what happened.

A journalist had been sent out to LA and sat down with my ex-husband. He'd proceeded to give her chapter and verse on our 23-year marriage. I had been invited to comment, but chose to say nothing. I could only sit back and read what he had to say, along with the rest of the country.

I barely had a wink of sleep that night. When the paper arrived in the morning, the first thing I spotted was my face on the cover, next to a *Strictly* judge's paddle with a big '10' on it. According to Corky, that was the numbers of lovers I'd had behind his back during our marriage. That might have looked funny to somebody picking up the paper, but to me it was devastating and untrue.

Well, as everyone knows, in a long marriage that goes wrong, there are three versions of everything, his story, her story, and then there's the truth. And his version was as unflattering as he could possibly make it. He didn't just catalogue all the lovers I was supposed to have had, in addition he blamed me completely for the breakdown of our marriage and found every way he could of describing me as a terrible wife it had been impossible for him to stay married to.

What pained me was that Corky and I had managed to maintain a civilised relationship in the years since we parted – he's Mark's father after all, and Mark is our greatest gift. Long after our divorce, Corky and I would spend Christmas together, and he would often be round at my house. He was very helpful, setting up my Netflix on my TV, sorting out my computer and anything electronic that I was unable to do. In return, I'd passed along to him a lot of teaching for him and his fiancée, and also judging jobs. I'd supported him when he was on *Dancing with the Stars*. It was a big deal when he got the call to dance alongside Mark and the other people on the show, and he was paired with American screen legend Cloris Leachman. I'd given him lots of training for such a high-profile gig. I'd even helped him with his Ballroom as he was not particularly experienced, and at the time he'd seemed very grateful. I'd always been there to help him, and now this was what I got back in return.

What he didn't mention in his article was that literally only a couple of weeks before it was published, he'd been sitting in my front room with me, chatting and having a coffee. We were extremely friendly and cordial, or so I thought.

He lived half an hour away from me in LA with his girlfriend, and I'd previously helped them out, supporting them in court over custody arrangements for her daughter, vouching for them as good parents. It was all as civilised as it was possible to be, but I have to say things had changed since I had been offered my *Strictly* job. When I called him to tell him I'd got it, he didn't seem particularly happy for me, and hadn't been in contact since.

I know my ex-husband: he has a lot of good points, but he's very competitive and I wasn't sure he was best pleased for me. Now, it was clear he'd been offered the chance to tell what he said was his side of the story and he'd just let rip. It was mortifying to read all the dirt and slop on the page, where he made it clear that, even after all this time had passed, he continued to blame me in every way for the breakdown in our marriage.

I was so shocked by what he had to say that I could barely speak. It was a sharp reminder of what my married life had been like with him for all those years, and how he used to talk to me. Of all his cruel barbs, the single aspect of the whole feature that hurt me the most was how cruel he was about my mother.

He blamed her for wrecking our marriage, and actually called her 'a termite'. He told the paper, 'Audrey was silent and deadly, and like a termite eating the house of our marriage – you don't know the threat is there then suddenly all the wood has disappeared.'

This was the woman who had given up her own life to come and help raise our son. She cooked, she cleaned, she ironed, she babysat and did everything she possibly could to make our lives easier, so that we could travel the world, pursue our dreams and become successful in our industry.

Corky and I were British champions twice over, due in every single way to the fact that my mother was keeping his own son safe and happy, often protecting him from the worst of our battles, and now this is what he had to say about her. It was that one word – 'termite' – about my mother in the middle of a six-page article all about how awful I was that cut me to the quick. I was beside myself with pain and anger on her behalf.

I didn't want to show my mother the article, but she could see how upset I was, and insisted on reading it. Next thing I knew, she was spending the day before her 80th birthday feeling disappointed and angry, because her former son-in-law of more than 20 years had called her a termite. She was only ever a help to us, and this was what he had to say about all that support. I was devastated for her.

Even Corky couldn't deny that I was the right person for the *Strictly* job, saying that I was always professional with my students and work, but even then, his comment came with a sting in the tail. He told them, 'I like her as a dancer and dance teacher far better than I ever did as a person.'

This made me realise I'd been right from the very beginning of our relationship, all those years before. He may have admired my dancing and respected all that I'd achieved, but he'd never really liked me as a person, and finally I saw it in print.

I'd been married to that man for 23 years and had his child, I'd done everything I could to make our marriage last, to bring up our son, to work back-breaking hours to bring in enough money for us all when we moved to England, to train him and take him to the top of the dance industry because it was our shared dream, and what did he have to say about me? 'I didn't ever like her.' Even though we had long since separated, I was doubled up with pain reading his words. I'd always feared he didn't love me enough to make it work between us, and now here it was, proof in black and white.

It took me a long time to come to terms with what he'd written and for me to realise, 'Hang on a minute, Corky. You were married for all that time to someone and now you're saying you didn't even like her? More fool you!' For myself, I adored that man, I would have done anything to make things work between us as husband and wife, and all the time he claims he didn't even like me? Now I say, that's on him.

When I first saw the article, I actually refused to believe Corky had said all those things because, I rationalised, we may have had our ups and downs but we were a formidable partner-ship for all those years and, more crucially, because I knew he loved Mark as much as I did, and hanging all this dirty washing out in public would inevitably hurt him. I tried to phone Corky at home in California but he wouldn't pick up, so I left a message in which I think I made my sentiments pretty clear! Then I got a message back from his girlfriend, saying, 'Stop hassling us.' And that was that.

Personally, it was a disaster for me to see my loved ones so upset – as well as my mother, there was Mark, caught in the middle, as shocked as I was, and embarrassed for me. But professionally, there was no fall-out at all. The BBC were great, saying they expected certain stories to come along, and the papers later put out another article, saying I'd taken the high road by choosing not to comment on what they called his 'explosive kiss and tell'. They called my lack of reaction 'a dignified silence'.

Unfortunately, to this day, Corky and I still haven't spoken, and subsequently he informed me I was no longer welcome at the family functions that he and his new partner planned to attend. Personally, I felt she had a big part to play in all this unnecessary drama. This was a body blow to me, because I'm so close to my former in-laws and I had always enjoyed Christmases and some holidays with them. I'm hoping and trusting that, one day, things will work themselves out. I've known Corky for nearly 40 years and we share the person in this world that we're both the most proud of, our son, as well as our love of dance. In 2019, when I was packing up my house in California to sell and move back to London, I came across lots of photos of our career and our lives together. I made up a big box of souvenirs for Corky, sent it over to him with a message, and he was polite enough to respond. So, perhaps, the healing has begun.

After reading this article and feeling so desperately upset, I quickly had to try to put it behind me and instead look ahead because I had an almighty task to accomplish – a dance to learn for my debut on *Strictly*. Louise had told me she thought it would be good for me if I opened the show by doing a Samba with the rest of the professionals.

This was completely uncharted territory for me, far beyond my comfort zone. Of course I knew how to dance, but I hadn't performed in public for 20 years. I couldn't sleep a wink the entire week before – still reeling with upset over what Corky had said about me and my mother, full of hurt for my mother as our family life and the tragedy of my brother was splashed all over the papers. Everything we'd spent years dealing with privately was suddenly laid out for all the country to see. I felt extremely exposed for the first time in years, with Mark warning me there could be more to come.

I felt as though I was heading for rough, unfamiliar waters. I feared more people jumping out of the woodwork to grab their 15 minutes of fame by saying who knows what about me. Meanwhile, I had to learn a dance that I was going to perform in front of millions. My past and future were crowding in on me like two walls closing in.

Even more pressure came with my realisation that, if I wanted make a success of my new job, I was going to have to do something that felt very unnatural to me, and that was opening myself right up to huge numbers of people.

All my life I'd put up walls and, to my mind, they had served me well. Now my son was telling me, 'Your mind is like a parachute, it'll work better when it's open.' I knew in my head he was right, but in my heart that felt like jumping out of an aeroplane without a parachute, open or not.

What did I fall back on during that wobbly week? My passion, my experience and the fact that, when it came to the dancing, I knew I was more than qualified for the role. For those two minutes that each couple danced, that dance floor was my bullring, my area of expertise. When it came to dance, I knew exactly what I was talking about, and that became my security blanket. I knew if it came down to it, my knowledge and love of dance would save me, as it had previously on so many occasions in my life.

Louise no doubt thought she was helping me relax when she suggested I perform a dance before I first sat down. What she probably didn't realise was that, while I'd been teaching every day for nearly 40 years, I hadn't actually been getting out there on the floor myself for more than two decades. Nor had I ever worn a pair of stiletto heels in all that time. You always teach in flats! But she said, 'Trust me, Shirley. Our *Strictly* audience will love it.'

The wardrobe department had made me a beautiful red dress, which they'd sewn without even taking any measurements, and it fitted me like a glove. They must have X-ray vision! My friend Jason Gilkison choreographed a piece for me to dance with the male professionals, and suddenly here I was, ready to make my *Strictly* debut. In my lovely dress, my makeup, my high heels, I looked every inch the confident former world champion dancer. On the inside, I felt like a vulnerable young girl.

As the music started for my big number, I was waiting in the wings, absolutely terrified. My knees were shaking, my heart was pounding a thousand beats a minute and I could feel the sweat pouring down my spine. Only the sheer force of the fact I no longer had a choice – it was lights, camera, action! – propelled me out there underneath those big bright lights, in front of all those faces in the studio, and that was without counting all the millions and millions sitting at home, watching from their sofas. I knew too they were all experienced viewers who'd watched the show year after year, so I considered them armchair experts and I was hoping they'd approve of me. I was silently whispering a prayer that I didn't fall over before I'd even danced a step.

I should have had more faith, both in myself and in the magic of dance. As soon as I took my first turn, I forgot about everything but the music. I let it take over my body and it felt euphoric, simply wonderful to be out there dancing again. I was grateful, confident and completely relaxed for the first time in years. Dancing really is like riding a bicycle. However long you're off it, hop back on and you're away.

Professionally, I think it was a clever decision by the BBC, proving to any doubters, 'Look, she can actually dance. Shirley knows her stuff.' Personally, it was a magical moment in time that I shall never forget, one of the undisputed highlights of my life.

Before I knew it, my dance was over. I came off the floor and somebody had filmed a video so I was able to have a quick look. I can be hypercritical of myself at the best of times, but even I was pleased with how my very first moments on *Strictly* had gone. I finally permitted myself a smile as I thought, 'With that lovely dress, those high heels, what can I say? Not bad for 57, Shirley. Looking good!'

CHAPTER 10
The Viennese Waltz

'The epitome of elegance, requiring an accuracy of footwork and foot placements throughout left and right turns with an immaculate posture and frame, also with flight and seamless weight transfer. This dance is one of sheer joy and exhilaration.'

Each *Strictly* judge brings something unique to the show. Bruno is a wonderful storyteller and wears his heart on his sleeve. Craig is like the pantomime villain, always the most critical but clearly with a heart of gold. When I first met Darcey Bussell in the BBC studio, I was pretty awestruck. She was so tall, slender and poised that I gazed up at her and thought, 'She's Snow White.' She was always there for me, and steered me in the right direction, on and off the set. It was great to have two women on the panel. As Darcey said to me, 'Strength in numbers, Shirley.'

We are very different people, from completely different worlds, facing different struggles in different disciplines. But we recognised in each other that quality of being absolutely driven and we soon found a way of communicating – our common language was a love of music and dance. Then when we went on tour together, she was a hoot. I used to walk into our dressing room, and she'd be perched in vertical splits while casually talking to me – a very bendy, beautiful woman indeed.

As soon as I joined the panel, everyone did their best to make me feel welcome and I instantly felt very comfortable. This meant I was surprised when, during my second series, I had to fly back from LA and as soon as I landed in London, I noticed I had a surprising number of missed calls from Craig. When I eventually had a chance to call him back, he seemed quite sheepish. He told me, 'I think I may have said a couple of things out of turn. I have a feeling it's going to run in an article tomorrow, but please don't worry about it.'

I said, 'Okay, no problem, I know how these things get misinterpreted.' And I thought no more about it, until the next day when I saw the article, and I have to say it just unleashed years and years of pain.

He'd apparently been at a dinner for his book tour when he'd remarked on my appearance, referring to my first audition with him. He commented to a room full of people, 'She came to the audition and literally had her thing open to her navel.' Presumably he was referring to my dress.

Then he went on, 'I am not joking. Her boobs were like La BaZooKa things hanging out.' La BaZooKa is a French dance troupe with inflatable breasts. 'So they came and sewed all that up. Then they had to push them down ... and they're fake.'

I can tell you, when a man makes remarks about a woman's appearance, what they don't realise is, they might think it's funny and other women may even laugh along, but actually it's not funny at all. Women don't need anyone else to make critical remarks about them, we're quite critical enough of ourselves without them chipping in. Then somebody comes along and makes you feel that you were right to feel so negative about yourself. You think you're crap, and then someone else endorses it. How are you meant to feel about yourself after that? It was awful, and very, very painful.

It brought up a lot of things from my past that I thought I'd dealt with. Once again, I was propelled back to my toughest days with Corky, when he would make comments about my appearance: my crooked teeth, my nose, my arse that was too big. All those insults just came flying back as I read what Craig had said, apparently in jest.

The first chance I had to speak to him about it, I told him exactly how I felt: 'I'm your colleague. I should feel safe around you. You should feel like a protector to me, and I should to you. If I have to worry every time you go out that you're going to talk about me, that doesn't make me feel good about being on this show.'

I'm glad to say we cleared the air. Craig couldn't apologise enough and immediately afterwards sent me the biggest bouquet of flowers I've ever seen. I just think it was an oversight on his part, but it just shows how easily it's done. Men (and women, for that matter) everywhere need to be careful what they say. Please think before you speak, because you can't take words back, and they can really hurt, sometimes more than a slap.

I was as shocked as anybody when Darcey announced she was leaving in 2019. I knew I was going to miss her tremendously and my mind began to race about who they were going to replace her with. Would it be a man? A woman? A dancer? An entertainer? The same process I'd gone through to become a judge kicked off again and the person who was chosen to fill the seat was Motsi Mabuse. The first thing that entered my mind when I found out was, 'Fasten your seat belts, people, and buckle up. You're going to have the ride of your life.'

When I'd been working as a judge at competitions all around the world, Motsi was a frequent competitor. I was a huge admirer of her work, and as a judge I always awarded her high marks. She had a unique musicality, rhythm, charisma, plus a great pair of legs. She was the complete package. Now we're on the panel together, I couldn't be happier. We have the same sense of humour and we speak the same language of dance. I think, together, we've become quite a lot to handle for those two boys on the panel with us — I hope so, anyway! We love to talk dance on the show, and always stay in touch in between. Now it's me who gets to say, 'Strength in numbers, Motsi.'

. . .

Way back before my very first live show, I had the good fortune to work with a top TV coach called Francesca Kasteliz. She helped me get to grips with how it would feel to be in front of the cameras, guided me on where to look for the little red light and in communicating my style.

It wasn't easy for her. She had a set of exercises, which involved putting something on screen and asking me to talk about it until I felt comfortable. When I first sat down in front of her, all the walls I'd put up through all those years of competitive dancing were in full force, and she said herself she needed a sledgehammer to tear them down. The more she pointed these things out to me, the more nervous I became, and the worse it got. I knew that the stern teacher I wore on the outside wasn't letting my true personality come out, but there was nothing I could do. Those walls had taken 40 years to build, so they weren't going to come down in one afternoon.

Finally, we took a break while we were waiting for some technical changes, and started chatting about different things – how it would be with the press, how the cameras worked, what to expect. I sat very seriously, absorbing all she was telling me like a sponge. It was only when she started asking me about my family that everything changed. My whole being lit up and I smiled naturally as I spoke about them all. Francesca looked astonished, then she told me, 'That's the person we need to see on the TV. You need to lose your armour, so everyone sees who you are inside.'

Then, in a moment of inspiration, she gave me some imaginary hats to keep on the table and decide which one to wear depending on what I wanted to say. I had the Teacher Hat, the Mummy Hat, the Caring Hat and the Strict Hat, all there in front of me.

Although I'd always had confidence in my ability as a dancer, Francesca gave me the confidence to speak more naturally, and I definitely revealed more of myself as the first two series unfolded. Now I go a lot more on instinct, inspired by the music and dance, and how it makes me feel. I love to give words of encouragement, a kind of verbal cuddle, to be strict when it's necessary, but also to be positive. I also like to push people beyond their own boundaries and see what they might be capable of.

What the audience doesn't always realise is that, on *Strictly*, it's not necessarily a competition between different contestants, it's about each person's individual journey and their own growth. I might give someone an 8, when the audience at home thinks they only deserve a 6, but I can see they've grown over that week in certain aspects, and their performance warrants that kind of encouragement. I've learned to be much more circumspect, even if sometimes the viewers at home disagree strongly with me, and often give us judges harsh abuse online.

After the first series, I went to the two people I can count on to tell me the truth: my son and my mother. 'Be honest with me. Francesca says I come across a little strict and scary on the show. What do you think?'

There was a pause before Mark said, 'You started nervously, I could see that. You were definitely leaning on your knowledge of technique because that's what you know, and that's why they hired you, after all. But you need to let your warmth come through.'

My mother was a little bit more blunt. She just said, 'Tell me about it. I turned on my TV and shuddered, I was so scared. And I'm your mother. You're very stern when you talk.' Don't hold back, Mother.

I've always been direct. It's just the way I was raised. The whole time I was a student taking private lessons, the teaching was all about what I could do better, and there was very little praise. There were also definitely times in my life when I taught people the way I had been taught, being super-critical. It was only later I realised how nice it was to be encouraged, and that constructive criticism can be given at the same time. It's about finding the right balance. It took years for me to get that balance right, so I took what my mother said on board. She and I sat down and watched the first few shows together and I started learning how to soften my edges.

Nobody likes criticism, but if you can also be encouraging, it gives people balance and a way forward. And anyway, it's show business, where a smile is just as important as a win. I'm still learning.

• • •

I always used to ask myself, why is *Strictly Come Dancing* so popular, both in Britain and all over the world? So many people have asked me the same question since I joined the show that I've been forced to consider it properly. I believe it's because when there is so much negativity going on around us, so many challenges for each and every one of us in our personal lives, when something like this show comes along on a Saturday evening, particularly during the long winter months, people treasure it and are willing to let it warm their hearts. It gives our Saturday evenings a thrill and something that we can all, as a family, sit down and enjoy. There is something in this show for everybody: a sensual appeal for adults, fun for children and nostalgia for older folk like me who can remember the days when we used to go courting and dancing. There's plenty of humour in it, too, and let's face it, in this day and age, we can all do with a smile.

Nobody could have predicted that this show was going to be as successful as it was. For sure, the producers put together a list of elements that seem really obvious now but which were completely visionary back then. They created a simple but stunning formula of glitz, romance, the drama of the dance routines – fast, slow, Ballroom, Latin – plus the celebrities themselves, with all their glamour, heartbreak, and often surprising, personal life stories.

For me sitting in the studio, what makes the show so spectacular in the UK is the fact we have a live orchestra. It could have been perceived as old-fashioned, but actually, it helps give the whole programme an extra slice of pizzazz, like a proper extravaganza. For me, having that live music transforms the show into a real event, as does having an audience there with us. Louise

Rainbow added a rule that, in my view, made a big difference too – she banned studio guests from wearing jeans. It makes being there feel like attending a special evening event, a big night out. If people want to come along, they have to dress appropriately and in return, they get to be transported back into the ballroom world of years ago. Wonderful!

Even with all those ingredients in place for launch, I don't think anybody had any idea the show would take off in the way it did, and end up becoming one of the most successful formats in TV history. In Britain, the first series, in 2004, had an audience of around 4.5 million viewers, whereas it can go up to anything like 15 million these days. The dancing standards, the budgets and the production values of *Strictly* may have all got bigger and better over the years, but I think the same qualities that made it such a hit nearly two decades ago are all still very much the same. With *Strictly* only running one series a year in the UK, there's always a huge sense of occasion leading up to it, and the producers are smart enough to make only the tiniest of alterations so that the show doesn't fundamentally change. I also like that it's very much a female-driven programme. Not to slam the men who are such a great part of it, but women are nurturers by instinct, they understand how to create a family unit, how to spread a warm, almost maternal feeling, and I'm convinced that comes through on screen.

You see it in the chemistry between the hosts, and I can tell you they are just the same people off screen as they are on. Claudia Winkleman is hilarious and Tess Daly is an absolute doll. They're both always smiling, always helping out behind the scenes. They're very kind to people, and I feel privileged to be in their company. They make all the competitors feel special, and when our comments about the routines have to be harsh, I look at their faces and I can tell they're really feeling it for the people who are dancing. They are definitely masters of their craft.

What people hadn't realised before the show really took off, although I could have told them right from the get-go, is that there's nobody more competitive on this planet than a Ballroom dancer. Right from the show's beginning, what the dancers were able to do was somehow share their ambition with the celebrities, and then on to the audience. As you'll know by now as you've travelled so far with me in this book, most professional dancers specialise in either Ballroom or Latin, one or the other. For the show, we manage to find high-level professionals who are trained in both disciplines and they're also brilliant teachers before they even come on the show. Because they care so much about their partners and invest so much time in helping them improve, the celebrities naturally start caring just as much and they all get better, week in, week out, so the competition heats up and starts meaning something.

Critics complain that some celebrities have an unfair advantage coming on the show if they've had a little bit of previous dance experience, like doing hip-hop or being in a band that dances. Trust me, nothing is as hard as training in Ballroom or Latin, so for everybody, it's a completely new experience.

Strictly seems to be a show where people come prepared to wear their emotions on their sleeves. The celebrities may be stars, experts or champions in their own fields, but entering this world of dance seems to bring something else out in them, a vulnerability, a truthfulness, and I think that translates to the audience. It certainly does to the judges, I can tell you.

As a judge myself, the most exciting thing about our show is the journey, watching the celebrities' confidence grow. In week one, you'll see a male contestant standing there nervously while the seamstress sews his shirt onto his trousers. By week four, that same man is suddenly requesting a routine where he gets to rip off his shirt on live TV in front of 10 million people. Meanwhile, the ladies' hemlines are getting shorter and shorter as they go further in the competition. All the celebrities get fitter, they get better at the dance, they get more ambitious and it's wonderful to watch. I've seen the standards get higher and higher every year. Just when you think it can't get any better, it does.

As well as the highly qualified professional dancers and the judges, the producers are astute in creating a mix of very different celebrities to keep the show interesting. If you only had celebrities who turned out to be good dancers coming on the show, imagine how much smaller and uninteresting it would be. We wouldn't have some of those great iconic moments from the show, such as Russell Grant shooting out of a cannon, John Sergeant coming back week after week due to popular demand, Ann Widdecombe being dragged around the floor by Anton du Beke – something I will never forget – and the jaw-dropping Ed Balls and his Gangnam Style moment. Sometimes, *Strictly* can change people's perceptions of someone forever, just as it did with Ed.

All these stars prove you don't have to be the best dancers in the world to be thoroughly entertaining and give the audience a great time. I had my own revelation about that during my very first series, when the Reverend Richard Coles suddenly appeared high up on the ceiling and descended to the dance floor on a cloud, with a celestial harp, as you do. Craig was ready with the perfect line when he told him, 'All the problems really began, darling, when the cloud actually landed.' It was wonderful entertainment, proper laugh-out-loud funny.

People like to talk about the *Strictly* curse and every year, it's a big topic in the press. What can I say about it? What we have to remember in our industry is that to entertain the audience, the pairs must have chemistry. Partnerships are crucial to the success of the show. I believe the BBC's producers have always been quite inspired in matching professional to celebrity partner in terms of height, personality, experience, confidence, and working out which professional will get the best out of their partner by nurturing and encouraging them. Everyone has their strengths, whether it's rhythm, music or comedy. Chemistry is everything. The *Strictly* workplace is no different from any other workplace where colleagues are together every day, friendships will flourish and sometimes romances are ignited. For up to four months, the couples are intensely involved with each other and it can be easy to become infatuated. Dance lends itself very easily to thoughts of romance and, with *Strictly*, everyone is under the microscope and the world is watching. I can only say that I know perhaps more than anyone just how intoxicating dancing can be.

And now here we are, in 2020, about to go into our 18th series. Week in, week out, people will start placing bets on who's going to win. The audience really cares. Last year, who'd have thought the actor Kelvin Fletcher would win? He only got invited on to the show because *Made in Chelsea* boy Jamie Laing injured his foot during the series launch. Kelvin was paired up with Oti Mabuse, they found their chemistry straight away and developed a great work ethic. He was a complete non-dancer who ended up winning the Glitterball trophy!

There were some great routines in that series, such as Michelle Visage's 'Vogue' with Giovanni Pernice, and Saffron Barker's Waltz with AJ Pritchard brought a tear to my eye. The moment that will go down in history, though, the moment that had me nearly peeing myself laughing, was when Anton du Beke danced the Salsa with his partner, Emma Barton. It was a fantastic routine, Anton was dressed up as Austin Powers, the wig and whole look was absolutely remarkable, but the thing that everyone, including me, will remember the most was when Craig complimented him on his fake teeth – except it turned out they weren't fake at all. Oops! At least they got through, and for the first time in 17 years, Anton got his first 10 at Blackpool and then made it all the way to the final. I'm sure one day soon, he's got to lift the trophy – my goodness, he's earned it! Every series, there are standout numbers and people we'll remember forever.

Strictly has given a new lease of life to the community of dance throughout this country. I love having one foot inside the *Strictly* bubble, but I'll always have my role as teacher and coach, and it's amazing to watch the huge numbers of new students coming in the door, many of them inspired by a TV programme. Twenty years ago, ballroom dancing was going through a bit of a dip when the show started; it was perceived as an old-fashioned hobby that you only saw going on in church halls. *Strictly* has been integral to its change in status.

You'll find social classes much fuller these days, and students much more enthusiastic. They want to go along and learn the basics, plus I find they all want to talk about *Strictly*. What's encouraging for the show's viewers is that they can watch the celebrity beginners and see them improve dramatically from week to week, so that inspires them to try. Ordinary people fantasise that they too might be able to master a sensual Rumba, and let me tell you, it is possible! Find yourself a good social class and get yourself out there. Particularly if you're on your own, it's a great way to meet new people. Thousands of beginners all over the country have discovered dance to be a gateway to a whole new world of exercise, music, friendship and so many other rewards. Why not have a go?

Millions of others are content to sit and watch on the TV, and it's clear the show's many viewers don't miss a thing. Everyone these days seems to know their Paso Doble from their Foxtrot, as I discover when people come up to talk to me in the street, or taxi drivers want to chat whenever I catch a cab. I love it. I've been having this conversation about Ballroom dancing all my life, but these days, everyone wants to join in.

I've heard that lots of people think I'm far too strict, but do they really? Everyone likes a little bit of controversy as well as encouragement, kindness, guidance. Every year, once we're a few weeks into the series, my Twitter and Instagram blow up after I've been the judge who's had to send someone home. Everyone latches on to their favourites so, no matter who I send home, there will be some fans left feeling unhappy. This all comes with the territory of being the head judge. Remember the hoo-ha when I had that run-in with one of the professionals, Brendan Cole, about his partner Charlotte's 'rise and fall'?

Brendan was dancing with Charlotte Hawkins and they performed the Tango. When it was time for the judges' remarks, I gave some positive comments and then I told them, 'There is no rise and fall in Tango, so we have to make a concrete decision not to use rise and fall.'

I thought I said it sweetly enough, but Brendan snapped straight back, 'I'm really sorry but there was no rise and fall in that whatsoever.' It was clear he wasn't sorry at all, so to my ears he sounded incredibly sarcastic. I learned later that it wasn't personal, that was just generally how Brendan spoke to all the judges, but at the time I have to say I was a bit surprised, as nobody else had spoken like that since I arrived on the show.

Instead of throwing me off my game, it actually fuelled my own competitive juices. After all my professional experience in more than 50 years of dancing, including many years of judging and more than a few occasions when I'd encountered Brendan himself in a competitive capacity, this was nothing new for me. It might have been new for the studio audience and the viewer at home, but his attitude was absolutely nothing I couldn't cope with.

I calmly replied, 'You should play it back, Brendan.'

But he kept going! 'I will, my dear, I will.'

Well, that was just patronising, to the extent that my fellow judge Bruno Tonioli actually told him off for being rude. He told Brendan, 'I'm not an expert, I've only done about 500 shows, and I think she's right, Brendan. You should be more respectful to a lady.'

That was that. There was no huge fall-out, as was depicted in the press, and even now, if Brendan and I bump into each other anywhere, we're quick to say hello. It's all perfectly civilised. To this day, I'm not really sure why he took such offence when I was only trying to be constructive, plus he knew it was one of my very first weeks on my first series. He might have thought I'd be a little intimidated, but what he didn't realise is that I've had men in the dance industry trying to undermine me for so many years that similar experiences with people like him were nothing new for me. To be honest, it was like water off a duck's back.

What comes through on the TV screen isn't what we get to see in the studio as judges. From where I'm sitting, I can see the whole thing. Dance is a non-verbal exercise, so the dancers have to communicate their emotions through movement without speaking. As the judge sitting there, I need to be able to understand what it is they're trying to say. Some people instinctively get that, and some people don't.

I remember when Simon Rimmer and his partner Karen Clifton danced a Waltz to the Liverpool anthem, 'You'll Never Walk Alone'. It was in my first series and only my second week of sitting on the panel, so I was still nervous, thinking about all the things I had to get right. I sat there, holding my pen to make notes, very aware of the cameras and lights everywhere, but despite all that, once I started watching them, their emotions got to me, the music got to me, the power of what they were trying to communicate completely caught me and, before I knew it, I had tears pouring down my face.

Even in my role as a judge, *Strictly* ticks every box, touches parts of me I thought I'd tucked well away, and lets me enjoy them. It really is one of the greatest privileges and pleasures of my life to be part of this family show and to know it is just as special to so many other people.

CHAPTER 11
The Rumba

'This is a vertical expression of a horizontal desire. It is the dance of love, with soft, hard, angry and passionate energy. It's not just "I've fallen in love with you", it's also "getting to know you", then it is "I know you, I hate you, I love you". It has all these different sentiments. Dancers must bring all of these emotions to their performance for a complete interpretation.'

Because I spent years travelling between the US and Britain and only properly settled in London once my work increasingly kept me here, my sense of being recognised out in public came very gradually over the course of my first two series. When I'm on the show, I'm all glammed up, but when I'm just out and about, I wear very little makeup and I frequently have a hat on, so I barely look like the same person everyone sees on the TV. By my second year on the show, though, people were definitely spotting me on the street – sometimes not even from my face, but from the way I walk, the way I stand, or when they hear my voice. I do my best to stop and chat to them if I have time. I've discovered lots of people want to talk about the show, why this person was eliminated or that person stayed in. It always ends up with me asking, 'Who is your favourite?' When they tell me, I remind them, 'Be sure to vote, and make sure your friends vote. Make my job easier!'

At first, being recognised on the street was something I found very daunting. I would be walking through the train station and I'd suddenly hear, 'Oh, it's that lady from the telly, that Shirley Ballas.' It took me a while to get used to it. If you're 22 years old when that happens to you, it probably feels fine, but at 57, as I was then, I can tell you, it feels distinctly odd – popping to the shops and having people wanting to stop me all the time, wanting to talk to me, or getting in a taxi in central London and having the driver turn round to me and say, 'Awful what your ex-husband had to say about you, wasn't it?' At first, I felt very exposed and very uncomfortable with people seeming to know so much about me and my life. I took to pulling down my hat, trying to rush along as quickly as possible to get back home. Gradually, I realised it was okay, people were just being friendly, and for the most part those I've met are lovely, even though there are some strange ones out there too. It was just something that I needed to get used to.

All the time I was living in LA, whenever I visited London I would often stay with my friend Terrie Martin. I need to tell you about Terrie, who I've known for 30 years. Our children went to school together, and that's how we first met in the playground all those years ago. One day, out of the blue, she said to me, 'Do you want to go to Hilton Head Island in America for a holiday?' So we did and that's when we became true friends, and have been ever since.

I often used to stay with Terrie when I travelled to the UK for work, and she was always incredibly supportive, 'You go off to work, do whatever you need to do, I'll be here.' She'd prepare meals for us, sort everything out and create a real home from home for me. When I got my job on *Strictly*, she carried on doing exactly the same thing, and her kitchen became a sweet sanctuary for me.

Terrie is one of those girls who always has your back. She's East End, properly street-smart and she takes no shit. As I got to grips with my new role, it gave me great comfort to go home to her, close the door and share a glass of wine with a much-trusted friend. With the increasing pressure and as my public profile began to grow, she became a wonderful sounding board at the end of those first, strange, days.

The path from Terrie's house to the train station includes a dark alley, and I became very wary of walking through it. I took to running from one end to the other, perspiration running down my back, my heart racing at a thousand beats a minute. It took me straight back to those days when I was 14, and I used to have to race through Liverpool in the dark from my dance classes. Forty years later, and here I was again with exactly the same fear, just desperate to get home.

If that was an age-old challenge I had to face again, the scrutiny that came with my getting the job on *Strictly* was a brand new one. And if having people know things about me took a lot of getting used to, I'm not sure my mother has ever come round to the fact that strangers were now aware of what she considered her personal business. My mother is a very, very private, independent person. She has never been particularly sociable; she prefers to have just one or two close, lifelong friends that she considers her inner circle, and she keeps everything to herself – as we learned when my brother was ill, she always wants to keep family business safely tucked away.

All this sudden attention on us came as a sharp shock to a woman intent on keeping her private life private. It didn't help that, right at the start of my time on *Strictly*, her former son-in-law wrote that damning portrait of our marriage and singled her out as a 'termite'. That very personal character assassination became a defining moment for her in terms of how she viewed any press about any of us.

It wasn't just rumours about me, it was the story of my brother and how he'd taken his own life that really got to her. They were really graphic in their description of what happened to him, which forced her to relive all those awful, dark days that she'd done her best to put behind her. In 2018, when she received her cancer diagnosis, I had to tell her that we needed to do our best to manage telling the story before it was spun into something beyond our control. Fortunately, her treatment was successful, but the extra attention was alien to her and she was, unsurprisingly, very distressed by it. In fact, she struggled so badly with the intrusion into her life once I got the *Strictly* job that, when I was offered my second series, I almost didn't accept it.

I explained to her, 'This all comes with my job. If you're not happy with it, then I just won't continue with *Strictly*. The choice is completely yours.'

I meant it, and she took some time to think about it. Eventually, she decided, 'You should continue with the job, and let's see if I can learn to cope with it.' And she has. It's started to feel a bit more normal to her now, and sometimes she can even have a laugh about it.

Another challenge for me is all the attention that comes my way on social media. Like anyone else, I get my share of messages that are beautiful and much appreciated, but also, at the opposite end of the spectrum, vile comments. Just like everyone else in the world, it's the insults that I remember a lot longer than the compliments. When I first started working on *Strictly*, I hadn't ever been on social media before, so I wasn't remotely prepared for how nasty some people can be. One of the first messages I ever received said, 'You're so ugly, you've got a chest like a Seville orange, it looks like it's been eaten by a thousand slugs. Die, you bitch.' I'll never forget that, as you can tell – I can quote it word for word to this day. It definitely took some effort on the part of the writer, and I believe it came the day after I'd cast a controversial deciding vote on *Strictly*. I'd probably sent home their favourite and that's what sparked them off to write such horrible words.

People are sometimes in a rush to express themselves when they don't agree with you. As soon as the show finishes, these keyboard warriors go straight to Twitter and spew out their feelings. If I don't respond, I'll often get another message later on, apologising, 'I'm so sorry, I said that in the heat of the moment.'

More recently, a death threat was delivered by hand to where I was appearing in pantomime. This one showed a figure of me digging my own grave, with the message, 'Do you realise how much you are hated? The country hates you. How did they ever give a job to someone like you, you old witch.'

What these people don't realise is that I come from a tough housing estate, and I've spent years many years being bullied in my industry, so I've developed an exterior shell as hard as a hob-nailed boot, those walls that my TV coach Francesca battled so hard to break through. Over the years, I've had to make myself immune to being vilified by professional rivals, having people smile to my face, telling me they're in my corner, and then slagging me off the minute my back's turned. Every time someone says something unkind, my heart breaks afresh, but I'll be damned if I'm going to show it, I wouldn't give them that satisfaction. The hurt goes deep, but I'm still standing. And all those nasty comments over the years have somehow set me up for all the crap I've received on social media. In a way, it's been good practice!

It's important for me to say, though, that, just because I can take it, doesn't make it okay. Just because I can cope, doesn't mean I should have to. And as we've seen too many times, there are plenty of people who also receive hate mail on Twitter who really can't cope with it, and for their suffering, I'm sorry. It's definitely far too high a price to pay for success.

These days, people ask me, 'Why are you so nice to people on Twitter, even if they're being rude to you?' For a start, I think it goes with the territory of having a public face, but more personally, I always ask myself, 'What if they're feeling suicidal, what if they're having a bad day?' They might just be reaching out for someone to listen. I give everyone three chances, then if they're still intent on being mean, I might eventually delete them, but often I get an apology. My brother David is never far from my thoughts, so if I can do some good for someone by reacting like this, then I feel I'm doing my bit to protect and honour his legacy. It's my way of trying to create something positive out of the biggest sorrow of my life.

Ever since I lost David nearly two decades ago, I've tried in every way I can to highlight the continuing problem of men's mental health. I know my brother felt he couldn't speak out about the extent of his suffering, and I fear that's the case for a lot of men in the world today. My brother was 44 when he died, and I've since learned that suicide is the biggest killer of men under the age of 45 in the UK, with around 16 men taking their own lives each day – a shocking statistic.

Men are also three times as likely as women to take their own lives. From what I've learned, and also experienced myself, I fear they feel embarrassed and judged for what they see as society's expectations of so-called masculinity, that they will appear weak in some way to have to admit to any mental health issues. That was certainly the case with my brother. I want to take all these men in my arms and tell them it doesn't make them weak, that they only have to speak up and ask for the help they deserve and need.

For my 50th birthday, I was living in LA at the time and I hosted a huge party at a hotel. My dance industry friend Michael Chapman designed the evening for me, and it was very special. Instead of presents, I asked for financial gifts, which I was able to donate to a charity working for suicide prevention. For a long time, I've supported the charity Campaign Against Living Miserably (CALM), which works to protect men's health. One of the most satisfying aspects of getting my role on *Strictly* and raising my profile has been the chance to bring more attention to all the tireless work they carry out.

The loss of David, and my sadness at feeling that I could have done something for him, is something I've carried with me for a long time, and I know it's the same for thousands of other people. You just never know what is going on behind closed doors, and what might be going on in the minds of those we care about the most.

This was brought home to me when I was invited to attend a Duke of Edinburgh Awards event at Buckingham Palace. I had my speech all ready to go, but as I began to speak, I felt compelled to share my brother's story. I had never spoken about him in public before, and I wasn't quite sure what made me do it then. All I can say is I had a sudden urge to share, so I took a deep breath and expressed it all – everything he suffered, plus what we went through as a family, and how important it was that we find fresh ways of looking after those who are suffering with fragile mental health, and their loved ones who suffer equally with their own feelings of sorrow and powerlessness through all the dark times.

It was a large crowd that day, but everything just poured out of my heart in a way I wasn't expecting. I finished, then sat down exhausted and feeling very emotional about everything I'd just expressed. A gentleman I didn't know came up and sat down next to me. He told me, 'When I saw your name on the list, I thought, "What's that dancing woman got to offer?"' He went on to reveal that he'd just lost his own son to suicide aged 12, which must have been unspeakably awful for his whole family. He told me, 'What you shared with the audience, I could see was extremely heartfelt. You served my family well today.'

It meant a lot to me that this man had stepped forward, particularly as it was the first time I'd spoken like that about David. What he told me opened my eyes to the fact that suicide has no age limits, and it lit a fire in me to do much more. I decided that day that, however long I have this high-profile job, and however long I'm graced with a public platform and people are interested in what I have to say, I will dedicate myself to doing whatever I can to highlight men's mental health, and to speak out every chance I get. Little did I know that I would soon be offered an extraordinary opportunity to do this on a grand scale.

• • •

Early in 2019, I was challenged to climb Mount Kilimanjaro for Comic Relief. I fast realised that this could potentially be the biggest platform I would ever have to do something to shine the torch on mental health, so I grabbed the chance with both hands.

I admit now I hadn't actually researched Kilimanjaro when I signed up for the trip. When I finally looked it up and found out just how high the mountain is, how difficult it would be to climb, I realised this was going to be without doubt the most terrifying thing I'd ever do in my life.

I didn't know any of my fellow climbers. We had two of the girls from Little Mix, Jade Thirlwall and Leigh-Anne Pinnock, Dani Dyer who'd just won *Love Island*, an American NFL player and sports pundit called Osi Umenyiora, TV presenters Dan Walker and Anita Rani, actor and comedian Alexander Armstrong, former politician Ed Balls and me. It was a pretty mixed bunch, and learning to get along with each other was going to be as much of a challenge as getting to the peak.

Prior to Kilimanjaro, I'd only had one experience of camping in my whole life and it hadn't exactly been an advert for sleeping out under the stars. When I was 16 years old, I went away with my boyfriend Nigel Tiffany and another couple. Four of us were cooped up in a tiny tent, and the other pair spent the night canoodling and fondling each other in their sleeping bags. Nigel and I tried to sleep, but we could hear every bump, groan and grunt going on next to us, which didn't make for a peaceful night. In the morning, they got up and the young man started cooking us all breakfast on the grill. There he was sorting out the bacon and sausages, and he hadn't even washed his hands! Well, that was enough to put me off camping forever, and I didn't get in a tent again for over 40 years, until the day I set out to climb Kilimanjaro.

I had absolutely no idea what to expect, and I'll admit now I thought we might stay in tiny little hotels or shacks, and that I'd be able to plug my hairdryer in somewhere. Fortunately, it turned out I wasn't the only one thinking like that – Jade from Little Mix admitted she'd brought her portable kettle along. And then Dani revealed, 'I've never even climbed a climbing frame.' What a bunch!

As we travelled in on the bus, we all reminded each other to use lots of positive words, and for that we were lucky to have Osi with us. He gave us a great pep talk when we got to the start of the trail. He kept it simple, saying, 'We have an obstacle. A lot of people depend on us getting up that hill, and a lot of people depend on us getting down this hill, let's get this thing done, let's raise a bunch of money, let's have a good time doing it.' Osi became an amazing support for me over that week. He said on camera at one point, 'I've got Shirley's back at all times.' And he really did.

We were going to pitch our first camp about five miles in, at 2,000 metres up, and from then on we'd have no running water or electricity for the next seven days. I wasn't too worried at first as we set off on the mountain path, all of us chatting, full of the joys of spring. The sun was shining, the trees were beautiful all around us and, initially, it felt like a gentle countryside walk. I thought, 'Well, this isn't too bad at all.'

Just then, the weather changed, the rains began to fall and the footpath we'd been strolling along turned into a mud bath that we had to struggle not to sink into. That went on for a few more hours, which meant the water got in all our clothes, and I began to get a bit cold and miserable. Then, all of a sudden in the pissing rain, they told us, 'You have to make camp here. Can everyone start pitching their own tent?' Well, with that, I looked down at the muddy ground, listened to the tree rats in the branches all around us, felt all the water inside my drenched clothes and burst into tears.

Fortunately, I had two very gallant men with me. Dan and Osi both helped me put up my tent, but soon another challenge presented itself – the bathing. At home, I generally jump in the shower about three or four times a day, but on Kilimanjaro, things were a bit different, with bugs everywhere. The prospect of washing my bits and bobs with a wet wipe was quite daunting for me. Dan couldn't have been nicer. He gave me a huge hug and said, 'You're going to be great. Why don't you harness Shirley Ballas, three times world champion?' Anita added, 'The badass that is Ballas,' and that made me smile.

I didn't even know why I was getting upset, mortified because I was aware all the time of how many people in the world have nothing, especially in Africa where we were, and here I was complaining about pitching a tent. I was just a very long way out of my comfort zone.

I went to bed that night exhausted, worrying that I wasn't going to be any good on this trip. The boots, the clothes, the walking, all of that I could cope with, but the camping seemed a challenge too far. I resolved to keep my brother David, the reason I was doing all this, at the forefront of my mind. If honouring him meant sleeping rough for a week and going without a bloomin' hairdryer, so be it. My love for my brother got me through that first wobbly night, and pushed me up the rest of that mountain.

The next morning I was determined to give everything a better shot. I remembered I was still the girl from Wallasey I'd always been, and if anyone on that mountain knew how to wash out of a small tin bowl, it was me. I ended up showing all the other girls how best to wash all the necessaries and even wash their hair in the freezing cold. That all came out of living on the estate, when we didn't always have hot water and often bathed in the sink, so I was more used to cold water than I remembered. After my initial freak-out on the mountain, I started finding my own way, and our harsh surroundings stopped bothering me, even having to go to the bathroom behind a rock. Well, if you're drinking four litres of water a day, it's going to happen. It's amazing what you get used to, and how quickly.

What did bother me? Knowing I was the oldest in the team and worrying that I might not be able to keep up with the rest of them. But what I'd never realised was just how fit all that dancing makes you, and I was soon striding out in front. Osi and I ended up leading the pack almost to the summit, but the organisers had to have a word in my ear: 'Shirley, you can't lead the pack because we need everybody to reach the top at the same time.' I'd been getting too far ahead!

A few of us suffered to varying degrees from altitude sickness, and I also slipped over on the narrow ledges several times. On one occasion, I would have gone tumbling over the edge if Osi hadn't caught me by the scruff of my coat collar and pulled me back up. Thank goodness for all those years of NFL training and his quick-as-a-flash reactions. Just as he'd promised, he had my back, quite literally.

There was a true spirit of teamwork between all of us, we all had a cry and a laugh, and it was properly bonding. We spoke about anything and everything, and some of the conversations were a bit surreal. At one point, I heard Ed Balls singing 'Shout Out to my Ex', but in a really posh voice, much to the surprise of Jade and Leigh-Anne. Then, when we all went off to bed, he called out 'Goodnight, John-Boy' and was really upset when no one answered!

As anybody who's ever gone up a mountain will know, though, there is plenty of time when it's just you and your thoughts. You walk for miles and miles and miles, often in perfect silence, too tired to chat, and that's when your thoughts and memories come flooding in – in my case, the cause of my life's greatest sadness.

Because I wasn't sleeping well, I was in a state of constant tiredness, and as we all know, when you're feeling like that, your mind can start playing tricks on you. A few days in, I suddenly started feeling very panicky, then before I knew it, I was having a nosebleed and starting to vomit. But what came into my mind was worse than anything physical. I couldn't control my emotions, and I can only assume it was the altitude having its effect on me, because I know the others were going through their own personal challenges as well. It plays tricks on your mind and makes for a very lonely, sad experience.

But something else happened too, which I found immensely comforting. On one of our final days reaching the summit, I distinctly heard my brother talking to me. All he said was 'Shirley', but it sounded exactly like him, and it was a reminder of why I was doing all this, just when I needed it most.

The final overnight climb to the summit proved to be the hardest stretch of all, and we were lucky to have Osi to give another one of his pep talks, which put fire in our bellies – just as well because it was minus 5 degrees outside, properly cold. The air was thin, oxygen was down to about half of what we were used to, and it was a very tough seven hours. We were clinging to each other as we finally reached the summit, where we all made sure to touch the board at the same time.

I can truthfully say that trip to Kilimanjaro was tough in every single way – mentally, physically, even spiritually – but I also gained an awful lot from the experience. It gave me the confidence to go out and do something on my own, without my comfort blanket of family, close circle of friends and work. Physically, it was the hardest thing I've ever done in my life, with the weather constantly changing, and learning how to camp. But the knowledge that I was doing this to raise the profile of a charity so close to my heart constantly kept me going. The satisfaction of reaching the summit was beyond immense. As I stood on the top of the mountain, I sent all the love in my heart out to my brother and I like to think that on that day, like every other day, I made him proud.

• • •

The year 2019 presented me with another physical challenge, just as immense but a little bit closer to home. A lot was written about my boobs, or rather the shrinking of them, when I had my implants taken out in October, but there was a whole lot more to that story.

I originally had them put in 17 years ago, and if I'm honest, it was because I hoped that they would make me appear more attractive as a wife to my then husband. My marriage was already failing, and I was desperate to see if there was anything I could do that could make a difference and help Corky to find me more attractive.

Throughout our marriage, he always had a thing about me looking as nice as possible, smelling nice, and looking perfectly groomed. He was such a perfectionist, he used to carry red nail varnish around with him in his pocket and, if I ever chipped a nail, he would be fast to the rescue to make sure my nails got quickly repaired. Even if he was teaching, he used to carry it with him in his pocket in case a girl got chipped toenails. He couldn't seem to handle it! So I really hoped the boobs might make a difference. They were a last-ditch attempt for me to try and feel better about myself.

I had them done in London. It was an expensive but straightforward procedure, but I realise now I didn't do anything like enough research before I had the operation. I didn't have a clue what could grow in and around those bits of plastic; I just had this simple idea in my head that I needed these big boobs. So I got them and, for a short period of time, I felt more confident but not in any meaningful way, and, unsurprisingly, it didn't make the slightest bit of difference to my relationship with my husband. Let's face it, unless you're centred and happy with who you really are, no amount of surgery is going to fix it. Equally, you can't make someone love you. If they don't love you, they don't love you, and Corky didn't love me. The boobs became a Band-Aid over a wound that was never going to heal.

A few years after that, my issues with my body hadn't gone anywhere, and I continued to have the same concerns regarding my weight. I was by then living in LA, working training dancers full-time but, however many hours of physical exercise I did every week and the healthy lifestyle I led, I couldn't seem to shift the extra pounds and bumps under my skin, and it played havoc with my confidence. I was approaching 50 and had all the concerns of many women of that age, looking in the mirror and wondering what I could do to improve my body and, with it, my self-esteem.

I thought I'd discovered the magic solution when I met Dr John Shieh and become good friends with him and his wife, Floy. I regularly used to visit him at his Rejuvayou Medical Spa clinic in Pasadena for small cosmetic treatments. When he offered me the chance to be treated with laser liposuction for a video he was making, I didn't do any research, but just jumped at the chance to remove some fat from my tummy and thighs.

Mark came along with me for support on the day and you can see from his face on the video – still somewhere on YouTube, I think – what he thought of the whole thing: that I was barmy for going through with it, or even thinking I needed it in the first place.

The treatment, a laser that went under the skin and then a machine that hoovered out the fat, was quite painful, but I thought it would be the miracle I was after and that I'd come out much thinner. Afterwards, I was a bit slimmer for a while, but what I fast realised is that you may be able to take the fat out, but if you continue to overeat, it's all going to go back in, and that's what happened.

We all think there's some secret magic formula out there, the secret to the perfect body and all the happiness that goes with it, but the fact is we already know what the answer is: good diet, exercise, drinking lots of water, going to sleep at a sensible hour and taking care of ourselves. That's it. There are no shortcuts.

For many years while I lived in the United States, I had a book-keeper called Christine Anderson. She was so thorough with all my accounts, she soon noticed that in among my other bills were frequent invoices for medical treatments. I often attended clinics for various procedures and to deal with scares, the removal of lumps and bumps, as well as extra procedures, including mammograms.

Christine was a long-time friend and she began to be very concerned for me. She said to me, 'Do you realise you are constantly sick? Doing your books, I can see you are. Could it be your boobs? I've read an article, and some women say their boobs make them feel tired and sick. Maybe it's worth getting them checked out?'

That was two or three years before I even thought about it, but she said it to me fairly regularly, and her words stayed at the back of my mind.

Taking part in *Who Do You Think You Are?* in 2018 and having the opportunity to conduct research into the history of my relatives soon made me realise how much cancer ran in both sides of my family. After that, I couldn't stop thinking about it.

It started to play on my mind what Christine had told me and, whether it was physical or psychological, I began to feel that my boobs were becoming increasingly heavy and uncomfortable, to the point where I couldn't even roll over in bed without wincing.

While I was in England, my GP suggested I had another mammogram because my boobs were looking very misshapen. When I went for the screening, the nurse told me, 'Well, everything appears to be fine. But I just want to check, you do realise that it's impossible to see behind the back of the implants?'

As I got back in my car following the examination, everything seemed to come together, all Christine's concerned words, conversations I'd had with my mother, the weight of these boobs, how uncomfortable they always felt. By now, they'd even separated to the point where my real boobs were in one place while the implants were in another, so everything was horribly misshapen. With my fears of any cancer lying behind them undiscovered, I decided it was time to find myself a good doctor and get those implants out of my body once and for all.

This time I decided to do my research, and find myself a great doctor. I visited one in Liverpool, and we discussed what it would involve to remove the implants completely. I not only wanted to remove them but also the capsules around the implants, the fibrous scar tissue that the body naturally forms around any object it recognises as foreign. I told him that if I was going to go under the knife and general anaesthetic, I wanted the lot gone! This was a more extensive operation than I believed the doctor in Liverpool would have been comfortable performing, and he referred me to a specialist in London.

By the time I met up with the specialist, Doctor Waterhouse, I was convinced I needed everything gone. From the moment I first walked into his office, I told him, 'I'm not here for your opinion, I've made my mind up. This is what I want to do. I want to take my breast implants out.' He told me he'd never had a patient walk through his door quite so fixed on one course of treatment, but by then I was absolutely determined. Nevertheless, he made me read up on all the medical literature before I confirmed I wanted the implants, the capsules, everything gone, even though it would mean being under the knife for four to five hours.

As the time loomed ever nearer for my operation, I have to admit that the anxiety I've struggled with all my life came back in full force – panic attacks, sleepless nights, the lot. Everything was rushing through my mind: how would my boobs look? Would I have scars? Would I feel attractive afterwards? How would I feel? I couldn't stop worrying. But the boobs had got far too heavy on me, emotionally and physically, so whatever happened, I knew it was time to take them out.

The BBC team was extremely supportive of any decision I made about the timing of the operation, and it helped me that I could talk to a team of women about this very sensitive subject. Meanwhile, Doctor Waterhouse made it clear he would have preferred me to take at least six weeks off and he also asked me, 'Do you think you should postpone things until after *Strictly*?'

We were right bang in the middle of my third series of the show, but I had decided I couldn't wait until after the final for my operation. I was having night terrors about having cancer, which meant that, as well as all the emotional anguish, the operation to have my implants removed had become, as far as I was concerned, a race against time.

The surgery was booked for the Tuesday and the BBC offered me the chance of taking as much time off afterwards as I needed to recover. But, in my own head, I vowed to be back at work in time for the show on the Saturday, and I made sure everyone knew that. Before the operation, I'd made it clear to everyone around me, 'I don't want anyone telling me I can't go back to work. If you plan to say that to me, don't call me for another six weeks.'

On the other hand, I told my mother, 'If there's anyone who can get me up and running and back on my feet after three days, it's going to be you.' She came and stayed with me and helped me recover from the operation.

As soon as I came round from the surgery, I realised I'd set myself a mammoth task. I'd had my share of dancing injuries over the years but this was a whole new level of pain. I forced myself out of bed 24 hours after the operation, but even just getting down the stairs was a challenge. As I prepared to climb in the car to take me to *Strictly* the following Saturday, I looked across at my mother and whispered, 'I'm in so much pain.' She replied, 'You made your choice, Shirley. Get in the car.'

I'd made a commitment to *Strictly* – the show must go on – but the BBC had made it clear I could take a break. Why was it so important to me to be back at my post without taking even one week off? I'll be honest, I wanted to see how strong my mind was. I wanted to test my boundaries. It was one more test I set for myself, to discover if I could deal with that kind of pain, and I'm glad I did it.

I couldn't have asked for more tender care than I got that evening from everyone at the *Strictly* studio. My dresser Alexandra, who's been with me from the very beginning, took me into the dressing room and said, 'I have a surprise for you.' She produced a stunning black trouser suit with a bow, and I was very moved. As well as making sure I was comfortable, Alexandra wanted to help me send a message: 'Here's a woman who's coming back to work four days after surgery. She's strong because she wants to be. I'm putting her in a power suit.'

As for the boobs, I'm more than happy that I took them out. Even though the scars will remain, I know it was the right thing to do. I feel a huge relief mentally and physically that they're now gone. I look at my scars in the mirror, and to me they look like two small smiley faces, and I choose to smile at them in return. If I could go back to my younger self, I would ask the question, 'What on earth made you do it?' Even though I know why I did it! My heartfelt advice to any woman, young or old, out there is, think before you do it and ask yourself why you're doing it. Also, make sure you do your research, make sure you get a good doctor and make sure you understand what's growing inside your body. Every woman must make her own decision. I made mine and I can live with that. I'm not saying don't do it, I'm just urging you to make sure you do it for the right reasons.

• • •

During that whole time, I had someone very special who was an incredible support to me. He said he didn't care what I looked like, it made no difference to him, he just wanted me to do whatever made me feel happy and, equally importantly, healthy. He said from the off, 'My opinion doesn't come into it. This is about protecting yourself, and that's the most important thing.'

Just before Christmas 2018, if you'd asked me if I was happy, I'd have replied with my usual, 'What is happy?'

All my life, I was never really sure what being happy meant, but at that point in time, I was certainly content. I had had many ups and downs throughout my life, but here I was aged 58, with a great job, a wonderful family and a busy, purposeful life. Who could ask for more? I'd pretty much come to the conclusion that I wasn't put on this planet for personal happiness, but to help other people move along the bus with their careers and other dreams.

As a woman in her late fifties, I thought personal happiness would have to elude me, especially in the form of romance. In today's society, as every woman will know, the older you get, the more invisible you start to feel as you battle the ravages of time. All we ever seem to get is messages that we're fast approaching our sell-by date. I have all the same insecurities as every other woman, plus a whole load of extra baggage based on two failed marriages with men who didn't make me feel good about myself, including an ex-husband who used to say, 'Get fat and I'll leave you' and then did. Plus, I have to say it doesn't help when that same ex-husband turns up with a new partner 20 years younger than him on his arm.

But what could I do? I had been blessed in so many other ways in my life, it would be greedy to think about asking for anything else. Famous last words ...

Much earlier in 2018, Craig Revel Horwood had convinced me to take part in a pantomime. He considered this would be a wonderful experience for me, being onstage and learning how to perform in front of a live audience. He also thought it would boost my confidence for any public speaking engagements that came my way.

I had several offers for pantomime that year, but the one that appealed to me the most was *Jack and the Beanstalk* at the Liverpool Empire, put on by Qdos Entertainment. I chose this one as it meant I could be close to my mother at Christmas time. She'd been having cancer treatment, so I wanted to make sure she was okay, and that I'd be able to invite her and her friends along to the show so everyone could have some fun. It felt fun and fitting to be going back to Liverpool to make my theatrical debut.

In the meantime, though, I was terrified. I can't tell you how scared I was of taking on this job. I'd always been a performer, but that was in the non-verbal language of dance. I'd never acted, never learned a script, never spoken someone else's words and it scared the living daylights out of me. As soon as I signed my contract in early March, I immediately asked for the script and started trying to learn it the moment I got home. I was panicking off the chart with every page and I even got myself some private acting lessons on how to deliver it. I was living with my friend Terri at the time, and she got used to playing opposite me, as I tried desperately to become word-perfect. I have to say I truly was regretting ever saying yes to the idea, but I knew I'd already signed the contract. There was no escaping it.

Later on in the autumn, we were still in the throes of my second series of *Strictly* when we started rehearsals for the panto in central London. The cast consisted of comic John Evans doing all the heavy lifting as Simple Simon, Alex James-Hatton as Jack, and a lovely girl I already knew called Clair Gleave was set to play the princess. Iain Stuart Robertson was the dame, and the villain of the whole piece, Fleshcreep, was to be played by an actor I didn't know called Daniel Taylor. Before I met them, I felt these actors all belonged to a very different world from mine.

I walked into the rehearsal room for our first day, my knees knocking and my heart pounding, exactly how I'd felt when I was waiting to go on for my debut on *Strictly*. For the first time in

30 years, I realised I didn't know another soul in the room, and I didn't have the foggiest idea what I was meant to be doing. We sat round a big long table and everyone introduced themselves. They all seemed smiley, friendly and extremely confident. I sat there and all I wanted was a bucket so I had somewhere to throw up with fear about the whole thing.

The first thing we had to do was a big read-through of the whole script. That was okay, I had the pages in front of me, but then, before I knew it, we each had to get up in turn and start acting out our scenes. It was like being back at school where you have to read out in class, and although I'd spent many months trying to get word-perfect, I might as well not have bothered. I was so terrified, all my lines immediately fell out of my head and I found myself blubbering. It was like one of those dreams where you're convinced you're walking down the street with no clothes on. All I could think about was how quickly I could get out of that room and see if I could somehow get out of my contract.

My role was Mother Nature, and most of her scenes were opposite Fleshcreep, so I had to stand up and start acting opposite this very experienced actor, Daniel Taylor. He seemed so confident and immediately powerful in his role that I found myself completely floored and unable to even say my lines, let alone start acting. I was just completely intimidated, and eventually the director, Bob Tomson, could see I was floundering. He took me out of the room and I shared with him my fears.

'I can't do it,' I told him. 'You're going to have to get someone else. This actor is obviously very experienced, and he's way too powerful. I've wasted everybody's time. I'm sorry.'

Bob didn't crack a smile. He was very strict as he replied, 'Shirley, you have to stand your ground. You've signed up for this and you have to do it. Go back in the room and continue your lines. You'll be just fine.'

I'd been performing in front of huge audiences for decades, but for the first time I realised how truly terrifying it is to step so far out of your comfort zone, and it reminded me of what all the *Strictly* celebrities must go through when they have to step out onto the dance floor for the very first time. I was absolutely terrified.

Eventually, after some more persuasion from Bob, I went back in, and I very slowly began to get better, but it was still terrifying and I wasn't happy for days. I wouldn't let go of my script, I considered it my security blanket, until Bob grabbed it off me. But eventually, I began to relax. What a way to begin my first season in panto! It was mortifying.

All the time I was fluffing my lines, Danny was the ultimate professional, offering to do scenes again and again until I found my feet. As I finally started to feel a little more confident, I couldn't help but start to notice this handsome man acting opposite me – very tall, tanned skin, jet-black hair and big blue eyes – so that meant I started forgetting my lines all over again. It was a disaster! Fortunately, if anybody noticed, they didn't say anything.

As the weeks went on, Danny and I got talking in between scenes. It was just idle chit-chat, and then I realised he was from the same part of the world as me, and he was also looking forward to spending time in Liverpool. I found myself being very drawn to his big blue eyes, honest and kind, so I later made a discreet enquiry about his situation. My friend Clair did some scouting around and she came back to tell me, 'Sorry, Shirley, he's not single.' And that was that, or so I thought.

A few weeks later, we all re-grouped in Liverpool, and this was where I got to catch up with Danny again. He revealed to some of the company that he'd been going through a painful breakup after his relationship of 15 years had fallen apart. By the time we got to the Liverpool Empire for our first dress rehearsals, I noticed that although he was always very nice to everyone, he wasn't in a good place. He seemed a little bit down on himself and this brought out the nurturing side of me, and I tried to help him in what small ways I could. I didn't want to say anything too personal as we weren't close enough friends for that, but I made sure to make him hot honey and lemon drinks backstage and invite him along with the rest of us for meals whenever we went out. By then, my only concern was that he was healthy and had someone to take care of him.

For our opening night, all my family turned up to support me, including my son Mark and BC Jean, who had travelled from LA. After all the effort I'd made to get word-perfect – literally practising my lines since March for goodness' sake – a few nerves still got the better of me, and I managed to make a few cock-ups onstage, but fortunately, I laughed along with the audience and the more mistakes I made, the funnier they found it! It was a great crowd at the Empire that night, and every night after, and we got some cracking reviews. I really couldn't have asked for a better pantomime debut experience. Not only was I back in my beloved Liverpool, but the show also included lots of *Strictly* moments, children holding judges' paddles, the show's theme music being played, and I even got the chance to dance the Samba. I found myself really starting to enjoy it, and comedian John Evans as Simple Simon was properly funny. For me, the hardest part was trying not to laugh whenever we were onstage together. His timing and delivery of his one-liners were second to none.

On opening night, after the show finished and we came offstage, we decided to go for drinks at the famous Cavern Club, and my son Mark and BC Jean came along as well. As I saw Danny chatting away to my family, I realised I'd started to look at him in a different light. Mark told me afterwards that he could tell something was up and that some kind of special chemistry was brewing.

Mark has always said to me that I should try to go out with someone not in the dance world. Well, if I'm honest, what he actually said was, 'You need to be dating somebody not in the same industry as you. There's nothing more boring than going out to dinner and talking shop all night. Boring, boring, boring!'

My son was probably more relieved than most when he met Danny and was able to talk about a whole host of other things going on in the world besides dance. Besides acting, Danny worked as a successful theatre producer and as a singer-songwriter, so he and Mark had plenty in common. Also, my son was very intrigued to see me accept a second gin and tonic from Danny when I hardly ever drink!

I could see that Danny definitely wasn't ready for any kind of relationship. He was in the darkest, lowest place of his life and, for myself, I hadn't been with anyone for a long time, so I was quite happy just to be friends. As good-looking as he is, it wasn't his looks that made me eventually fall in love with Danny, it was his warm, kind attitude to everybody he met. Despite everything he was going through in his life and all the personal heartache he had experienced, he always had time for other people.

After pantomime season finished in early 2019, I found it quite tough saying goodbye to everyone I'd been working with. We'd spent almost all of our time together for weeks, performing two shows every day, getting to know one another very well in the hours in between, and I found it very strange to be leaving behind what had become a very tight-knit community of wonderful people. We created a WhatsApp group for everyone to make it easy to stay in touch.

As the months went on, Danny and I stayed in touch, sending texts just to see how each other was, meeting up for the occasional cup of coffee whenever we were in the same neck of the woods. He came along with me when I had to buy my hiking boots for my trip to Kilimanjaro, then he invited me to see him onstage in *Blood Brothers*. We slowly got to know each other and there was no pressure.

It was around the time I watched him perform in *Blood Brothers* that I began to feel there might be something in this. Round about March, he revealed he'd started to have feelings for me, and by May, we had become quite serious about each other.

When I first met Danny, I'd thought I must be quite special to him, because of how well he treated me, and it came as quite a shock to realise that I wasn't actually that special – at that point anyway – he treated everybody the same way. There is an expression that I learned from my old student and friend, Lester Smith. He always said, 'Watch out for how people treat other people, because if they're nasty to them, at some point that's how they'll be with you. It's not if, it's when. But if they're kind to other people, that's a very good sign.' And that's how it was with Danny. He was kind to everybody he met and always positive. I watched how he treated his mother, his friends, and the crew on his show and I thought, 'Wow, if I had someone treating me that well, it would be pretty amazing.'

Despite everything Danny's gone through in his life, the ups, the downs, none of it has made him remotely bitter; he's just worldly wise, and he's a little bit more laid-back than me. To me, he's like a worn shoe, an old, comfortable leather boot that's gone really soft. It doesn't sound sexy, but trust me, it is. He's street-smart but warm. I've never been an emotional sharer, but I soon realised that perhaps I'd met someone I could share my most personal feelings with.

You'll have realised by now I've never been scared of an age gap, but because Danny was becoming so important to me, I was more worried about the years between him and me than I cared to admit. Danny doesn't seem to notice any faults with my looks or my body, but I probably do enough worrying about all those things for both of us. I believe, if they're honest, most women care about things like that. Whenever I admit to having any insecurity as a woman in her late fifties, Danny always reassures me, 'We'll never lose the humour, because as we get older, we're going to bloody well need it!.' I'm going to have to remind him of that! He just tells me, 'Age is a case of mind over matter. If you don't mind, it doesn't matter. Shirley, love knows no age.'

One of the first nights I ever spent with Danny, it was after I'd been at a big *Strictly* event, which meant I was wearing a gold, sequinned gown, and lots of stage makeup. I've always been very self-conscious about my body and my looks, but Danny unzipped my dress and he even wiped all the makeup off my face. He said to me, 'There she is, the girl I fell in love with.'

Danny didn't realise it but, with that one simple gesture, he began to undo years of damage that I had stored inside me, both through having such critical partners in the past, and also because of my own deep self-doubt. His actions meant a lot to me, and it made a huge difference to our relationship.

I like to think that I've learned something from everyone who's passed through my life, and Danny has already taught me many lessons in the time we've been together. Never go to bed fighting. See the humour in everything. Think before you speak, because words can be accidentally hurtful. That one took me a while to come to terms with as I was used to speaking straight away, but Danny likes to take his time to process his thoughts. He explained it to me, 'Words you can't take back, so let's always think before we say anything that might be hurtful.'

Something that is huge for me, and something I've often missed out on in my life, is that date nights are important, carving out special time just for Danny and me. Fortunately, he agrees with that, and sometimes he's even taken my phone off me if we're heading out for the evening, so that we can fully focus on each other. It's the same late at night, which he reminds me should be a time of rest and that I need to switch off. He's even made me close the pages of my beloved diary. It takes a brave man to do that!

Our first year together was everything I'd always believed a relationship should be but had never personally experienced myself. At Christmas, my son sent Danny a card, in which he wrote, 'Thank you for making my mum happy again, and for looking after my nan.' I think Mark's very grateful that Danny has appeared in my life.

A few months after we got together, Mark asked me, 'How is your life going, Mum?'

I told him, 'Pretty good actually, thanks.'

He said, 'I can tell.'

'Oh, really? How?'

'Cos you're not bothering me every five minutes.'

LOL. So there you go. Everyone's a winner.

• • •

I think one of the people who was most relieved that I'd finally got myself a nice boyfriend was my friend Terrie. She'd always been concerned that I never had enough fun. In fact, she once told me, 'I'm going to slide into my coffin sideways, Shirley, and I'm going to shout out, "I had a ball."' Then she looked at me and added, 'And you're going to slide in your coffin sideways and say, "And I worked myself to death."' Well, that told me!

I've always known that, when your time on earth is complete and it's time for you to leave, you're taking nothing with you. There are no pockets in the coffin, no luggage rack on the end. What will you be left with? I've worked extremely hard all my life, and it's brought many wonderful things that I will never fail to appreciate. But perhaps my dear friend Terrie was right, perhaps it's time now for me to sit back a bit more often, make some time for myself, pour another coffee and smell the flowers.

If I'm not dancing so much, what would I like to spend my time doing? At this point where I'm learning to relax just a little bit more, with a great partner at my side, I have several things on my bucket list I would still like to do. I'd love to jump out of an aeroplane, have some adventures with my son and his wife, and travel the world properly. I'd like to visit all those countries that I went to when I was dancing, when I only ever saw the inside of departure lounges and ballrooms. Now I'd like to go back and experience them all properly.

I know I have to find some me time, I can't keep trucking on at the rate I have been doing. It's time for some balance. I said to Mark recently, 'I might need to have a break,' and he replied, 'No shit, Sherlock, we've all been saying that for years.'

I know that, whatever else comes my way, I'll never give up the thing I still love best, which is teaching, coaching, guiding people to a place of success.

People see the person on the TV, dressed up in a nice frock, lots of makeup, great hair, glitz, glamour and sequins. As we all know, all that came very late in my life. I was a fully formed person long before that, and that person is a mother, a teacher and a coach first and foremost. All that glamour is fabulous – there isn't a girl who doesn't like the chance to dress up – but it's no longer the biggest part of me. That person is stripped down in a studio, trying to inspire someone who's going through all the battles and struggles that we all have to face every single day – dealing with illness, family, insecurity, grief, heartbreak, whatever it is – and help them escape into a world of dance.

Obviously, what I have to impart is all the steps and techniques, but they're just the tools of the trade. What is really important is helping people to get the best out of themselves. I'd like my legacy to be that I helped a lot of people, on and off the dance floor, fulfil their ambitions and dreams.

Have I made mistakes? Absolutely, just like everybody else. I would say my biggest mistake was not finding self-belief and confidence in myself earlier in my life. All those years, it just felt like I was trying to swim upstream to reach my goals, fighting to be better, fighting for recognition, fighting for approval. It was tough, and a lot of the time, I made things a lot harder for myself than it needed to be.

Had my father stayed with us all those years ago, would I have been the same person, doing the same things with my life? Well, my mother says he'd have never let her spend the money she did on my dancing, so that's a no. Plus, had he been the kind of father who drove me everywhere like my friend Karen's, I might never have become so resilient. I might have been a happy little kid, but not gone on to achieve very much. The truth is, I'll never know. What I do know is that, if I hadn't been so driven, I wouldn't be where I am now, and I wouldn't change that for the world.

My rewards have come in lots of different ways: in seeing Mark so happy, so busy and fulfilled following his musical dreams with his wife at his side, and my niece Mary doing so well and embracing her future; watching Derek and Julianne enjoy such brilliant careers; helping my students get better results than they ever thought possible; being able to take care of my mother and be there for her 24/7; getting a text message from Danny to say he's on his way home. Then there's having the *Strictly* contestants smile with delight as they get better, or even the shock when someone goes home; knowing that so many viewers embrace the show, those same people sharing their stories with me when I bump into them on the street. Plus, being able to do so much work for charity and for mental health ... I look at all of this and I realise, that little girl from Wallasey, she's done all right. And if seeing me on a TV show inspires the next young girl to think, 'I can do that', even if she's from a block of flats on a housing estate somewhere in the north of England, then that makes me very happy and warms my heart.

Even now though, I struggle to relax. Last night, I sat at my kitchen table, looked at my long list of to-dos, and realised I'd done everything on it. So I thought, 'Okay, I'll sit still for five minutes and do some deep breathing.' Well, I managed all of two minutes before I got a bit restless, so I came to the conclusion I should try and have an early night. Off I went for a quick shower and tucked myself into bed. After about five minutes, I decided I'd do just one more thing, so I got back out of bed, went into my office and started doing some filing. Two hours later, I finally took myself back to bed.

I'm very satisfied with all the wonderful things I've achieved so far in this life, but I know the biggest challenge I have yet to master is the elusive art of standing still.

Epilogue

How Dance Rewards

Dance has given me the opportunity to express myself in an extraordinary way. When I was a young girl growing up on a housing estate, it gave me my way out into a bigger world, then it gave me the opportunity to prove my abilities twice over in a super-competitive environment against the greatest talents in the industry and all the odds. Later, it brought me the respect of my teachers, my rivals, my students and my peers. It brought me financial independence and the chance to travel the world, sharing my knowledge with people hungry for it and helping to prepare the next generation to follow their own dreams. It brought me the chance to appear on a TV show beloved by millions and to spread my joy for something I'm still so passionate about.

Now I'm nearly 60, it continues to nourish me, giving me the platform to remain creative, physical and expressive, and to push my body as far as I can. Dance is always evolving in what it means to me, but it has been a constant in my life, and brought me more treasures than I could possibly have imagined.

Ballroom gave me my start. It gave me my tools, my steps, my techniques. Latin gave me my language, my colour palette, my story.

Now whenever a new couple comes to my studio and asks whether they should choose Ballroom or Latin, I just say, 'Don't worry, one of them will choose you.' But whichever path they take, as long as they're prepared to step out and work hard, then I want to make sure I give them my all, so that one day they can sit down with their children and know they've achieved their dreams like I achieved mine.

I can teach them the steps, show them how to hold their arms, their feet, their heads, but really, it's very simple. All I need to do is share that one instruction my wise teacher once gave me, that has guided me and never failed me through all my years of dance:

'Listen carefully to the music. Learn your technique. Marry the two together and perform from your heart.'

Acknowledgements

I am hugely grateful to have had the help and support from a wide range of family, friends and colleagues during the time it's taken to write my story.

My life has been a whirlwind of adventures. Emotionally, I've gone through so many ups and downs throughout my 60 years. Now, I am just looking for peace and tranquility, which I believe I have finally found. Writing this book was a lot harder than I ever thought it would be, more rewarding than I ever imagined, and of course, great therapy.

I want to dedicate my book to my amazing and beautiful mother Audrey for all her hard work in raising me, and for believing in my talent from the very beginning when no one else did. For standing by me through thick and thin, and being a constant help and support in my life. Thank you for sitting up all night to read my early drafts of the book and then re-reading them again and again. It's because of your efforts and encouragement that I have a legacy to pass on to my family where one did not exist before.

It was so difficult to write about you, David, but in some strange way I found some comfort realising you are no longer suffering. You have always been my rock and my go-to person, and I think about you daily. I miss you so much. You inspired me to share my journey. Thank you for 44 years of being the best brother a girl could ask for. I know we will be together again one day. RIP. X

Mark, I feel so blessed for having a son like you. You truly are the best thing that ever happened in my life and the day you came into the world will be forever etched in my mind. Thank you for reading through the drafts and encouraging me to write an interesting journey of my life from my perspective, and for calling me daily all the way from Los Angeles to check how the book was shaping up.

I'd like to thank my ever-patient manager, Ashley Vallance, for his constant kindness and never-ending support. Thank you to my literary agent, Jo Bell, who has been with me since the beginning of this journey, and to Caroline Frost for helping me bring magic to my story and finding the best way to help me express my thoughts and feelings. Caroline, thank you for your patience in going over the book with me so many times. Your editorial help, keen insight and ongoing support really brought my stories to life. To the team at BBC Books and Penguin Random House, Yvonne Jacob, Nell Warner, Alice King and Abby Watson, who guided me through the publishing process. To Laura, my publicist and dear friend, for sitting with me for hours and hours, and guiding me through my career on *Strictly* – I have learnt so much from you. You inspire me daily with your wisdom and knowledge, and I really can call you a true friend.

To Sammy, who gave me an opportunity for my big break in the Ballroom industry. You taught me discipline and guided me through five tough years. Thank you for making me stand on my own two feet – in more ways than one. You took a chance on an 18-year-old unknown dancer from a single-family home on the Leasowe estate. Through all our ups and downs, you've always had a very special place in my heart.

I'll always be eternally grateful to Nigel Tiffany and his family for allowing me to move into their home at 14 years old. Sharing your family with others is not easy. Thank you for understanding all these years later why I left to dance with Sammy. I respect you so much and I'm so happy you are in my life as my financial advisor. I sincerely love you.

Corky, our marriage of 20-plus years produced a wonderful son, who is the most beautiful creation from our time together. I'm grateful for the opportunity you gave me in taking an inexperienced competitive dancer on a journey of a lifetime. Along the way I learned so much more about attitudes, good and bad, in the industry. You had a steel spine and a mental attitude that I had never before encountered in a dancer, and have never seen since. We had some difficult times, but some beautiful times too. And of course TWO Open to the World British Championships.

Terri, I fall short of words to express how grateful I am for having you in my life for over 30 years. I appreciate your caring and loving attitude towards me. We have always been there for each other throughout the years. I'm so blessed to be able to call you a friend.

Karen – over 40 years of friendship. We have toured the world together in dance, and even lived next door to each other. I feel incredibly blessed to have this wonderful woman in my life. Our friendship has stood the test of time and we have been a constant source of support for each other. We have listened to each other and truly supported each other's dreams.

Denise Weavers, thank you for standing by me from day one through all the dramas and struggles, and for being such a positive and calming friend. Thank you for all the laughs we had travelling the world in dance. You truly are a great friend.

Ruud Vermeij, I may have met you later on in my career, but what a difference you made in our dancing. Your wealth of knowledge and the fact you shared your brilliant mind with us was absolutely the most beautiful experience of all time. Thank you for believing in our team.

To Michael Stylianos and Lorna Lee for helping us when we moved back to London and for always being kind and giving so much of yourselves to my family. I will be forever in your debt.

Last, but not least, to a very special man in my life, Daniel Stuart Taylor. Thank you for sitting up with me night after night until the book was completed. Thank you for your positive feedback and for truly understanding my journey.

Index

SB indicates Shirley Ballas.

INDEX